Developing Three-Dimensional CAD Software with the IBM PC

MECHANICAL ENGINEERING

A Series of Textbooks and Reference Books

EDITORS

L. L. FAULKNER

Columbus Division
Battelle Memorial Institute

and

Department of Mechanical Engineering
The Ohio State University
Columbus, Ohio

S. B. MENKES

Department of Mechanical Engineering
The City College of the
City University of New York
New York, New York

Mechanical Engineering Software

Developing Three-Dimensional CAD Software with the IBM PC

C. STAN WEI

Polytechnic University
Brooklyn, New York

MARCEL DEKKER, INC.   New York and Basel

Library of Congress Cataloging-in-Publication Data

Wei, C. Stan [date]
   Developing three-dimensional CAD software with the
IBM PC.

   (Mechanical engineering ; 59)
   Bibliography: p.
   Includes index.
   1. Computer graphics. 2. Computer-aided design.
3. IBM Personal Computer--Programming. I. Title.
II. Title: Developing 3-dimensional CAD software with
the IBM PC. III. Series.
T385.W45   1987   006.6'765   87-15444
ISBN 0-8247-7791-3

MARCEL DEKKER, INC.
270 Madison Avenue, New York, New York 10016

Current printing (last digit):
10 9 8 7 6 5 4 3 2 1

PRINTED IN THE UNITED STATES OF AMERICA

remembering grandma

Preface

Built on powerful 16- and 32-bit microprocessors, today's micro-
or personal computers (PC) have come of age as a viable engineering tool for numerous applications. These machines have
powers equivalent to the minicomputers manufactured just several
years ago and command sufficient software support for taking up
three-dimensional (3-D) computer-aided design (CAD) applications.
This book presents a system-oriented approach to learning how
to develop 3-D CAD software systems on microcomputers.

An objective of the book is to implement a 3-D CAD system on
an IBM PC, PC/AT, or PS/2 level machine that integrates computer-
aided drafting with polyhedral solid modeling. The integration of
theory and practice is emphasized throughout the book: practical
program modules and their embodied mathematical principles are
presented side by side. The reader may progressively integrate
these building blocks into a basic, open system, and enhance
his or her understanding of CAD by practicing it on a microcomputer. The included source code of the open system may also
serve as a foundation for building systems with greater facilities.

The mathematical principles for the design and display of polyhedron relevant geometric entities, including points, lines, polygonal circles and arcs, plane polygons, and polyhedra, will be
delineated. The data base for the geometric entities of interest
will be constructed in compliance with the standard IGES definition. Workable FORTRAN program modules will be developed,
utilizing the Microsoft FORTRAN compiler, in the form of building blocks from which practical CAD systems can be constructed.

v

A development system, named CAD-PS, will be built using these building blocks.

Computer-aided design is destined to be an important part of most creative professions. Although being a user of CAD systems does not require a thorough understanding of their design principles, being a student of CAD does. This book is tailored to the need of educators and students of CAD for a system-oriented CAD textbook or reference book.

The book can be used as a textbook for a second course on CAD for senior- or graduate-level students in a mechanical or aerospace engineering or computer science curriculum, following an introductory computer graphics course. It can also serve as a reference book for CAD practitioners who require an in-depth knowledge of how a CAD system is implemented, and for motivated microcomputer users who are interested in taking on a new adventure.

The text begins with an introduction to microcomputing. Chapter 1 provides a brief review of the basic elements of microcomputing and CAD. They include the inner workings of a microcomputer, memory addressing, registers, I/O peripheral devices, machine instructions, assembly languages, high-level computer languages, and the working of a CAD system.

Chapter 2 focuses on microcomputer graphics and computer generated geometric data bases. Their roles in CAD are elaborated. A generic graphics interface and the role of the system-independent IGES specification as a guidepost for computer-based geometric data base design are delineated. Also presented there are the concept of model space and definition space, and its implementation in a PC environment.

Chapter 3 deals with the design and display of planar geometric entities. Practical FORTRAN modules are implemented for the interactive design of points, lines, and polygonal arcs and circles as parts of 2-D wire-frames. A versatile viewing system is presented to provide the user of the CAD-PS system with convenient visual access to the computer-generated 3-D geometric data base. A filing mechanism for storing and retrieving geometric models is also presented.

Chapter 4 discusses topics related to 3-D drafting and interactive design of 3-D wire-frame models. Subroutine modules for switching definition spaces and transforming polygonal shapes and for forming polygonal face entities over existing wire-frames are incorporated in the CAD/PS system. This chapter also examines the uses of CAD-PS in finite-element mesh generation and in forming surfaces of revolution. Practical algorithms for evaluating the area of closed polygons and for computing hidden lines removed images of a geometric model are elaborated.

Chapter 5 presents the subroutine modules for forming polyhedral volume or solid entities from existing polygonal face entities. An extension of the volume formation algorithm for generating volumes of revolution is examined, and a module for analyzing the geometric entities created with CAD-PS is implemented. This chapter also presents a Boolean processor that offers simple geometric set operators by which complex shapes can be formed from solid primitives. The chapter concludes with an algorithm for computing realistic, perspective images of solid entities.

In presenting the CAD program modules, I assume that the reader is familiar with the FORTRAN language and reads simple assembly-language routines for the IBM PC. For those readers who would benefit from a brief review or introduction of the two computer languages prior to learning the design of CAD modules, Appendices A and B offer a concise account of the basic elements of assembly-language and FORTRAN programming in a typical PC environment. For readers interested in pursuing further the courses of microcomputer architecture, computer graphics, geometric modeling, and computer-aided design and manufacturing, the Bibliography at the end of the book provides some pointers to the published literature.

Although developed on the PC, the software modules presented in this book may also be implemented on other computers. Today, mainframe computers and minicomputers are the mainstay of industrial CAD applications. Their speeds and memories are much superior to those of the PC. The performance of PC-based CAD systems, in terms of response time, problem size, and system versatility, is no match for large-scale computer-based CAD systems. However, if the past path of evolution of microprocessor technology may be extrapolated, tomorrow's PC should gain enough power to take on tasks that are being performed on today's large computers. PC-based CAD will become an essential part of automated design before long, and modern engineers should be prepared for it.

A few words of caution on the computer programs included in this book are in order. Like authors of the majority of computer programs in service today, I fell short of being able to extend a bug-free warranty. However, the CAD-PS system has been implemented on the IBM PC and PC/AT and the TI PC and

extensively tested.   I welcome any comments or bug reports on
the programs, but would retain the rights to any commercial uses
of the programs.   A set of two disks containing the source code
and a compiled, ready-to-run version of CAD-PS is also available
directly from the author, who can be reached at P.O. Box 7860,
Flushing, New York 11352.

   Finally, to Rich, Mansuk, and Rocky, my thanks for all that
friendly, unreserved support.   To my family, my love.

                                                                C. Stan Wei

Contents

Chapter 1

Elements of Microcomputing and CAD

This chapter provides a brief account of microcomputing and its current applications in computer-aided design (CAD). These basic elements are to serve as a steppingstone into the subject of microcomputer-aided drafting and design of polyhedral solids.

1.1   THE HARDWARE AND SOFTWARE OF A COMPUTER

From a user's standpoint, a digital computer may be viewed as merely a tightly structured mass of electronic circuits put together to process information. The electronic computation and information processing performed by computers is actually a master and slave act. And fortunately, we, as users, play the role of the master in the act.

   In a closer look, a computer is an information processing machine consisting of central processing units (CPU), banks of memory cells, and peripheral devices. It can be used to perform scientific calculations, to write and edit reports, to monitor inventory, to forecast the rise and fall of the stock market, to control the burning of fuel in automobile engines, to aid in architectural and engineering designs, and to perform many other tasks.

   The CPU in a computer is designed to recognize a limited set of coded commands or instructions. Channeling these machine instructions, usually stored in a disk-like magnetic medium and copied to the memory bank when needed, to the CPU will direct

the electronic circuits in the CPU to carry out predefined operations on information pieces stored in the memory bank or
acquired from the environment. By rearranging the machine-
readable instructions, we can *program* a computer to execute
specific tasks.

Electricity gives life to a computer through a system clock
generating stable electric pulses in mega hertz (10^6/second) fre-
quencies. The system clock coordinates all activities occurring
within the CPU. The organization of the electronic circuits in
a computer is the *hardware* of the computer. The *software* of
the computer refers to the various arrangements of machine
instructions, or programs.

A special-purpose computer like the one used in monitoring
the burning of fuel in automobile engines is expected to carry
out only one particular sequence of instructions during its en-
tire service life, thus the machine instructions may be perma-
nently stored in the memory bank and no further programming
will be allowed. In this application the driver should not expect to be able to prepare his or her tax returns using the computer under the hood.

Most computers are general-purpose, programmable machines,
however. In order to perform various user-specified functions,
the computer often comes with mass information storage devices,
such as electromechanical drives for magnetic tapes and disks
for depositing large amounts of programs and data, and with
other input/output (I/O) devices, such as typewriter-like keyboards, printers, and cathode ray tube (CRT) video displays
for communications between the human user and the machine.
The term "hardware" is often extended to include all such peripheral devices.

1.2   CLASSIFICATION OF TODAY'S COMPUTERS

It is intuitive to attempt to classify computers according to the
capacity of the CPU. The processing speed and the size of man-
ageable memory banks are two conspicuous factors. However,
because of the ever increasing rate of advancements in microelectronics and software engineering, the boundaries for classi-
fication based on absolute speed and memory alone are inherently
unstable. It is now more common to classify computers based on
their relative sophistication and costs. Within the next decade

or so the computer industry can be expected to continue to make available four major classes of computer:

Supercomputer. This term has evolved into a generic one that stands for the most powerful computing machinery at any point in time. Today's supercomputers are represented by machines like the CRAY-2 and the CYBER 205. These machines may cost tens of millions of dollars. Their major uses are in the areas of weather forecast, aircraft design simulation, and nuclear physics. In order to achieve extreme speeds, supercomputers often carry unorthodox architectural designs and require special programming techniques.

Mainframe computer. A mainframe is a large, general-purpose computer system capable of performing complex tasks such as banking, business administration, and modeling of physical systems. Examples include International Business Machines (IBM) Corp.'s 3090 series and Control Data Corp.'s CYBER mainframes. These machines cost around a million dollars.

Minicomputer. A mini is a general-purpose system, capable of supporting multiple users. A mini may be used as a satellite station remotely supported by a mainframe. Minicomputers are mostly used in laboratories for specific applications and cost between $50,000 and $300,000. Today's typical minicomputers include Digital Equipment Corp.'s VAX-11/780 and Data General's Eclipse series.

Microcomputer. A micro is a small-size personal computer (PC) system that can be put right by or on a desk. It is typically a single user system, although a small group of users can share some specially configured micros. Examples include Apple's Macintosh, IBM's PC, PC/AT, and PS/2, and Texas Instruments' Professional Computer and Business-Pro. These machines cost between $1000 and $10,000

Because of current rapid developments in the microelectronics industry one should not expect the above categorization to precisely identify every available machine. Terms like super-microcomputer and super-minicomputer have already been used to refer to the in-betweens.

Although the architectural design and electronic circuits may differ for different types or brands of computer, the principles of computing and programming are universal. Since this chapter is to provide the basic elements of microcomputing, from here on we shall be concerned only with microcomputers.

1.3   A USER MODEL OF THE MICROCOMPUTER

A simplified model of how a computing machine works is essential
in learning to understand and command the machine. At the core
of a microcomputer is, in most cases, a microprocessor. Some
machines utilize more than one microprocessor. The microprocessor is the central processing unit (CPU) of the machine,
it usually takes the form of a densely packed rectangular chip
about the size of a postage stamp. In a typical CPU chip there
exist 100,000 or more integrated transistors. These very large
scale integration (VLSI) circuits form the nerve center for the
channeling and processing of information entities.

1.3.1   Microcomputer System

A CPU cannot perform by itself. To construct a functional computer system, banks of memory cells and necessary input/output
devices are tied around the CPU for storage and transmission of
information.
   Computers are adept at binary arithmetic, while we humans
are more used to the decimal system. It seems natural for us to
count things in the tens, hundreds and millions. But not for
the computer. Computers are designed to handle masses of two-
state or *binary* information pieces. Consider a bank of eight
electric bulbs individually controlled by eight flip-switches, as
illustrated in Figure 1.1a, as a simple model for the binary system. Each bulb can be at only two possible states, either ON
or OFF, correspondent with the position of the controlling switch.
A two-state or binary device like the bulb may be used to store
or represent two pieces of information. Arabic numerals 0 and 1
can be adopted to represent the OFF and ON states. Thus the
state of each bulb may be represented by a *binary* digi*t*, or a
bit for short.
   The eight bulbs can be used as a counter. Here the principles we developed for decimal numbers apply except that the only
legitimate digits are 0 and 1. Therefore 00000000 is zero,
00000010 is two, 00000011 is three, and 11111111 will be two hun-
dred and fifty five, or 255 in decimal. The same eight bits can
also be used to represent non-numeric information. If we attach
a piece of non-numeric information, an alphabet for instance, to
a particular pattern displayed by the eight bulbs in Figure 1.1a,
the bit patterns of all possible combinations can be a coding system for 256 different alphabets. The two bit patterns in Figure

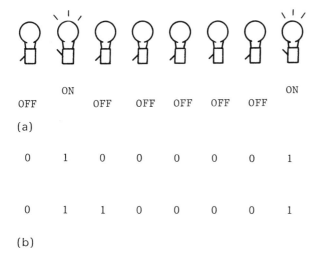

ON   ON
OFF   OFF   OFF   OFF   OFF   OFF

(a)

0   1   0   0   0   0   0   1

0   1   1   0   0   0   0   1

(b)

Figure 1.1   A simple model for the binary system.

1.1b are, in fact, well-established symbols for letters "A" and
"a." They are part of the American Standard Code for Information Interchange (ASCII). Analogously, the eight bits may also
be used to code 256 different machine instructions.

Of course, there are no bulbs in the computer. Instead small
electronic gates responsive to two levels of voltage, LOW and
HIGH, are used to represent the zeros and ones. It should now
become obvious that certain consensus must be established between human and computer as to how information is embedded in
the bit patterns, so the computer will be able to make the right
sense out of encoded programs.

A common practice by the industry is to refer to a group of
eight bits as a convenient unit known as *byte*. The ASCII system utilizes seven bits of a byte space to define 128 standard
characters including letters, numerals, and special symbols.

Today's microelectronics industry can pack 256K bits into a
memory chip no larger than a postage stamp, and eight such
memory chips can be connected to form a memory bank of 256K
bytes. The "K" unit is another industrial jargon referring to
the number of all possible combinations with a string of 10 bits,
which is exactly 1,024. Thus 1K bytes is approximately one kilo-
byte and 256K is equivalent to 262,144 in decimal. At the time
of writing, a few lead computer chip manufacturers already are

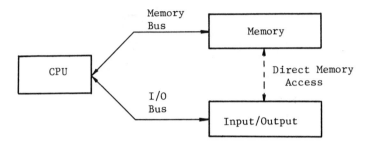

Figure 1.2   Elements of a computer system.

turning out one-megabit (1,048,576-bit to be precise) memory chips.

The hardware of a typical computer comprises CPU, memory, and input/output peripherals, a simplified schematic of which is shown in Figure 1.2. A microcomputer's memory usually takes the form of banks of Read Only Memory (ROM) and Random Access Memory (RAM) chips. The CPU can write to or read from its RAM space, but can only read from its ROM space. The memory is attached to the CPU through a memory bus. A memory or data bus is just a group of fine conductors for transmitting electrical signals within the computer system. The input/output peripherals are attached to the CPU through an I/O bus, another data bus. In many cases memory and I/O buses share the same physical conductors.

To transmit a datum between memory and an I/O device, the CPU can be instructed to fetch the datum from the transmitter and pass it on to the receiver. When large blocks of data need to be transferred between memory and I/O devices, this approach would tie the CPU down for just moving the data. The need for CPU's intervention on every transmission also limits the rate of data transfer. For more efficient use of the CPU and higher rates of data transfer, direct memory access (DMA), a special link connecting a peripheral and memory that allows data transmission without CPU's intervention, may be applied.

1.3.2   Inside the CPU

A simple model of a typical processor consists of an arithmetic logic unit (ALU), special-purpose and general-purpose registers,

and timing and control circuits. The ALU performs basic arithmetic and logical operations such as addition, subtraction, multiplication, division, and Boolean OR and AND operations on numeric data stored in registers or memory. Registers are built-
in temporary storage cells. The contents of the registers can
be accessed by the ALU in a much shorter time than it takes to
read the contents of the attached memory. For instance, to add
two numbers stored in memory cells 1 and 2 and store the result
in cell 3, the CPU will first channel the contents of cells 1 and
2 to registers A and B, so the ALU can quickly add the contents
of A and B and put the result in A. Then the CPU will copy
the contents of A to cell 3 to complete the operation. Later it
will become clear that programming a microcomputer is no more
than telling the CPU how to process information through manipulation of its registers.

The control circuits and the address and I/O data buses are
there to bridge the CPU circuitry with the outside world including the memory and the peripherals.

1.3.3   Memory and I/O Peripherals

The memory of a microcomputer is generally arranged into a long
array of bytes. The size of a memory is known as the *actual
address space*. Each 8-bit byte bears a unique *address label*.
The control circuits and data buses allow the CPU to write to or
read from any particular byte within the address space by first
sending a binary-number address, usually through an address
register, on an address bus to the interfacial control circuits of
the memory, which then opens the gate to the addressed byte
and passes the data through a data bus. The largest memory
space a microprocessor can address at any given time constitutes
its *physical address space*. A 16-bit wide address bus allows the
CPU to address 65,536 (2^{16}) or 64K bytes of memory, and a 20-
bit address bus is able to handle around one megabyte (2^{20}
bytes) of memory. Today's professional microcomputers are typically capable of manning one megabyte or larger physical address
spaces.

The input/output peripheral devices attached to the processor,
such as keyboards, CRT displays, printers/plotters, and mass
storage units like floppy and hard disk drives, all interact with
the processor in a way that is similar to the interfacing between
the memory and the processor. Every I/O device bears a unique
identification number and communicates with the processor through

an I/O port of one or two bytes wide. Data are sent from the
processor to an I/O device in a way that is analogous to writing
to a memory cell, while obtaining data from an I/O device is analogous to reading from a memory cell. In fact, some systems
implement the so-called memory-mapped I/O, which reserves a portion of the total address space for I/O ports, thus memory cells
and I/O devices may be addressed through the same channel.

1.4 MICROCOMPUTER SYSTEM SOFTWARE

What can one do with the hardware alone? Not much. To get
the machine to perform we need software or programs. A program is always made up of two parts: *instructions* and *data.*
The organization of the instructions and data dictates the performance of the computer system. To enhance the utility of a
computer system, the system manufacturer always makes available a system program called Operating System (OS).

The OS performs system housekeeping tasks such as handling
of various I/O devices, servicing of user's requests, and loading
and executing of programs, thus providing the user with a convenient, functional interface to the innards of the computer.
With the aid of the OS program, we, as users, are spared of the
tedious chores of programming every bit of the control routines
for the I/O devices every time we turn the machine on to perform useful work.

A computer program is an organization of instructions and
data. The instruction set of a particular processor is specified
by the processor designer. Each instruction is encoded into two
parts: opcode (*operation code*) and operand(s). An instruction
may be of one to several bytes long, and may take one to several
clock pulses to execute. Some instructions may have only the
opcode. Both the opcode and the operands are mere groups of
zeros and ones.

The opcodes for a microprocessor are defined by the chip
designer for all machine operations. Some instructions tell the
processor to manipulate data stored in particular memory locations
indicated by the operands, some others instruct the processor to
treat the operands themselves as data. Thus at the processor's
viewpoint, a program is just one long string of bytes filled with
zeros and ones. Programs in this barebone format are known as
machine-language programs since the electrical signals represented
by the zeros and ones are a natural language to the electronic
circuits. In the current microprocessor industry, the laws of

capitalism dictate that every manufacturer design and practice
a unique machine language for its own family of processors.

Writing programs in any machine language is difficult and
error prone because of the lack of logical inference from numbers
to physical machine operations. Debugging or correcting them
is even more tedious. To facilitate development of application
programs, the processor manufacturer often provides a translation program called *assembler*, usually a machine-language program itself, that would translate assembly-language programs
into machine instructions.

An assembly language is an abstraction of the machine language through use of mnemonics. To instruct an Intel 8086
microprocessor (see next section) to add the contents of register
BX to the contents of register AX, for example, we may write
down, symbolically, in assembly language:

ADD AX,BX

which would be translated by an 8086-assembler into a machine
instruction coded in two bytes:

00000011 11000011

The moment the CPU processes these two bytes, the desired operation will be carried out in order.

Assembly-language programmers familiar with a particular
processor can select instructions one at a time to produce very
efficient programs. However, an assembly language deals strictly
with basic machine operations available in a particular machine,
using it to develop large application programs would not be a
simple task because each high-level function would require coordination of a large number of machine instructions. Moreover,
such programs are usually very machine-dependent, they would
not work on other processors. The need of higher level computer instructions for developing machine-independent application software had led to the invention of numerous high-level
computer languages.

FORTRAN is a mature high-level computer language widely
used by scientists and engineers for more than thirty years.
The goal achieved by FORTRAN, a contraction of *FOR*mula
*TRAN*slation, was providing a convenient set of keywords for
coding scientific and engineering calculations. After that Lisp,
BASIC, COBOL, Pascal, APL, C, and many other languages
were introduced for various purposes.

The first generation of microcomputers was produced, about ten years ago, in garage-converted laboratories and supported only BASIC and assembly languages. They were made for and used by hobbyists. Their capacity was very limited because of severe shortage of memories. The last ten years have witnessed an exponential growth of micros, from virtually nil. They have now evolved into a miracle tool in financial offices, scientific laboratories, design and manufacturing firms, and many other professional applications. Today's micros support virtually every high-level language in existence.

Ever since its introduction, FORTRAN has been the mainstay of computer applications in virtually all physical sciences. The language has gone through several revisions in order to provide up to date programming facilities to scientists and engineers. The fact that FORTRAN has been widely used in scientific and engineering applications and extensive resources have been committed to the language firmly establishes it as an indispensable facility. The majority of existing computer-aided design (CAD) and computer-aided manufacturing (CAM) software is written in FORTRAN.

1.5   ENGINEERING MICRO WORKSTATIONS

Ever since its inception in early 1981, the IBM PC has set standards for today's desktop microcomputers. The IBM PC standards have also created a so-called IBM compatible PC market crowded with PC clones built on the same CPU chip, managed by the same operating system, and designed to emulate the performance of the IBM PC and tap the vast applications software resources developed around the IBM PC.

The PC family are built upon the Intel CPU chips. The other notable contender in the general-purpose microprocessor market, now dominated by Intel Corp., is the 68000 CPU family manufactured by Motorola Inc. Apple's Macintosh is a well known personal computer designed on the 68000.

The first generation of the IBM PC and its compatibles utilize the Intel 8088 CPU chip or its cousin, the 8086. The original PC was based on an 8088 CPU and designed to operate under a 4.77 meta hertz system clock providing pulse cycles of 210 nanoseconds or billionths of a second.

The primary I/O devices supported by the original PC design include an alphanumeric keyboard, a monochrome or color display,

two disk drives for 5¼-inch floppy diskettes (each stores up
to 360 kilobytes of data or programs), an interface port to a
dot-matrix printer, and standard RS-232C communication ports
for modems or graphic input/output devices. A modem is a
device that converts data to a form that can be exchanged,
usually through telephone lines, between data-processing machines; a graphic input device allows the user to indicate specific locations on the display to the computer. Typical graphic
input/output devices designed for the PC are light pen, digitizing tablet, mouse, and line plotter. An enhanced version of
the original PC which supports a hard disk, capable of storing
up to 20 megabytes, was later introduced by IBM as the PC/XT.

The 8086/88 family are 16-bit CPUs because their internal
registers are 16-bit long, and they are able to process 16 bits
of data within a single machine instruction. The 8086/88 family
support up to one megabyte of actual memory through a segment-
ed 20-bit address line. The accompanying Math Coprocessor, the
8087, is designed to handle the arithmetic of floating-point values
represented by up to 80-bit wide data.

The second generation IBM PC was introduced as the PC/AT
in 1984 and is based on the intel 80286 CPU, an 8086-extended
CPU, and the 80287 Math Coprocessor. Naturally, a great number of PC/AT clones became available soon after. The PC/AT
is powered by an 80286 operating under an 8-mega hertz system clock. The improved memory architecture of the IBM PC/AT
extends the one megabyte (2^{20} bytes) memory limit to 16 megabytes (2^{24} bytes) and provides a virtual memory capacity of
one gigabyte (2^{30} bytes). Virtual memory addressing is a memory management scheme that uses the physical address space
as a relocatable *window* over a much larger virtual memory space
residing in a mass storage device such as a Winchester hard
disk. With virtual memory, programs may be designed to address spaces larger than the available memory space.

The 80286 is upward compatible with the 8086/88 family in
that the 80286 supports the 8086/88 instructions as a subset of
its instruction set. Although the new architecture includes a
so-called Protected Mode featuring a sophisticated memory
management and multilevel protection mechanism, a seasoned
8086/88 programmer should have little difficulty with the 80286
chip.

In April, 1987 IBM Corp. introduced its third generation PC as
the Personal System/2 (PS/2), which offers four distinct models
based on the 8086, 80286, and 80386 CPU chips. The 80386 CPU

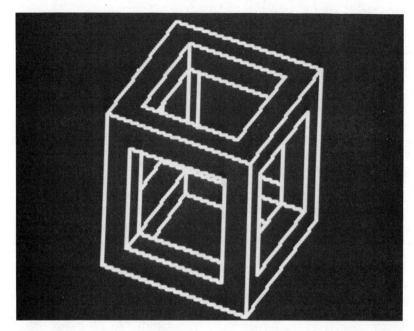

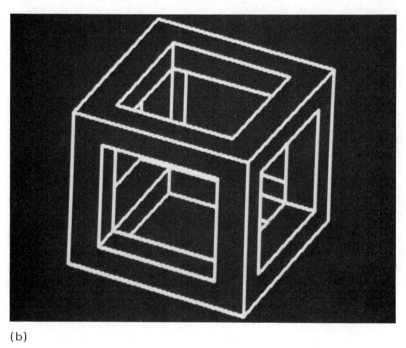

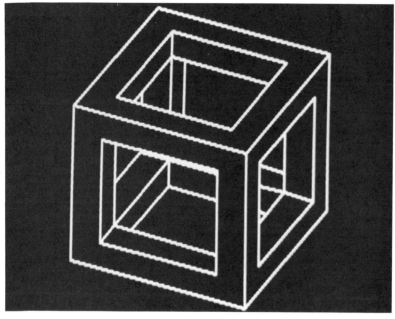

(c)

Figure 1.3 Images of a solid model displayed on (a) IBM CGA display; (b) IBM EGA display; (c) TI PC color display.

is Intel's most recent offering which supports advanced *multi-tasking;* it is also upward compatible with the 8086/88.

The graphics capability or resulution is an important factor in selecting a microcomputer for use in CAD. Most microcomputers present graphics on a raster CRT screen consisting of a fixed number of picture elements or *pixels.* Images are generated by a display controller scanning through a specific part of the memory space where the display signals or images (ON or OFF) of all the pixels are stored.

The original IBM PC is equipped with a Color Graphics Adapter (CGA) which offers two graphic modes: a four-color medium resolution of 320 by 200 pixels and a black and white, high resolution of 640 by 200 pixels. Recently IBM has added two higher resolution displays and controllers for the PC and its successor the PC/AT: the Enhanced Graphics Adapter (EGA) with 16 colors for 640 by 350 pixels and the Professional Graphics Adapter (PGA) with 256 colors for 640 by 480 pixels.

The ability to display CAD images in various colors adds significantly to the effectiveness of the user interface of a CAD system. The four-color mode of the IBM PC/CGA with only 320 by 200 pixels is marginal for displaying CAD images (see Fig. 1.3a). Of the two higher resolution adapters, the EGA (see Fig. 1.3b) has gained wide acceptance and seems to be emerging as a de facto PC graphics standard.

It is notable that, among currently available non-IBM PC and PC/AT level machines, the Texas Instruments Professional Computer (TI PC) and Business-Pro Computer, based on the 8088 and the 80286 respectively, offer a considerably higher graphics resolution than IBM's CGA. The TI standard color graphics card is not compatible with any of the IBM PC's graphics adapters. It offers 720 by 300 pixels with eight colors (from three colored planes) for each pixel, which more than trebles the pixel resolution of IBM's CGA and rivals that of IBM's EGA.

Figure 1.3 shows a geometric model displayed on the CGA and the EGA color displays and on the TI PC color display. The extent of staircasing or jaggedness due to a CRT's finite resolution is most conspicuous on the CGA display. The IBM EGA and the TI PC displays are comparable in this respect.

The geometric design related algorithms discussed in this book will be implemented in FORTRAN on the IBM PC and the TI PC. The program modules presented can easily be installed on an IBM PC/AT or PS/2 level machine. The portability of the FORTRAN language will also allow the programs to migrate to other computing systems that support the FORTRAN standard.

1.6   MICROCOMPUTER PROGRAMMING IN ASSEMBLY LANGUAGE AND FORTRAN

The proliferation of the microcomputer workstation is changing the working relationship between engineers and computers. Prior to the advent of the microcomputer, an engineer working with a mainframe or minicomputer seldom was required to program in anything other than FORTRAN. All the tedious system management chores having to do with assembly-language programming were left to the corporate computing center. Most computer users at that time were quite isolated from the inner workings of computers.

The invention of the desktop microcomputer presents, for the first time, the whole body and soul of the machine to a single user. An off-the-shelf personal computer can be, and has many times been, customized to perform wonders. But such

developmental work often requires an understanding of the
machine at a very intimate level.

Although versatile and machine-independent, a high-level
language like FORTRAN does not permit direct control of the
CPU and I/O devices of particular computers. On the other
hand, programming in machine-dependent assembly languages
alone can be very labor-intensive and inefficient in implementing
sophisticated algorithms.

The goal of this book is to develop a machine-independent
or *portable* CAD software system for the IBM PC, PC/AT, and
PS/2 level machines. We shall *divide* the software system into functional units or modules and *conquer* them individually. Those
modules involving specific I/O devices will be implemented in
the 8086/88 assembly language, while those involving geometric
design algorithms will be implemented in FORTRAN. The
assembly-language modules will be linked to the FORTRAN modules to form a complete CAD system.

The CAD system will function on most 8086/88, 80286, or 80386
based microcomputers. To port the software to other computers,
one would adjust the assembly-language modules so identical
I/O routines can be performed on the particular target computer,
recompile the same FORTRAN modules, and link the two sets of
modules together to yield the same CAD software system for the
target computer.

In the next chapter we will present several 8086/88 assembly-
language routines to demonstrate the use of a device level language in coordinating basic I/O devices. All the other number
crunching procedures required in the CAD applications to be
discussed in the following chapters will be implemented in standard FORTRAN. The computer program modules will be presented
with the assumption that the reader is fluent in FORTRAN and
reads simple assembly-language routines for the IBM PC.

For those readers who would benefit from a review or introduction of the two computer languages prior to delving into
specific CAD applications, Appendices A and B offer a concise
account of the basic ingredients of assembly-language and
FORTRAN programming in a typical PC environment, with special
emphasis placed on the integration of the two languages.

1.7   COMPUTER-AIDED DESIGN

In the computing world computer graphics is generally recognized
as the most effective and versatile communication medium between

man and machine. A formal definition of computer graphics was
established by the International Organization for Standardization
(ISO) in 1982 as: Methods and techniques for converting data
to and from a graphic display via computer. Today computer
graphics is used in varied fields ranging from machine design
and manufacturing, to commercial media arts, to medical imaging
and diagnoses, and to flight and space journey simulations.

An early application of computers and computer graphics in
the design and manufacturing industry was computer-aided
drafting. The field began to develop in the early 1970's and
today computer-aided drafting is widely accepted as an effective tool for all drafting professionals. Until recently these
automated drafting tools were developed on mainframes, minicomputers, or special graphics workstations and available only to
highly capitalized industries. The advent of graphics-capable
microcomputers has allowed users of these inexpensive workstations
to begin tapping the automated drafting technology.

A typical computer-aided drafting system or program would
run on a mainframe or minicomputer and support multiple users.
A user interacts with the computer through I/O devices such as
keyboard, CRT text and graphic display, graphic input device
(pointing light pen, digitizing tablet, or mouse), text printer,
and plotter. The automated drafting system would assist the
user in creating two-dimensional (2-D) engineering or architectural drawings composed of geometric lines and curves and other
non-geometric textual information, by providing realistic images
of the drawings on a graphic display.

The form of a drawing is sotred in the computer memory as
defined by the program. The drawing data base may, at any
time, be sent to a plotter to produce the required drawing.
As a result of being able to see the drawing data base on a
graphic display in real time, the draftsman can produce and edit
drawings more efficiently than he or she could with traditional
drawing tools.

During the development of the computer-aided drafting technology, other design and analysis features have been added
which allow designers to create and analyze geometric objects
in the three-dimensional (3-D) domain, thus creating true 3-D
data bases. While computer-aided drafting systems enhance
draftsmen's productivity in documenting the designer's conception of 3-D objects in 2-D drawings, a 3-D computer-aided design system allows the designer to experiment with his or her
creativities right on the computer display. A 3-D solid object
can be simulated on the computer, manipulated on the display

screen through a pointing device, analyzed numerically in terms of its functional requirements, and rapidly redesigned to satisfy relevant functional or manufacturing constraints, all without the designer's leaving the computer workstation.

As distinct from computer-aided drafting which provides drafts-men with a modern tool, computer-aided design emphasizes the automation of the conceptual design and engineering analysis processes in developing original ideas. While productivity increase is a major achievement of computer-aided drafting, the facilitation of creativity is an even more notable characteristic of computer-aided design.

The development of 3-D CAD may be divided into three stages. The first stage is the modeling of an object or solid in the form of its shape-bounding points and their connections. A 3-D object is represented by mere points and linear and curved edges connecting the points, no information about its surface and volume is included in the representation. Such computer generated geometric models are known as *wire-frame* models. Practical applications of wire-frame modeling systems include 3-D drafting and finite-element engineering analysis.

Although not able to render realistic images of 3-D objects, nor provide volumetric properties of the represented objects such as surface area, volume, center of mass, and moments of inertia, wire-frame modelers are still widely used by the industry as an extension of computer-aided drafting systems. Several wire-frame modeling systems have already been implemented on the IBM PC and PC/AT level machines.

The next stage in 3-D CAD is the modeling of surfaces. A surface modeler represents a 3-D shape in the form of a space region bounded by specific faces. Surface modelers are instrumental in automating the design and manufacture of crucial curved shapes such as aircraft fuselage, car body, and propeller. Precise representation of arbitrarily shaped or sculptured surfaces is the key to a successful surface modeler. In general, these surfaces are represented in the form of joined *patches*, each defined by a set of boundary curves and shape-controlling parameters.

An early commercial application of sculptured surfaces modeling is the UNISURF system developed by Bezier, using Bezier curves and surfaces, for Renault's car body design [1971]. More recently, rational B-spline curves and surfaces have been used in the GEOMOD system developed by Structural Dynamics Research Corp. Because of the large data base and sophisticated algorithms involved in implementing surface modeling

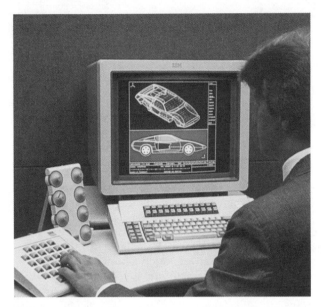

(a)

(b)

18

(c)

Figure 1.4 Examples of contempory CAD systems. (Courtesies of IBM Corp., Dassault Systems USA, Intergraph Corp., and Micro control Systems, Inc.)

principles, their practical applications are still limited to large-scale computing environments. Presently only a few experimental systems have been implemented on the microcomputer.

The third stage in 3-D CAD is solid modeling. Ideally, a solid modeler not only is able to define unambiguously a wide spectrum of solid shapes as required in design, but should also provide a mechanism to deal with dimensional tolerances so a class of solid objects can be defined based on each underlying exact shape, as required in manufacturing interchangeable, but not identical, parts.

Solid modeling has just begun its commercial application phase. Current solid modelers are limited to basic shapes, such as blocks, cylinders, spheres, cones and tori, or combinations of these basic shapes. The potential uses of solid modelers include design and assembly simulation, manufacturing processes simulation, visual communication of original design concepts, and simulation of interferences between robot manipulators and machine parts. However, precise definition of sculptured solids and provision for design tolerances are still unresolved problems.

Figure 1.4 shows representative CAD systems operating on today's mainframe, mini, and micro computers.

1.8   MODELING OF POLYHEDRAL SOLIDS

The majority of today's solid modeling systems deal specifically with polyhedral solids or solids bounded by flat faces. Unlike the case of curved, sculptured solids, the algorithms for computing the intersections and volumetric properties of polyhedral solids are well established. These systems handle curved faces by approximating them with joined, flat polygonal faces.

Polyhedral solid modeling has found numerous applications in the areas of robotics and flight simulations, animated motion pictures and video arts, design of product styling and packaging, and development of original design concepts. Interactive design of polyhedral solids is a major concern of this book.

Practical implementation of CAD on microcomputers has just begun. Because of the potential of the new micro-CAD marketplace, there are already dozens of micro-CAD systems available commercially. Most of these systems are limited to 2-D drafting or $2\frac{1}{2}$-D wire-frames, however. The term $2\frac{1}{2}$-D is used to refer to systems capable of forming 3-D like models by lifting a planar cross section into the perpendicular direction. These systems do not permit construction of models with non-uniform cross sections. Much of the developmental work to implement full 3-D solid modeling capacity on the microcomputer is still under way.

The mathematical Principles of CAD have been well published. However, very little has been published to account for the know-how of implementing CAD systems. This is primarily due to the lack of affordable computer workstations during the major development phases of the CAD technology, only a relatively few groups of specialists had access to the able computer on which the art of CAD could be performed. An additional reason for the general lack of system-oriented CAD texts may be the potential capital values associated with the implementation of CAD systems. The wide acceptance of powerful microcomputer workstations by engineering professionals has now rectified the former cause. However, the capitalistic spirit stands unshaken, and knowhow of implementing CAD software still flourishes in the form of trade secrets.

This book is to present a system-oriented approach to learning how to develop 3-D CAD software systems on the microcomputer. The focus is on the basic ingredients of 3-D CAD software, with a specific interest in the design of a microcomputer-based polyhedral solid modeling system. The essential software modules for constructing such a micro-CAD system, from modules for basic user-machine interactions to those for designing and displaying 3-D models on a 2-D CRT screen and for computing volumetric properties of computer generated polyhedral solids, will be presented in the form of modular building blocks. In addition, practical algorithms for advanced solid-modeling facilities such as hidden lines removal and Boolean set-operations will also be presented.

The rest of the book is arranged into four parts: micro-computer graphics programming, design of 2-D geometric models, design of 3-D drafting and wire-frame models, and design of polyhedral solid models. To develop a micro-CAD system, one first has to understand the graphics facilities on the micro workstation which make it possible to provide a friendly man-machine interactive environment, as well as the basic structure of a 3-D geometric data base. The next chapter will present a generic graphics interface for the IBM PC and PC/AT level machines, along with a simple CAD data base that is compatible with the Initial Graphics Exchange Specification (IGES), a standard data format specification for computer generated geometric models.

Microcomputer Graphics and CAD Data Base

An objective of this book is to present and demonstrate the practicality of developing solid-modeling CAD software on an engineering micro workstation. Simply stated, a CAD software system is a modular computer program for modeling geometries representing certain design concept in a man-computer interactive environment. A complete geometric data base for a conceptual product design is created through the stages of construction, display, and analysis of the component geometric entities. Figure 2.1 illustrates the basic elements of a micro-CAD system.

A micro-CAD workstation must process large amounts of geometric and non-geometric data, and perform intensive numerical calculations. A practical micro-CAD hardware system should include 512K bytes of RAM, two floppy disk drives, an RS-232C serial communication port, a graphics board, a dot-matrix printer, a line plotter, and a math coprocessor.

Typically a component geometric entity is created as a result of interactive model definition, model visualization, and model representation. The definition of various CAD entities required in constructing 3-D polyhedral solid models will be dealt with in the chapters to follow. This chapter is to present the graphic facilities for displaying geometric entities in a PC environment, a recently established national standard for representing CAD entities, and a basic data base for a micro-CAD system.

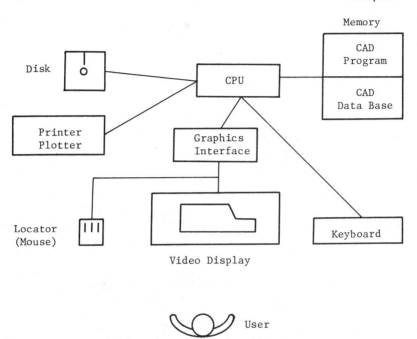

Figure 2.1   Elements of a micro-CAD system.

2.1   MICROCOMPUTER GRAPHICS

An ideal interactive graphics environment for developing CAD
systems is a standard, hardware-independent graphics interface
for all types of graphics workstations. The graphics interface
is to provide the CAD system, usually written in a high-level
programming language, with a library of *callable* routines for
manipulating the image or video display controller of the workstation. Most microcomputer displays present graphics by
scanning the rasters on a virtually flat surface, hence the displayed images are inherently two-dimensional. With a standard
graphics interface, portable CAD systems can be designed to
work on any computer systems supporting the standard graphics
interface. The construct of the CAD software, graphics interface, and graphics workstation can be symbolically described
with the block diagram in Figure 2.2.

The Graphical Kernel System (GKS) is such a standard graphics interface proposed by the International Organization for

Standardization (ISO) in 1982. The CKS is essentially a merger of two graphic interfaces independently developed in the U.S. and West Germany. It is composed of about 200 interface routines that allow a programmer to perform graphics I/O with a variety of graphic devices supporting the GKS. The formal definition of the GKS is expected to provide the computer graphics industry with guidelines for the architectural design of future graphics workstations. Nevertheless, there are several other notable graphics interfaces designed specifically for the PC workstation that have emerged as viable contestants for the champion of PC graphics applications.

The HALO graphics system published by Media Cybernetics, Inc. offers a collection of graphics subroutines for programs written for a variety of PC workstations in various high-level languages including BASIC, FORTRAN, Pascal, C, and Lisp. The definition of HALO routines is somewhat similar to that of the GKS, though not in strict compliance with the GKS. The HALO system achieves machine-independence by configuring itself for a particular workstation environment at the beginning of a graphics session. Thus an application program developed on a PC can be ported to another PC by changing only the workstation identifier in the configuration command.

Two more recent entries on the micro graphics market are the VDI-based graphics interface produced by Graphic Software Systems (GSS) and the Graphics Device Interface (GDI) published by Microsoft Corp. VDI stands for Virtual Device Interface. The two systems are similar. Both are compatible with the GKS definition. These interfaces offer machine-independence by providing a virtual interface between the PC and all of its graphics generators such as printers, plotters, and video displays.

To form the virtual graphics channel, the graphics generators as well as the application program must be equipped with device-specific software drivers. An application program in a

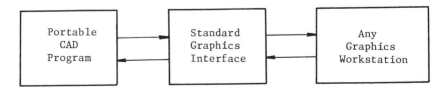

Figure 2.2   Use of a standard graphics interface.

virtual graphics environment generates graphics by sending
machine-independent graphics commands to local software drivers
attached to individual graphics generators which in turn drive
the graphics circuits, thus avoiding the need to modify the
application program when it is ported to other PC environments.

Each of the three PC graphics interfaces mentioned above
is able to provide a machine-independent environment for a
variety of application graphics software to be transported across
a variety of PC workstations. However, the only common feature
found in these interfaces is the concept of machine-independency,
their implementations are largely incompatible with one another.

We may select any of the interfaces to be the graphics interface between the CAD system to be developed and the typical
PC workstation. But it appears that any such choice would
hamper the flexibility of the CAD modules since no single interface has proved to be pervasively dominant across the whole
spectrum of personal computers. It seems sensible that we
should not bind the CAD modules to be developed to any of
these interfaces.

In order to allow maximum flexibility in implementing the
program modules presented in this text on any particular PC
workstation, by not locking into one of the contesting interfaces, we shall utilize the Generic Graphics Interface (GGI) to
develop a solid-modeling CAD system in a typical PC environment. The GGI facility consists of only a minimum number of
basic graphics utilities which can be found in any of the full-
scale graphics interfaces discussed above. Thus the developed
CAD system will be readily adaptable to any of the available
interfaces and PC workstations the reader chooses to work with.
The GGI graphics routines will be delineated in Section 2.1.3.

Today's microcomputer graphics rely mainly on raster technology which requires dedicated memory areas (video RAM) for
storing the digital input to a video display controller. The
controller is made to display an image by turning corresponding
picture elements or pixels on or off according to the image map
stored on the video RAM. However, disparities can be found
in the way a PC handles text and graphics displays.

Typically a PC uses a single video RAM area for both text
and bit-map graphics: pixels forming the shape or font of
textual symbols are intermixed with other pixel-based designed
images. The IBM PC's Color Graphics Adapter (CGA) and
Enhanced Graphics Adapter (EGA) are two typical text-in-
graphics display controllers. Another family of displays use
separate video RAMs for text and graphics: the text and

graphics images on the display, although overlapped, can be manipulated independently of each other. The TI PC is equipped with such a text-on-graphics display.

In this book we shall utilize graphics routines defined in the GGI to perform all image display tasks required by the CAD system, which will be implemented on the IBM PC and the TI PC. However, the CAD system can be integrated with another graphics interface, such as the HALO interface, the GSS/VDI graphics system, or the GDI system from Microsoft Corp., by simply replacing the GGI commands with corresponding commands of that interface.

As a preparation for developing CAD program modules on the PC, let us first examine the coordinate systems and various cursors defined within the GGI interface, as well as the concept of *window* and *viewport*. We then will describe the GGI interface in detail.

2.1.1   World, Device, and Normalized
Device Coordinates

If we view a 2-D computer image as a picture captured by a camera hung over a sheet of drawing paper affixed to a drawing board, then there are naturally two separate coordinate systems: one attached to the drawing paper and the other to the image.

For 2-D planes, a practical coordinate system can be defined by affixing a pair of joined, right-angled reference axes to any convenient point (the origin) in the plane, thus all points in the plane can be identified by measuring the perpendicular distances between the points and the reference axes, and represented by pairs of values or *coordinates* with a selected unit such as inch, millimeter, or pixel.

The coordinates in the drawing paper are called *world coordinates*; while those in the image are called *device coordinates*. These two coordinates are very different in that world coordinates are limited by the size of the drawing paper which varies between drawings and can be very, very large; but device coordinates are limited by the resolution of the display which is fixed when the display was built. Additionally, world coordinates are real values measuring the continuum in the drawing paper, while device coordinates are used to identify the finite number of displayable pixels on a display screen and therefore they always have integer values.

There always exists a binding relationship between a world
coordinate system in a drawing paper and a device coordinate
system in a corresponding image plane, similar to one between
the location of the drawing paper and that of the camera that
took the picture. Such bindings may be looked at more closely
with the coordinate spaces shown in Figure 2.3. The left, external rectangular box represents the theoretically infinite
drawing paper; the upper right one represents the full display
surface of an IBM PC's EGA display (640 × 350 pixels); and the
one at the lower right represents the display surface of a TI
PC display (720 × 300 pixels).

The X and Y reference axes are affixed to the center of the
drawing paper and the rectangular *window* defines a visible area
over the world coordinate space. The image taken within the
window is to appear in a display area or *viewport* on a computer
display. In Figure 2.3 we utilize whole displays as viewports.
In general any rectangular enclosure on the display can be defined as a viewport. The mathematical expressions for the binding between geometric entities in the drawing and their images
on the computer display are simply the one-to-one mapping
transformation between a *window* and a *viewport*.

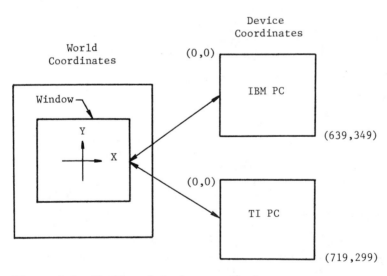

Figure 2.3   World and device coordinates.

Notice the difference in the direction of the vertical Y-axis in the world and the device coordinate planes: in the world coordinate plane the Y-value increases in the upward direction; while in the device coordinate plane the Y-value increases in the downward direction. The world coordinates utilize the conventional notation in dealing with analytical geometry; while the device coordinates are prompted by the inherent scanning sequence of a raster display which normally starts at the upper left corner and ends at the lower right corner.

In Figure 2.3 the mapping between a world coordinate *window* area and a device coordinate *viewport* area apparently varies with the arrangement of pixels on the display. In order to provide a display-independent relationship between window and viewport, the GGI graphics library defines a *normalized device coordinate* system in which a unit square region bounded by the opposite corners at (0.0, 0.0) and (1.0, 1.0) is mapped to the full display area of a GGI workstation. Although most PC displays are rectangular, not square, any point in the normalized device coordinate region is mapped to a specific physical location on the CRT display, regardless of the arrangement of pixels.

The above definition of normalized device coordinates is similar to one given in Foley and Van Dam [1982], but the latter maps the unit square region to the largest square area of a display surface, thus resulting in an inaccessible area in a nonsquare display surface.

The normalized viewport is defined in a normalized device coordinate plane in which the X and Y directions are identical to those in the world coordinate plane. The intermediate normalized device coordinate system makes it possible to form a set of device-independent *window* and *viewport*, as illustrated in Figure 2.4. The mappings between corresponding points in the window, the normalized viewport, and the device viewport may be obtained through simple similar-triangle relationships.

As illustrated in Figure 2.5, we divide the display into three regions in the normalized device coordinate plane: the region defined by the opposite corners at (0.0, RATIOY) and (RATIOX, 1.0) will be used as the viewport for image display; the region defined by (RATIOX, RATIOY) and (1.0, 1.0) will be used for menu display; and the region defined by (0.0, 0.0) and (1.0, RATIOY) will be used for interactive dialogues. We will also display the size of current window and other miscellaneous messages at the top of the viewport. (See subroutine SETUP in Sec. 2.1.4 and subroutine WSIZE in Sec. 3.1.2.)

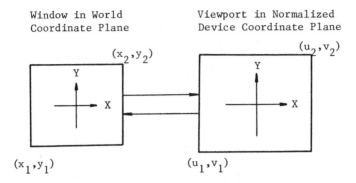

Window in World   Viewport in Normalized
Coordinate Plane   Device Coordinate Plane

Figure 2.4   Device-independent window and viewport.

In order to maintain a uniform scale in the image plane along
the displayed X and Y axes, the aspect ratio, width divided
by height, of the rectangular window must always be kept
identical to that of the rectangular viewport on the display.
In practice, the physical size of the window can be assigned to
be identical to that of the viewport on the display to achieve a
1:1 scale between objects drawn in the world coordinate plane
and their images in the device coordinate plane.   Such a default
window is implemented in subroutine SETUP in Section 2.1.4.

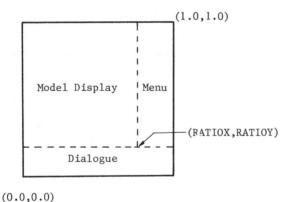

Figure 2.5   Display surface is divided into three regions.

The menu area is for displaying available design options so the user can organize his or her own design procedure by selecting desired functions with a graphic input or locating device such as mouse. This type of interactive design process is often described as being *menu-driven*. The dialogue area is for displaying system prompts and echoing the user's keyboard input.

2.1.2 Graphic, Text, Crosshair and Menu Cursors

We shall utilize four types of cursor to track and identify information displayed on the screen. The Graphic, Text, and Crosshair Cursors are defined within the GGI. The GGI library maintains two Graphic Cursors which point to a pair of corresponding locations within the world and the device coordinate planes from which graphic elements can be generated. The location of the Graphic Cursor in the normalized device coordinate plane can be obtained through a mapping subroutine. Although either Graphic Cursor can be obtained from the other through similar mapping routines, the GGI provides both cursors explicitly to allow the programmer to switch between the two planes more efficiently.

The GGI library defines three Text Cursors: a world Text Cursor indicating a point in the world space at which texts can be drawn, a device Text Cursor indicating the pixel position in the device space at which texts can be drawn, and a text-plane Text Cursor indicating the character position (row and column) at which texts are to be displayed. The typical PC can display 2000 characters in one full screen, which is arranged into a matrix of 25 rows and 80 columns. It ought to be noted that, at its medium resolution graphic mode, the IBM CGA screen can display only 25 rows by 40 columns of characters. In the GGI environment, the two Graphic Cursors in the world and the device planes are identical to, respectively, the world Text Cursor and the device Text Cursor.

Also defined in the GGI is a Crosshair Cursor serving as a tracking symbol which is driven by a graphic input or locator device such as mouse or digitizing tablet. At present the three-button mouse seems to be the most popular graphic input device in the micro environment. It is a puck-like device with three buttons which is manipulated by hand on either a plain flat surface (mechanical mouse) or a special grid pad (optical mouse)

and usually connects to a PC workstation through an RS-232C
serial communication port.

In a typical interactive environment, the user is prompted
by the CAD system, which usually displays a tracking symbol
on the screen, to maneuver the tracking symbol across the
screen by moving the mouse device and to press a button on
the mouse to select a command or indicate a location on the display to the CAD system.

For the divided display surface defined in Figure 2.5, there
is a need for a non-crosshair Menu Cursor for selecting a menu
item from the list displayed in the menu area.   In Section 2.1.4,
we shall develop a locator-input subroutine to customize the PC
workstation to support both the Crosshair and the Menu Cursors
through a three-button mouse.   The symbols <L>, <M>, and
<R> will be used in the program modules to refer to, respec-
tively, the Left, Middle, and Right button on the mouse.   The
GGI library also supports an Arrow-Key locator, which utilizes
the four arrow keys on the keyboard to control the movement
of the cursors, for use as a substitute for a mouse.

The machine-independence of graphics interfaces like GGI is
achieved by providing a uniform subroutine library to the application program and, in the same time, tending the specific
hardware design of a particular workstation.   Very often this
other side of a graphics library involves use of specific machine
instructions and thus can only be programmed in assembly languages.   As an illustration of how such a graphics library may be
built, we shall examine two assembly-language procedures for
manipulating the text-plane cursors of the IBM PC and the TI
PC.

Typically, the display controller, as well as other I/O peripherals, of a PC workstation can be programmed by invoking the
Basic I/O System (BIOS) routines in an assembly-language procedure.   The BIOS routines for the IBM PC are listed in its
Technical Reference Manual.   The following procedure IBMLOC
is designed to be attached to FORTRAN modules to allow
FORTRAN CALL-statements to move the text-plane cursor to a
desired location.   In IBMLOC, the interrupt routine 10H (or 16
in decimal) is part of the BIOS which moves the text-plane cursor to the location stored in registers DH and DL (see Appendix
A).   Text strings can be displayed at the text-plane cursor
location through other interrupt routines.

```
;   FORTRAN ->   CALL  IBMLOC(ROW,COLUMN)
;                      ROW:  1-25
```

```
;                   COLUMN: 1-80
;
        PUBLIC   IBMLOC
ICODE SEGMENT  PARA PUBLIC
        ASSUME   CS:ICODE
;
IBMLOC PROC    FAR
        PUSH     BP
        MOV      BP,SP
        PUSH     ES
        LES      SI,DWORD PTR [BP+10]  ;Get First Argument, ROW
        MOV      DH,ES:[SI]
        LES      SI,DWORD PTR [BP+6] ;Get Second Argument, COLUMN
        MOV      DL,ES:[SI]
        DEC      DH                      ;Adjust ROW to 0-24
        DEC      DL                      ;Adjust COLUMN to 0-79
        XOR      BH,BH                   ;IBM PC's graphic mode
        MOV      AH,02H
        INT      10H
        POP      ES
        POP      BP
        RET      8
IBMLOC ENDP
;
ICODE   ENDS
        END
```

Although the TI PC carries a different hardware design from the IBM PC, it provides a similar BIOS routine for relocating its text-plane cursor. The following procedure TILOCA would relocate the text-plane cursor of the TI PC to the location indicated by the least-significant bytes of the input arguments.

```
;  FORTRAN -> CALL TILOCA(ROW,COLUMN)
;
        PUBLIC   TILOCA
;
TICODE SEGMENT PARA PUBLIC
        ASSUME   CS:TICODE
;
TILOCA PROC FAR
;
; Relocate text cursor position (25 rows by 80 columns)
;
        PUSH     BP
        MOV      BP,SP
        PUSH     ES
        LES      SI,DWORD PTR [BP+10]       ;Get first argument, ROW
        MOV      DL,ES:[SI]
        LES      SI,DWORD PTR [BP+6] ;Get second argument, COLUMN
        MOV      DH,ES:[SI]
        DEC      DL              ;Adjust ROW to 0-24
        DEC      DH              ;Adjust COLUMN to 0-79
        MOV      AH,02H
```

```
          INT      49H
          POP      ES
          POP      BP
          RET      8
TILOCA ENDP
;
TICODE ENDS
          END
```

IBMLOC and TILOCA are two machine-specific I/O routines
performing the same function on two different PCs. To provide a machine-independent text-plane cursor control routine
to an application, we may maintain a machine identifier in the
graphics library and, in the control routine, activate the appro-
priate procedure accordingly. This can be achieved by programming directly in assembly language. However, the following
FORTRAN module, GTTCSR, is more illustrative in showing the
nature of machine-independency. In GTTCSR, the text-plane
cursor will be properly relocated according to the machine identifier, IDPC, stored in the graphics library.

```
*
*    Machine-independent routine for relocating text cursor
*    IDPC=1 -> IBM PC
*    IDPC=2 -> TI PC
*
      SUBROUTINE GTTCSR(IROW,ICOL)
      COMMON /GGPCID/ IDPC
      IF(IDPC.EQ.1) THEN
        CALL IBMLOC(IROW,ICOL)
      ELSE IF(IDPC.EQ.2) THEN
        CALL TILOCA(IROW,ICOL)
      ENDIF
      RETURN
      END
```

2.1.3   The GGI Library

The GGI graphics library was written by Mr. H. Shiotsuki and
the author for the IBM PC and PC/AT, and the TI PC. It is
composed of basic 2-D graphics subroutines that can be attached
to portable FORTRAN modules. The library is described as
being *generic* because all the graphics procedures can be
achieved by similar graphics routines found in other 2-D
graphics interface systems.
  Since the GGI library is only to serve as the display screen
input/output controller in the development of a solid-modeling

CAD system, we shall not discuss the implementation of the GGI library but only describe in the following the functions of the GGI routines needed to implement the CAD system. For the interested reader, the complete GGI library is available from the author.

GINIPC(IDPC,IERR)   Initiates the GGI interface, with IDPC indicating a particular PC system. The GGI library currently supports the IBM PC and PC/AT configured with the CGA or the EGA graphics card, and the TI PC configured with its standard graphics card. (The screen graphics mode is specified through subroutine GSCRN.) At initiation, window is set to be identical to the normalized viewport; device viewport is set to be the default full screen; color is set according to IDPC; and the XOR and Line Type parameters are set to be 0 and 1 respectively. GINIPC returns a non-zero integer through IERR when the PC system cannot be initiated.

GSCRN(IDSCRN)   Specifies the operating mode of the graphics board.

GINILO(IDLOCA,IDPORT,IERR)   Initiates the graphic input or locating device. IDLOCA specifies the attached locator and IDPORT specifies the I/O port number used by the locator. The GGI library currently supports a number of three-button mice. In the absence of such input devices, the GGI can be prompted to convert the Arrow Keys on the keyboard to simulate a graphic input device. GINILO returns a non-zero integer when the locator cannot be initiated.

GGCLS   Clears the graphics planes of the screen.

GTCLS   Clears the text plane of the screen. This subroutine is effective only for machines with an extra text plane, e.g., the TI PC.

GWINDO(X1,Y1,X2,Y2)   Declares the range of a new window by its two opposite corners in the world coordinate plane: lower left corner at (X1,Y1) and upper right corner at (X2,Y2).

GNVIEW(X1,Y1,X2,Y2)   Declares the range of a new device viewport by its two opposite corners at (X1,Y1) and (X2,Y2) in the normalized device coordinate plane: lower left corner at (X1,Y1) and upper right corner at (X2,Y2). All graphic elements displayed are clipped against this device viewport automatically.

GCOLOR(IC)   Sets active color to be IC. All graphic and
text elements will be displayed in the active color unless otherwise specified.

GPALET(IC1,IC2)   Assigns color IC2 to the palette index IC1.
This routine provides a tool for redefining the relationship
between an integer color code and an actual color.

GXOR(MODE)   Turns off XOR mode when MODE = 0; turns on
XOR mode otherwise.

GLNTYP(MODE)   Sets current Line Type to MODE. (MODE = 1
for solid line, MODE = 2 for dashed line, and MODE = 3 for
dotted line.)

GWPSET(XW,YW)   Plots the point at (XW,YW) in world coordinate plane in current color.

GDPSET(IXD,IYD)   Plots the point at (IXD,IYD) in device coordinate plane in current color.

GWGCSR(XW,YW)   Moves the world Graphic Cursor to (XW,YW)
in world coordinate plane.

GWLINE(X2,Y2)   Draws a line of current Line Type from current world Graphic Cursor to (X2,Y2) in world coordinate plane
in current color and moves the world Graphic Cursor to (X2,Y2).

GWTEXT(STR)   Displays the text string STR less the bounding
delimiters starting at current world Graphic Cursor in current
color, e.g., STR='\The back slashes will not be displayed\'.

GDGCSR(IXD,IYD)   Moves the device Graphic Cursor to (IXD,
IYD) in device coordinate plane.

GDLINE(IX2,IY2)   Draws a line of current Line Type from current device Graphic Cursor to (IX2,IY2) in device coordinate
plane in current color and moves the device Graphic Cursor to
(IX2,IY2).

GDTEXT(STR)   Displays the text string STR less the bounding
delimiters starting at current device Graphic Cursor in current
color.

GTBCSR(ISTAT)   Turns OFF the text-plane blinking Text
Cursor if ISTAT is zero; turns ON the text-plane blinking Text
Cursor otherwise.

GTTCSR(IROW,ICOL)   Moves the text-plane Text Curosr to
(IROW,ICOL).

GTTEXT(STR)   Displays the text string STR less the bounding delimiters starting at current text-plane Text Cursor in current color, and advances the Text Cursor to the end of STR.

GWBOX(X1,Y1,X2,Y2)   Plots a rectangular box defined by the corner points at (X1,Y1) and (X2,Y2) in world coordinate plane in current color.

GDBOX(IX1,IY1,IX2,IY2)   Plots a rectangular box defined by the corner points at (IX1,IY1) and (IX2,IY2) in device coordinate plane in current color.

GWBOXF(X1,Y1,X2,Y2,IC)   Fills the rectangular box defined by the corner points at (X1,Y1) and (X2,Y2) in world coordinate plane with the color specified by IC.

GDBOXF(IX1,IY1,IX2,IY2,IC)   Fills the rectangular box defined by the corner points at (IX1,IY1) and (IX2,IY2) in device coordinate plane with the color specified by IC.

GWTON(XW,YW,XN,YN)   Maps the point at (XW,YW) in world coordinate plane to a point at (XN,YN) in normalized device coordinate plane.

GNTOD(XN,YN,IXD,IYD)   Maps the point at (XN,YN) in normalized device coordinate plane to a point at (IXD,IYD) in device coordinate plane.

GDTON(IXD,IYD,XN,YN)   Maps the point at (IXD,IYD) in device coordinate plane to a point at (XN,YN) in normalized device coordinate plane.

GNTOW(XN,YN,XW,YW)   Maps the point at (XN,YN) in normalized device coordinate plane to a point at (XW,YW) in world coordinate plane.

GWTOD(XW,YW,IXD,IYD)   Maps the point at (XW,YW) in world coordinate plane to a point at (IXD,IYD) in device coordinate plane.

GDTOW(IXD,IYD,XW,YW)   Maps the point at (IXD,IYD) in device coordinate plane to a point at (XW,YW) in world coordinate plane.

GLDTCH   Terminates the communication channel between the Locator and the application program.

GLENAB   Enables interrupts from the Locator.

GLDISA   Disables interrupts from the Locator.

GLCOLO(IC)   Changes the color of the Tracking Crosshair
Cursor to IC.

GLCLRB   Clears all Locator status parameters.

GWLMOV(XW,YW)   Moves the Tracking Crosshair to (XW,YW)
in world coordinate plane.

GDLMOV(IXD,IYD)   Moves the Tracking Crosshair to (IXD,IYD)
in device coordinate plane.

GWLSTA(XW,YW,IBUTT)   Inputs the Locator status. The routine
reads the Tracking Cursor location (XW,YW) in world coordinate
plane along with IBUTT which indicates the Button status. IBUTT
returns zero when no button is pressed, 132 when <L> is pressed,
130 when <M> is pressed, and 129 when <R> is pressed.

GDLSTA(IXD,IYD,IBUTT)   Inputs the Tracking Cursor location (IXD,IYD) in device coordinate plane along with IBUTT
which indicates the Button status.

GINQLO(IDLOCA)   Returns current locator identifier.

GINQPC(IDPC)   Returns current workstation identifier.

GINQSC(IX,IY)   Returns screen resolution with (IX,IY) indicating the device coordinates of the lower right corner.

2.1.4   The SETUP and USELOC Modules

The first FORTRAN module and CAD building block on our way
toward a practical micro-CAD system will now be presented.
The SETUP module is to initiate either an IBM PC or PC/AT or
a TI PC workstation, and delineate the viewport defined by
RATIOX and RATIOY as shown in Figure 2.5. It also sets the
limits of the 3-D design space to be provided by the micro-CAD
system. Other initial configurations are described in the comment lines in the following listing.

```
*
*   SETUP initiates a micro-CAD interactive environment
*
      SUBROUTINE SETUP(IERR)
      COMMON /DEVICE/ IDPC,IDSCRN,IDLOCA,IDPORT
      COMMON /UNITS/ IUNIT
      COMMON /SCRN/ RATIOX,RATIOY,IXD,IYD,IXMAX,MENUDY
      COMMON /MSPACE/ XMIN,YMIN,ZMIN,XMAX,YMAX,ZMAX
      COMMON /WINDOW/ XW1,YW1,XW2,YW2
*
*   Initiate the PC workstation
*
```

```
      CALL GINIPC(IDPC,IERR)
      IF(IERR.NE.0) RETURN
      CALL GSCRN(IDSCRN)
*
*  Clear graphics planes and text plane (if any)
*
      CALL GGCLS
      CALL GTCLS
*
*  Initiate the locator interface
*
      CALL GINILO(IDLOCA,IDPORT,IERR)
      IF(IERR.NE.0) RETURN
      CALL GINQSC(IXMAX,IYMAX)
*
*  Define Viewport area on the display
*
      RATIOX=0.9
      RATIOY=0.1
*
*  Menu area is widened for IBM PC's 320*200 screen mode
*
      IF(IDPC.EQ.1 .AND. (IDSCRN.EQ.4.OR.IDSCRN.EQ.13)) RATIOX=0.8
*
*  We shall use only four colors: Black, Magenta, Cyan and White
*
      IF(.NOT. (IDPC.EQ.1 .AND. IDSCRN.EQ.4)) THEN
        CALL GPALET(1,3)
        CALL GPALET(2,5)
        CALL GPALET(3,7)
      ENDIF
*
*  Set default color to be White
*
      CALL GCOLOR(3)
*
*  Default Window centered at Origin
*
      XCTR=0.0
      YCTR=0.0
*
*  Set default Window size to be identical to Viewport size:
*  RATIOX*9.0 in. wide and (1-RATIOY)*7.0 in. high
*  (the display surface is assumed to be 9 in. X 7 in.)
*
      WIDWIN=RATIOX*9.0
      HEIWIN=(1.0-RATIOY)*7.0
      IF(IUNIT.EQ.2) THEN
*
*  Convert Inch to Millimeter
*
        WIDWIN=WIDWIN*25.4
        HEIWIN=HEIWIN*25.4
      ENDIF
      XW1=XCTR-WIDWIN/2.0
```

```
      YW1=YCTR-HEIWIN/2.0
      XW2=XW1+WIDWIN
      YW2=YW1+HEIWIN
*
*  Prepare for menu display and delineate Viewport
*
      MENUDY=(IYMAX+1)/25
      CALL GNTOD(RATIOX,RATIOY,IX,IY)
      IXD=IX+1
      IYD=IY+1
      CALL GDGCSR(IXD,0)
      CALL GDLINE(IXD,IYD)
      CALL GDLINE(0,IYD)
*
*  Set the limits of the 3-D design space
*
      XMIN=-10000.0
      YMIN=-10000.0
      ZMIN=-10000.0
      XMAX=10000.0
      YMAX=10000.0
      ZMAX=10000.0
*
*  Set default Window and Viewport
*
      CALL GWINDO(XW1,YW1,XW2,YW2)
      CALL GNVIEW(0.,RATIOY,RATIOX,1.0)
*
*  Center the Crosshair Cursor
*
      CALL GWLMOV(0.,0.)
      RETURN
      END
```

Next we will develop a general locator-input FORTRAN routine using the GGI routines described in the preceding section. Since we are more interested in the world or design coordinate plane where geometric models are built than the device coordinate plane where images of the models are displayed, the locator-input routine USELOC is to provide the caller module with the location of the center of the Crosshair Cursor in the world coordinate plane.

Considering that the same locator will also be used to select user-commands from the screen, we will establish a Menu Cursor in USELOC in the form of a small moving box in the menu region. The Menu Cursor can be maneuvered to enclose any item listed in the menu region through the *Up* and *Down* movements of the locator. The provision of two different cursors in USELOC should eliminate the ambiguity that may arise if the user was given a single cursor for both indicating a location in the viewport and selecting a menu item in the menu region.

USELOC automatically transforms the Crosshair Cursor into a Menu Cursor when it is moved into the menu region, and vice versa. This subprogram provides a controlled locator-input procedure in which the user is prompted to maneuver the attached locating device to either locate a point in the active window or select a user command from the menu region.

It ought to be noted that the USELOC routine presented here does not support text string input from the keyboard. A more sophisticated user input routine could be implemented which would allow the user to use, at all times, either a locating device or a text string entered from the keyboard to specify a user command or supply desired coordinate values. Such a routine must perform a device interrupt-monitoring procedure to determine which of the two possible input devices is active.

```
*
*    USELOC provides an interactive user interface by establish
*    ing a link between a Locating device, may it be a mouse or a
*    numeric keypad on a keyboard, and a graphic display.  The
*    user is to manipulate the hand-operated device to maneuver the
*    tracking Crosshair Cursor or the Menu Cursor on the screen.
*    After reaching the desired location, the user is expected to
*    press and then release a button on the locator.  USELOC then
*    returns with the World coordinates of the cursor and an
*    integer value representing either a mouse button (132 for <L>,
*    130 for <M>, or 129 for <R>) or a menu item (1-23).
*
      SUBROUTINE USELOC(X,Y,IBUTT)
      COMMON /WINDOW/ XW1,YW1,XW2,YW2
      COMMON /SCRN/ RATIOX,RATIOY,IXD,IYD,IXMAX,MENUDY
      DATA IC0/0/,IC1/1/
      CALL GXOR(1)
      CALL GLENAB
      CALL GLCOLO(IC1)
10    CALL GWLSTA(X,Y,IBUTT)
      IF(IBUTT.NE.0) GOTO 40
*
*    Change Crosshair to a menu box when entering menu region
*
      CALL GWTOD(X,Y,IX,IY)
      IF(IX.LT.IXD-1) GOTO 10
      CALL GLCOLO(IC0)
      CALL GNVIEW(0.,0.,1.,1.)
15    IMENU=IY/MENUDY*MENUDY
      MENUY=IMENU+MENUDY-1
      CALL GDBOX(IXD+1,IMENU,IXMAX,MENUY)
20    CALL GDLSTA(IX,IY,IBUTT)
      IF(IBUTT.NE.0) GOTO 30
      IMENU0=IY/MENUDY*MENUDY
      MENUY0=IMENU0+MENUDY-1
```

```
      IF(IX.GE.IXD-1) THEN
        IF(MENUY0.EQ.MENUY) GOTO 20
        CALL GDBOX(IXD+1,IMENU,IXMAX,MENUY)
        GOTO 15
      ENDIF
*
*   Change menu box back to Crosshair Cursor
*
      CALL GDBOX(IXD+1,IMENU,IXMAX,MENUY)
      CALL GNVIEW(0.,RATIOY,RATIOX,1.0)
      CALL GLCOLO(IC1)
      GOTO 10
30    CALL GDLSTA(IX,IY,IBUTT)
      IF(IBUTT.NE.0) GOTO 30
      IBUTT=IMENU/MENUDY+1
*
*   Delete Menu box, set normalized viewport, and adjust cursor
*   center
*
      CALL GDBOX(IXD+1,IMENU,IXMAX,MENUY)
      CALL GNVIEW(0.,RATIOY,RATIOX,1.0)
      CALL GWLMOV(0.99*XW2+0.01*XW1,Y)
      CALL GLDISA
      CALL GXOR(0)
      RETURN
40    CALL GWLSTA(X,Y,I)
      IF(I.NE.0) GOTO 40
      CALL GLCOLO(IC0)
      CALL GLDISA
      CALL GXOR(0)
      RETURN
      END
```

The utility of USELOC may be demonstrated with a simple MAIN program module. The following MAIN program would produce the image shown in Figure 2.6 when run on an IBM PC/EGA. The reader should note that pressing any button on the mouse will terminate the program.

```
PROGRAM MAIN
COMMON /DEVICE/ IDPC,IDSCRN,IDLOCA,IDPORT
COMMON /UNITS/ IUNIT
COMMON /SCRN/ RATIOX,RATIOY,IXD,IYD,IXMAX,MENUDY
COMMON /MSPACE/ XMIN,YMIN,ZMIN,XMAX,YMAX,ZMAX
COMMON /WINDOW/ XW1,YW1,XW2,YW2
*
*   IDPC=1     -> IBM PC
*   IDPC=2     -> TI PC
*   IDSCRN=3   -> IBM PC alphanumeric (A/N) mode
```

```
*   IDSCRN=4   -> IBM PC resolution: 320*200 (4 colors)
*   IDSCRN=13 -> IBM PC resolution: 320*200 (16 colors)
*   IDSCRN=16 -> IBM PC resolution: 640*350 (16 colors)
*   IDLOCA=2   -> SummaMouse of Summagraphics Corp.
*   IUNIT=1    -> Inch
*
      IDPC=1
      IDSCRN=16
      IDLOCA=2
      IDPORT=1
      IUNIT=1
      CALL SETUP(IERR)
      IF(IERR.NE.0) THEN
        WRITE(*,*) ' '
        WRITE(*,*) ' Workstation initiation fails...'
        WRITE(*,*) '  IDPC   -> ',IDPC
        WRITE(*,*) '  IDSCRN -> ',IDSCRN
        WRITE(*,*) '  IDLOCA -> ',IDLOCA
        WRITE(*,*) '  IDPORT -> ',IDPORT
        STOP
      ENDIF
*
*   Disable Blinking Text Cursor in Text Plane
*
      CALL GTBCSR(0)
      CALL USELOC(X,Y,IBUTT)
*
*   Clear screen
*
      CALL GGCLS
      CALL GTCLS
*
*   Restore Blinking Text Cursor in Text Plane
*
      CALL GTBCSR(1)
*
*   Detach Locator interface and switch to A/N mode
*
      CALL GLDTCH
      IF(IDPC .EQ. 1) CALL GSCRN(3)
      STOP
      END
```

Later we shall expand the above MAIN module to coordinate all the component modules required in building a workable CAD system. The ability to display CAD entities in various colors is crucial in highlighting user selected entities in an interactive environment. Although the black and white picture shown in Figure 2.6 does not tell the whole story, the CAD modules will use four basic colors (Black, Magenta, Cyan, and White) in displaying or highlighting CAD entities.

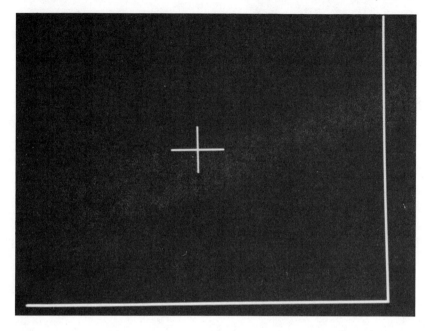

Figure 2.6   Viewport and Crosshair Cursor in CAD-PS.

2.2   CAD DATA BASE

Having a firm grip of the coordinate systems involved in the
design and visualization of geometric entities is a prerequisite
to understanding CAD.   In the practical world we never design
anything truly two-dimensional.   The space we live in is three-
dimensional.   In the past, designers used to consolidate a design concept by drawing a number of projectional views of the
3-D conception on paper to help communicate and document their
creation.   On the design drawing dimensions were marked, specific requirements for material selection and processing were detailed.   The drawing was then transferred to the manufacturing
end where craftsmen would read the drawing and apply appro-
priate tools to shape raw material into parts or products specified by the design drawing.
    With 3-D CAD, products can be designed in a virtual 3-D
space, visualized through 2-D computer generated images, and

individually selected and edited through a designer-operated locating device. The interactive graphics allows the designer to probe into the design space via the viewport-window setup. (The topic of how 2-D windows can be used to visualize a 3-D design space will be discussed in Section 3.1.) At the end of a design process, the completed product model can be documented in actual 3-D coordinates.

This section is to present the coordinate systems to be used in developing a practical CAD system, their transformations in the design space, and a standard format for documenting 3-D geometric entities.

2.2.1   3-D Model Space and Definition Space

Any set of three joined and mutually perpendicular coordinate axes (X, Y and Z) can be used to define a linear 3-D space. If one aligns one's thumb, first finger, and middle finger along three mutually perpendicular directions and labels them as the X, Y and Z axis respectively, then a 3-D space described with the right hand system is known as a *right-handed* Cartesian space and a 3-D space described with the left hand system is known as a *left-handed* Cartesian space.

The construction of a geometric model of a part or product typically involves defining component geometric entities and assembling them into one complete model. The 3-D coordinate space in which a model resides is known as the *model* space. Although component entities may be defined directly in the model space, it is often found convenient to define component entities in more intuitive local coordinate spaces that are themselves defined in the model space. Such indirect definitions also allow the coordinates of an entity within the model space to be evaluated when needed. The simplifying effect is most apparent when defining those entities which can be constructed in a single plane. Such entity-dependent coordinate systems are known as *definition* space coordinate systems.

It is common to use a right-handed Cartesian X. Y. Z coordinate system to define a model space and right-handed Cartesian XT, YT, ZT (just to avoid confusion with the model space axes) coordinate systems to define definition spaces. The model space in which a particular geometric model is defined is fixed and provides a set of *global* reference axes, while the definition space may vary from entity to entity.

2.2.2 Coordinate Transformations in 2-D Planar Space

Let us take a close look at the planar space defined by the X-Y plane in a Cartesian space. As shown in Figure 2.7a, point P_1 in the plane can be uniquely identified by its coordinates (x_1, y_1, z_1), or simply (x_1, y_1) since z_1 for all the points in the plane is zero. Translating the X and Y axes to a new location would result in new coordinates for P_1. Suppose we move the axes by a vector (u,v) so point O', located at (u,v), becomes the new origin. Figure 2.7b shows the translated coordinate plane. The relation between the new and the old coordinates is simply:

$$x_1' = x_1 - u$$

and

$$y_1' = y_1 - v \qquad\qquad (2.1)$$

Next, we consider rotation of the X and Y axes about the origin by Θ-angle measured counterclockwise from the positive X axis, as shown in Figure 2.8. It is sometimes convenient to represent a planar space in polar coordinates in which a point is represented by the distance from the origin to the point (r) and the angular orientation of the point with respect to the X

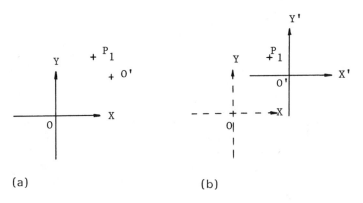

(a)   (b)

Figure 2.7 Translation of coordinate axes.

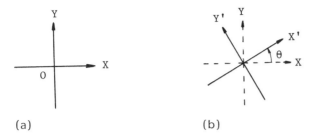

(a)   (b)

Figure 2.8   Rotation of coordinate axes.

axis (ϕ). The polar coordinates of P_1 can readily be related to its Cartesian coordinates as follows:

$$x_1 = r_1 \cdot \cos \phi_1$$

and

$$y_1 = r_1 \cdot \sin \phi_1 \qquad (2.2)$$

The relation between the new and the old coordinates of P_1 can be derived from its polar coordinates in the new and the old systems, namely

$$x_1' = r_1 \cdot \cos(\phi_1 - \Theta)$$

and

$$y_1' = r_1 \cdot \sin(\phi_1 - \Theta) \qquad (2.3)$$

which can be expanded and simplified to

$$x_1' = x_1 \cdot \cos \Theta + y_1 \cdot \sin \Theta$$

and

$$y_1' = -x_1 \cdot \sin \Theta + y_1 \cdot \cos \Theta \qquad (2.4)$$

Equations 2.4 can be put into a matrix form:

$$\begin{bmatrix} x_1' \\ y_1' \end{bmatrix} = \begin{bmatrix} \cos \Theta & \sin \Theta \\ -\sin \Theta & \cos \Theta \end{bmatrix} \cdot \begin{bmatrix} x_1 \\ y_1 \end{bmatrix} \qquad (2.5)$$

where a point is represented in the form of a column position
vector (from the origin to the point).

The elements of the square rotation matrix depend only on
the θ angle, thus a rotation matrix can be denoted as $R(\theta)$.
Note that boldfaced symbols are used to denote vectors and
matrices throughout the text. The advantages of expressing
geometric transformations and related operations in matrix forms
include flexibility in establishing definition space coordinate
systems and ready use of matrix algebra in combining various
geometric transformations.

Consider re-scaling the X and Y axes so a unit length on
an axis has a new dimension in physical units. Suppose the
X axis is re-scaled such that the old mark for x_1 units becomes
the mark for $x_1 \cdot S_x$ units and the Y axis is re-scaled by an
S_y factor, then the new coordinates for point P_1 become

$$x_1' = x_1 \cdot S_x$$

and

$$y_1' = y_1 \cdot S_y \qquad\qquad (2.6)$$

The scaling transformation can also be expressed in a matrix
form:

$$\begin{bmatrix} x_1' \\ y_1' \end{bmatrix} = \begin{bmatrix} S_x & 0 \\ 0 & S_y \end{bmatrix} \cdot \begin{bmatrix} x_1 \\ y_1 \end{bmatrix} \qquad\qquad (2.7)$$

The square scaling matrix is denoted by $S(S_x, S_y)$. Among
the three transformations just mentioned, only translations cannot be expressed as a matrix operation in its present form, thus
a composite transformation like a translation of the X and Y axes
to the X' and Y' axes followed by a rotation about 0' to the X"
and Y" axes cannot be expressed simply as the product of a
two by two rotation matrix on the left and a two by two translation matrix on the right. Notice that matrix multiplication is
not commutative, thus the order of multiplying matrices cannot
be arbitrarily reversed.

Homogeneous coordinate transformation is a tool of many uses
in computer graphics and computational geometry. One of its

uses is to allow a matrix formulation for coordinate translations. The utility of the theory of homogeneous coordinates can be realized without going over a rigorous analysis of the theory. We may regard the transformation as simply an extension of the two-element position vector representing a point in the X-Y plane to a three-element *homogeneous* position vector representing the same point, namely

$$\begin{bmatrix} x_1 \\ y_1 \end{bmatrix} \longrightarrow \begin{bmatrix} x_1^* \\ y_1^* \\ h \end{bmatrix} = h \cdot \begin{bmatrix} x_1 \\ y_1 \\ 1 \end{bmatrix} \tag{2.8}$$

The extra coordinate h is known as a *weight* which is homogeneously applied to the Cartesian components. Notice that a point in the X-Y plane can be represented by many forms in homogeneous coordinates, depending on the selected value of h. For now we only need the special form where h has a value of one, which results in an *extended* position vector with the first two elements being the X and Y coordinate values and the third being one.

The utility of the formation of extended position vectors is clearly shown in the following expression:

$$\begin{bmatrix} x_1' \\ y_1' \\ 1 \end{bmatrix} = \begin{bmatrix} 1 & 0 & -u \\ 0 & 1 & -v \\ 0 & 0 & 1 \end{bmatrix} \cdot \begin{bmatrix} x_1 \\ y_1 \\ 1 \end{bmatrix} \tag{2.9}$$

by which we have expressed a coordinate translation by (u,v) in a matrix form. The three by three matrix is called a translation matrix, $T(u,v)$.

The two by two rotation and scaling matrices derived earlier may be modified to account for the extended position vector, namely

$$R(\theta) = \begin{bmatrix} \cos\theta & \sin\theta & 0 \\ -\sin\theta & \cos\theta & 0 \\ 0 & 0 & 1 \end{bmatrix} \tag{2.10}$$

and

$$
S(S_x, S_y) = \begin{bmatrix} S_x & 0 & 0 \\ 0 & S_y & 0 \\ 0 & 0 & 1 \end{bmatrix}
\qquad (2.11)
$$

Now composite transformations can be achieved through multiplication of square matrices. Note that, in Equations 2.9–11, the linear transformation matrices have the same bottom row. This ensures that the product of any combinations of these transformation matrices will invariably have the same bottom row. Thus an extended position vector can only be transformed into another extended position vector under these linear transformations.

2.2.3 Coordinate Transformations in 3-D Space

The 2-D transformations presented in the preceding subsection may be regarded as special operations carried out in the X-Y plane of a 3-D Cartesian space. Thus the transformation matrices derived there can be extended to represent 3-D coordinate transformations. We first consider a translation of the X, Y and Z axes by a vector (u,v,w), as illustrated in Figure 2.9. The relationship between the new and the old coordinates of point P_1 is clearly

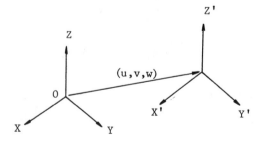

Figure 2.9　An isometric view of 3-D coordinate translation.

$$x_1' = x_1 - u$$

$$y_1' = y_1 - v \qquad (2.12)$$

and

$$z_1' = z_1 - w$$

which can be expressed in homogeneous coordinates in a matrix form as follows:

$$
\begin{bmatrix} x_1' \\ y_1' \\ z_1' \\ 1 \end{bmatrix}
=
\begin{bmatrix}
1 & 0 & 0 & -u \\
0 & 1 & 0 & -v \\
0 & 0 & 1 & -w \\
0 & 0 & 0 & 1
\end{bmatrix}
\cdot
\begin{bmatrix} x_1 \\ y_1 \\ z_1 \\ 1 \end{bmatrix}
\qquad (2.13)
$$

The translation matrix $T(u,v,w)$ is now a four by four matrix.

Since coordinate rotation about the origin in the X-Y plane is equivalent to coordinate rotation about the Z axis in the X-Y-Z space, the 2-D rotation matrix can be readily extended to a 3-D rotation-about-Z matrix:

$$
R_z(\Theta) =
\begin{bmatrix}
\cos\Theta & \sin\Theta & 0 & 0 \\
-\sin\Theta & \cos\Theta & 0 & 0 \\
0 & 0 & 1 & 1 \\
0 & 0 & 0 & 1
\end{bmatrix}
\qquad (2.14)
$$

Rotations about the X and Y axes can be derived by first formulating the 2-D rotation matrices in the Y-Z and the Z-X planes and then extending the 2-D rotations to the X-Y-Z space. The rotation-about-X matrix thus obtained is the following:

$$
R_x(\Theta) =
\begin{bmatrix}
1 & 0 & 0 & 0 \\
0 & \cos\Theta & \sin\Theta & 0 \\
0 & -\sin\Theta & \cos\Theta & 0 \\
0 & 0 & 0 & 1
\end{bmatrix}
\qquad (2.15)
$$

with the angle of rotation defined as positive when rotated from the positive Y axis to the positive Z axis. And the rotation-about-Y matrix is:

$$
R_y(\Theta) = \begin{bmatrix} \cos\Theta & 0 & -\sin\Theta & 0 \\ 0 & 1 & 0 & 0 \\ \sin\Theta & 0 & \cos\Theta & 0 \\ 0 & 0 & 0 & 1 \end{bmatrix}
\qquad (2.16)
$$

with the angle of rotation defined as positive when rotated from the positive Z axis to the positive X axis.

Extending the 2-D scaling matrix to 3-D should lead to:

$$
S(S_x, S_y, S_z) = \begin{bmatrix} S_x & 0 & 0 & 0 \\ 0 & S_y & 0 & 0 \\ 0 & 0 & S_z & 0 \\ 0 & 0 & 0 & 1 \end{bmatrix}
\qquad (2.17)
$$

With these 3-D coordinate transformation matrices, composite transformations can be expressed in the form of matrix multiplication. For example, the following matrix M:

$$
M = T(a,b,c) \cdot R_x(d) \cdot R_z(e) \qquad (2.18)
$$

can be used to describe a composite transformation consisting of a coordinate rotation about the Z axis by e-angle, followed by another coordinate rotation about the new X axis by d-angle, and then followed by a coordinate translation by (a,b,c). It is worth noting that every transformation matrix implies a particular orientation of the coordinate axes, thus in a composite transformation expression the parameters in a transformation matrix are always defined with respect to the axes implied by the immediate right hand side matrix. The order of multiplication corresponds to the order of transformation.

Following are listings of three FORTRAN modules for preparing a four by four matrix for each of the linear transformations, and a module for multiplying two four by four matrices.

```
*
*   Prepare matrix for translation by (U,V,W)
*
      SUBROUTINE TRANSL(U,V,W,T)
      REAL T(4,4)
      DO 20 I=1,4
        DO 10 J=1,4
          T(I,J)=0.0
10      CONTINUE
        T(I,I)=1.0
20    CONTINUE
      T(1,4)=-U
      T(2,4)=-V
      T(3,4)=-W
      RETURN
      END



*
*   Prepare matrix for rotation about X (N=1), about Y (N=2),
*   or about Z (N=3); THETA is the rotation angle in radians
*
      SUBROUTINE ROTATE(N,THETA,R)
      REAL R(4,4)
      DO 20 I=1,4
        DO 10 J=1,4
          R(I,J)=0.0
10      CONTINUE
20    CONTINUE
      R(N,N)=1.0
      R(4,4)=1.0
      N1=MOD(N,3)+1
      N2=MOD(N1,3)+1

      R(N1,N1)=COS(THETA)
      R(N1,N2)=SIN(THETA)
      R(N2,N2)=R(N1,N1)
      R(N2,N1)=-R(N1,N2)
      RETURN
      END



*
*   Prepare matrix for scaling by (SX, SY, SZ)
*
      SUBROUTINE SCALE(SX,SY,SZ,S)
      REAL S(4,4)
      DO 20 I=1,4
        DO 10 J=1,4
          S(I,J)=0.0
10      CONTINUE
20    CONTINUE
      S(1,1)=SX
      S(2,2)=SY
```

```
      S(3,3)=SZ
      S(4,4)=1.0
      RETURN
      END

*
*   Calculate  C = A * B
*
      SUBROUTINE MULT(A,B,C)
      REAL A(4,4),B(4,4),C(4,4)
      DO 30 I=1,4
        DO 20 J=1,4
          C(I,J)=0.0
          DO 10 K=1,4
            C(I,J)=C(I,J)+A(I,K)*B(K,J)
10        CONTINUE
20      CONTINUE
30    CONTINUE
      RETURN
      END
```

The foregoing matrices for *coordinate* transformations may be used to represent *object* transformations as well. The effect on the coordinate values of an object point from translating it by a translation vector in the existing coordinate space is equivalent to that from translating the coordinate axes by the reverse of the translation vector. The same reciprocal relationship exists in rotations. The new coordinates of an object point after being rotated about a principal axis are identical to those obtained by rotating the coordinate system about the same axis by the same angle in the opposite direction. Note that $R(-\theta) = R^T(\theta) = R^{-1}(\theta)$.

2.2.4 Definition Space versus Model Space

The relation between the coordinate values of a geometric entity defined in a definition space and those of the same entity measured in the model space can be represented by the product of a translation matrix and a rotation matrix. These two transformations are to retract the definition space axes back to the model space coordinate axes. In other words, the combined rotation and translation should put the XT, YT and ZT axes at exactly the position occupied by the model's X, Y and Z axes. Thus the coordinates of a geometric entity constructed in a definition space can be converted to those of the same entity with respect to the model space by pre-multiplying the definition coordinates first with the rotation matrix then with the translation matrix.

Any arbitrarily oriented XT, YT, ZT axes may be rotated to the X, Y, Z directions in at most three steps: first rotate about the XT axis until the YT axis is parallel to the X-Y plane; then rotate about the new YT axis until the ZT axis lies along the Z direction; finally rotate about the new ZT axis until the XT and YT axes lie along the X and Y directions. The order of rotations may vary, but it always takes at most three basic rotations. Since translations do not participate in the realigning of axes, the resultant matrix, product of possibly three rotation matrices, must be of the following form:

$$
\begin{bmatrix}
R_{11} & R_{12} & R_{13} & 0 \\
R_{21} & R_{22} & R_{23} & 0 \\
R_{31} & R_{32} & R_{33} & 0 \\
0 & 0 & 0 & 1
\end{bmatrix}
$$

The translation required to merge the realigned XT, YT, ZT axes with the X, Y, Z axes is a translation matrix $T(-T_1, -T_2, -T_3)$, where (T_1, T_2, T_3) is simply the coordinates of the origin of the current definition space with respect to the model space axes. The resultant transformation matrix from a definition space to the model space is thus

$$
\begin{bmatrix}
R_{11} & R_{12} & R_{13} & T_1 \\
R_{21} & R_{22} & R_{23} & T_2 \\
R_{31} & R_{32} & R_{33} & T_3 \\
0 & 0 & 0 & 1
\end{bmatrix}
$$

In addition to the relation between a definition space and the model space, useful information on the orientation of a definition space coordinate system within the model space can be readily acquired from the elements of the composite rotation matrix. By multiplying the composite rotation matrix with a unit vector along XT direction, namely

$$
\begin{bmatrix} R_{11} & R_{12} & R_{13} & 0 \\ R_{21} & R_{22} & R_{23} & 0 \\ R_{31} & R_{32} & R_{33} & 0 \\ 0 & 0 & 0 & 1 \end{bmatrix} \cdot \begin{bmatrix} 1 \\ 0 \\ 0 \\ 1 \end{bmatrix} = \begin{bmatrix} R_{11} \\ R_{21} \\ R_{31} \\ 1 \end{bmatrix} \tag{2.19}
$$

we obtain the orientation of the XT axis within the model space. Similarly the first three non-trivial elements in the second and third columns of the rotation matrix can be shown to indicate, respectively, directions of the YT and ZT axes within the model space.

2.2.5   IGES as a Benchmark for CAD Data Base

The last ten years have seen significant growth in applications of computer-aided design and computer-aided manufacturing (CAD/CAM). During the development of turnkey CAD/CAM systems, gaps in the communication of product definition data between various systems have become an inhibiting factor in the integration of existing CAD/CAM systems. The incompatibility in CAD/CAM data bases adopted by various systems does not allow product models to be directly transferred from one system to another. The CAD/CAM industry has recently found a remedy for the information clogging: the Initial Graphics Exchange Specification (IGES), a standard format specification for entities generated with computer-aided geometric modeling. IGES product geometry files can be exchanged between different CAD/CAM systems, provided that these systems support the IGES definition.

The IGES version 3.0 document was released in April, 1986 by the National Bureau of Standards. The standard establishes information structures for use in the digital representation and communication of product definition data, particularly for those product data generated by various CAD/CAM systems. The representation of product definition data in IGES is extensible and independent of the geometric modeling methods used.

The current version of IGES allows application-independent definition of 2-D and 3-D edge-vertex or wire-frame models and simple surface-based models. The geometric entities specified in IGES include points, lines, arcs, cubic splines and parametric surfaces. A number of non-geometric entities are also provided for dimensioning, drafting notation, text, and specific properties associated with individual or collections of data entities.

An IGES product file is composed of six major sections: flag (F), start (S), global conditions (G), directory entry (D), parameter data (P), and terminate (T). The flag section is optional and used to indicate the storage format of the file. The file is entity-based. Each entity is represented by two entries in the file: one in the fixed format D-section, with an index and other descriptive attributes about the entity stored in 20 eight-character long fields; the other entry is placed in the free format P-section which is pointed to by its counterpart in the D-section and provides the specific entity definition.

All geometric coordinates recorded are defined with respect to individual definition space coordinate systems established for individual entities, along with a pointer to a transformation matrix entity which consists of the rotation and translation matrices relating a definition space to the global model space (see Sec. 2.2.4).

The other three sections provide administrative information for the handling of the product model. The S-section provides a human-readable prologue to the file which may probably be a description of the part represented. The G-section contains statistical information of the product model such as product name or symbol, the particular software which generated the product, the scale and unit of the coordinates, date and time of file generation, minimum user-intended precision, approximate maximum coordinate value, and the name and organization of the author. The T-section records the end-of-file and provides an account of the number of entries in each section. Readers interested in the exact specification of IGES entities should directly consult the official IGES document available from the National Technical Information Service [1986].

A CAD system has to have a data base for recording the digital representation of geometric and non-geometric entities created. The data base to be defined during the construction of a micro-CAD system in the following chapters will be structured with IGES in mind. All CAD entities generated will be IGES compatible in the sense that they can be readily converted into IGES entities.

2.2.6   COMMON Blocks as CAD Data Base

To allow common access to designated groups of data among
various program modules, FORTRAN provides named COMMON
blocks. A number of COMMON blocks are introduced here before we close this chapter and embark on the designing of CAD
program modules.

The following data block will be used to record coordinates of
geometry points:

```
COMMON /POINTS/ NPTS,XT(300),YT(300),ZT(300),IPTDEF(300)
```

which defines a data area for three real and one integer arrays
each having 300 elements. The integer NPTS is to serve as a
counter for the number of existing point entities. The XT, YT
and ZT arrays allocate a block of static memory cells for storing
up to 300 geometry points defined in various definition space
coordinates. The data block is readily expandable when more
point entities need to be accommodated. But the size of such
static data blocks is always limited to what the available CPU
memory can accommodate.

Not all points are defined with respect to a single definition
space, however, they can be stored in the same arrays as long
as we keep a precise account of which belongs to what. The
IPTDEF array will be used to store integer identifiers indicating
particular definition spaces for each point entity. Point entities
will mostly be used as pivots or references of other CAD entities.

It should be noted that the finite-size data arrays declared
in /POINTS/ place only a physical limit on the number of point
entities that can be stored at run time. Logically, the system
can be programmed so that, when these data storages in the
memory are used up, the data elements can be swept to a secondary storage medium such as a floppy or hard disk. These
buffered data may be retrieved from the disk when required.
Such a data-buffering technique may be adopted to increase the
virtual size of the data base without breaking the limit of the
available memory space. However, this can only be achieved at
the expense of total system performance since managing the buffered data would be an extra burden on the CPU.

The next simplest form of a geometric entity is line segment.
A line segment is bounded by two end points. The following
COMMON block will be used to record line entities:

```
COMMON /LINES/ NLNS,IDPT1(400),IDPT2(400),LNFONT(400)
```

Notice that in stead of directly storing the coordinates of end points, the above declaration reserves cells for storing the identifiers which point to the individual end-point entities stored in the /POINTS/ block. This arrangement allows sharing of points between entities, thus avoiding unnecessary expense of memory cells for duplicate information. The integer array LNFONT is for storing the *font* or *type* number of line entities.

The transformation matrix entity, or the nine R_{ij} and three T_k elements as defined earlier, specifying the location and orientation of a definition space may be recorded in the following COMMON block:

```
COMMON /MATRIX/ NMAT,R(3,3,50),T(3,50),IDEF
```

Again there is an integer counter, NMAT, for the number of existing transformation matrix entities. The above COMMON block provides static storage for up to 50 different definition space coordinate systems. The integer variable IDEF is to record a pointer to the currently active definition space.

All the geometric entities to be created will be built upon the point entity. Since coordinates registered in /POINTS/ are defined with respect to entity-dependent definition spaces, caution must be exercised when performing calculations on these coordinate values. A secure approach is to convert all definition space coordinates into model space coordinates before intermixing the coordinate values.

In the next chapter, the three COMMON blocks /POINTS/, /LINES/, and /MATRIX/ will be incorporated in the design modules to keep track of all the point and line entities.

2.3   SUMMARY

This chapter introduces a 2-D graphics interface that is capable of supporting 3-D CAD applications on the IBM PC and PC/AT level machines, and a recently established system-independent data base format for geometric modeling. The various coordinate systems to be used in the design and display of computer generated geometric models are presented. A number of functional subroutine modules are designed to set the stage for the building of a 3-D CAD system.

Chapter 3

Design and Display of Planar Geometric Entities

With the stage set for a graphics-based interactive design environment, the rest of the book shall focus on the development of practical CAD program modules on the PC. The goal of this chapter and the next is to build a 3-D drafting environment within which polyhedral wire-frame models consisting of points, lines, and polygonal circles and arcs can be constructed. Modules for forming polygonal face entities from 3-D wire-frames will also be presented in the next chapter.

Additional modules will be implemented in Chapter 5 to mold such surfaced wire-frames into polyhedral solids. A more advanced solid-modeling approach, which combines primitive polyhedral solids into solids with complex forms through Boolean operations, will also be discussed in that chapter. The program modules will be presented in the form of building blocks and incorporated in a development micro-CAD system. The name CAD-PS shall be used to refer to this open system.

The first step in building a 3-D drafting facility within a model space is building a 2-D drafting facility within any selected plane in the model space. This chapter deals specifically with problems associated with the design and display of 2-D polygonal shapes in an XT-YT plane. Such 2-D shapes may later be extended to form 3-D wire-frames. The 2-D design options developed in this chapter are actually 3-D drafting tools because, as we shall investigate in Section 4.2, any plane in a model space can be transformed into an XT-YT plane.

The most discernible contributing factor to the success of a CAD system often turns out to be its user interface. At the top of such a user interface is a mechanism for presenting geometric data to the user via computer graphics. Interactive computer-aided design owes much of its strength to the versatility of computer graphics as an effective communication medium between man and machine. The orchestrated interplay of the user's creativity with generic computer-based design procedures is made possible by efficient graphics algorithms that are able to generate realistic images of inherently numerical product models on the graphic display.

We therefore begin this chapter with discussions on a user-oriented display system.

3.1 PROJECTION OF 3-D MODEL SPACE

On the graphic display of a PC, a 3-D model space can only be visualized in the form of 2-D projections. Images are collected on a *window* in a projection plane and mapped on to a *viewport* on a display screen. Here we have generalized the concept of a rectangular *window* in a 2-D drawing space being mapped on to a rectangular *viewport* on a display screen, described in Section 2.1.1, to a 3-D design space where a projection plane is used to collect images of 3-D drawings and a rectangular *window* is placed on the projection plane to define a finite regions for viewing.

The two projection schemes often used in engineering applications are parallel and perspective projections. Both schemes require a projection plane which can be any plane in the model space. A projectional image is obtained by projecting the 3-D product model with straight lines known as *projectors* on to a 2-D projection plane. The image of an object point in the model space is the intersection of the projector passing through the object point and the projection plane (see Fig. 3.1).

In parallel projections, all projectors are parallel to one another. When the direction of all projectors is perpendicular to the projection plane, the resultant parallel projection is called *orthographic* or *axonometric* projection. Since any projection plane placed along the projector direction would produce the same image, there is no need to specify a particular location for the projection plane. Only a projector or viewing direction need be specified for a particular projection.

Traditionally only orthographic projections are used by draftsmen in producing the top, front, side, and isometric views of a product model. Suppose we use the Z axis to designate the vertical direction in the model space, and the X-Y plane to

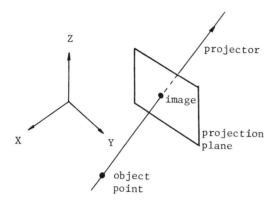

Figure 3.1   Projected image of an object point.

designate a horizontal base plane, then a top view of a product
model may be obtained by specifying the positive Z axis as the
viewing direction. In a top view, images of the unit vectors
along the X and Y axes would appear perpendicular to each other
and have their true lengths shown; while the image of the Z axis
would become a single point overlapping on the image of the
origin.

At other viewing orientations, images of the unit vectors along
the X, Y, and Z axes may appear skew and shorter than their
true lengths. When viewed from directions making identical angles with the X, Y, and Z axes, images of the three principal
unit vectors would appear to have the same length. Such symmetrical views are known as *isometric* views. Since there are
eight such viewing directions in the eight octants defined by the
X, Y, and Z axes, eight isometric views can be defined in a
model space.

In perspective projections, all projectors are originated from
a single point, the *eye* point. (A parallel projection is a special perspective projection with eye points in an *eye* plane located
at the infinity.) A projection plane for perspective imaging is
usually placed between the eye point and the product model.
Perspective projections result in images similar to those perceived
by human eyes. But perspective images are not suitable for
interactive design of 3-D wire-frames because important geometric
features like parallelism and perpendicularity are generally not
obvious in such images. However, they serve well in rendering

realistic images of complete solid models. Thus discussions on
the display of perspective images are deferred to Section 5.4
where we will have created complete solid models.

3.1.1   Display of 3-D Model Space

In order to provide a flexible viewing environment for orthographic projections, we first construct a right-handed viewing
space coordinate system, defined by the XV, YV and ZV axes,
which relates to the model space's X, Y and Z axes through a
viewing transformation matrix. The XV—YV plane will be used
as a projection plane with XV pointing to the right of the horizontal axis of the window and YV indicating the upward vertical axis of the window. Thus the ZV axis would lie along the
viewing direction. It follows that the viewing space can be regarded as a definition space for the projection plane and the
attached window. In fact, in CAD-PS the viewing space is
registered as a special definition space (see listings of the VIEW
and PROJTR modules below).
    The image of an object point (x,y,z) is displayed as a point
in the projectional XV-YV plane whose XV and YV coordinates
are results of multiplying the inverse viewing matrix with its
position vector in the model space. Note that its ZV coordinate
does not affect the projection, it only indicates the distance of
the object point from the projection plane.
    The viewing transformation matrix between the model space
and the viewing space can be determined by a viewing or projector direction. By using the orgin of the model space as a
reference point, the viewing system needs only another point in
order to specify a viewing direction. Figure 3.2 shows a viewing
space defined by a user-specified reference point E in the model
space, with OE pointing to the viewing direction. The transformation matrix can be obtained from the coordinates of E as
the product of rotation matrices which relates the XV, YV, ZV
axes to the X, Y, Z axes defining the model space.
    Consider again a model space with its Z axis in the vertical
direction. If we let a default viewing space's XV, YV, ZV axes
be identical to the model space's X, Y, Z axes, the default
viewing direction will lie along the positive Z axis and the viewing
transformation matrix will simply be an identity matrix. By
specifying a rectangular window in the XV-YV plane, we can
present a top view of the model space as shown in Figure 3.3
with the origin being located at the center of the window.

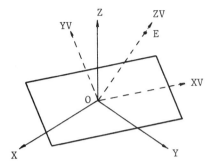

Figure 3.2   Orthographic viewing space for given E point.

In order to maintain a uniform scale along both XV and YV
directions for the displayed image, the aspect ratio (width
divided by height) of the window must be identical to that of
the viewport area on the display screen. The default size of
the viewport area as shown in Figure 3.3 is defined in the SETUP
module in the preceding chapter. The constancy of the aspect
ratio is maintained by module SCAWIN, listed below, which scales
up or down the active window.

With the aid of the GGI graphic routines, the image displayed
in the viewport, showing the part of the geometric model projected inside the window, may be scaled up or down by simply
changing the size of the window. The window can also be moved
around in the projection plane to show images projected in other
parts of the projection plane. These image manipulations are
known as, respectively, *zooming* and *panning*.

Various orthographic views of the model space are obtainable
through rotations of the model space about the default XV, YV,
ZV axes. Note that changes of images displayed on the screen
are direct results of *relative* movements between the model space
and the viewing space.

An orthographic projection that maintains all vertical directions
in the model space as vertical in the displayed image would present to the designer a properly oriented picture of the developing
product model. This can be achieved by a rotation of the model
space about the default ZV axis followed by another rotation of
the rotated model space about the default XV axis.

This maintain-the-vertical scheme leads to a singularity, however,
since in the default viewing space where XV, YV, ZV axes are
identical to the X, Y, Z axes, a vertical direction is projected

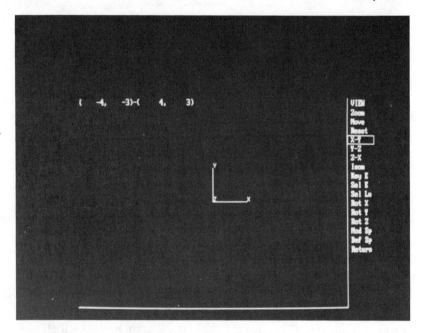

Figure 3.3   Default X-Y view of model space.

into a single point.   Fortunately this singularity can be treated
separately in a maintain-the-vertical algorithm (see subroutine
PROJTR below).   A closer look at Figure 3.2 is needed to derive
the required viewing transformation matrix.

Figure 3.4 shows the two stages of model space rotations
leading to the viewing space depicted in Figure 3.2.   The first
transformation is to rotate the model space about the ZV axis
until the reference point for the viewing direction E lies in the
YV-ZV plane, with XV axis pointing to the right of the desired
window when looking from E toward O.   This object rotation,
with respect to the viewing axes, is equivalent to a coordinate
rotation of the XV, YV, ZV system about the ZV axis in the
reversed direction, which is shown in Figure 3.4a to maintain
an orientation that is similar to Figure 3.2.

The second transformation is to further rotate the model space
about the XV axis until point E lies on the ZV axis, thus providing a maintain-the-vertical viewing orientation.   Again this is
shown in Figure 3.4b in the form of a coordinate rotation of the
XV, YV, ZV system about the XV axis.

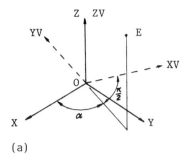

(a)

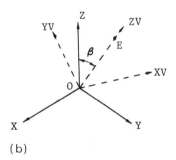

(b)

Figure 3.4   Construction of Viewing matrix (a) $R_z\left(\alpha + \frac{\pi}{2}\right)$; (b) $R_x(\beta)$.

The viewing matrix that would retract the viewing space axes to the model space axes is thus the inverse of the product of the above rotation matrices. An object point can be displayed by invoking GGI's GWPSET routine with its XV and YV coordinates as arguments. (See subroutines PROJTR and REDRAW given in Sec. 3.1.2.) It ought to be noted that the projected image of a 3-D straight line segment is the straight line segment joining the projections of its two end points. Figure 3.5 shows two different views of the model space axes.

3.1.2   The VIEW Module

The viewing environment discussed in the preceding subsection is implemented in a subprogram module called VIEW, a listing of which along with listings of relevant functional modules called

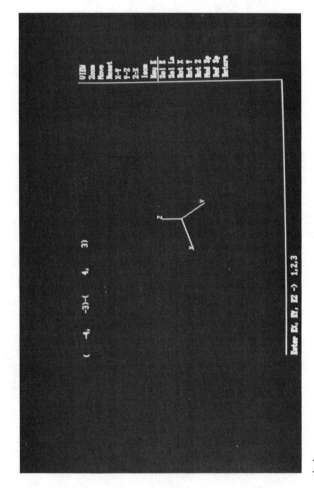

(a)

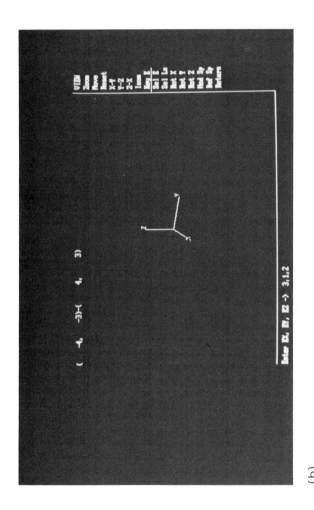

(b)

Figure 3.5   Two orthographic views of the model space axes.

by the VIEW module are given at the end of this subsection.   In
order to avoid unnecessary complications while developing algorithms for the interactive design of planar geometric entities, we
shall focus only on the XT-YT plane of the default definition
space, which is equivalent to the X-Y plane and the XV-YV plane
in the default viewing space.

The issue of how CAD software may be *menu-driven* seems to
be a timely topic now.   As we shall learn later, module VIEW is
one of four major building blocks to be discussed in this chapter.
In the beginning of a design session with CAD-PS, the system
will display a Main Menu in the menu area of the screen which
contains a number of user commands including "View," "Point,"
"Line," and others.   To initiate a particular design option, the
user is required to manipulate the locating Mouse Cursor into
the menu area and use the Menu Cursor box to enclose an active
menu item, then select the menu item by depressing any button
on the mouse.   This action causes the locating device routine
USELOC, discussed in Section 2.1.4, to return to the MAIN
module (see Sec. 3.5) an integer value indicating the order of
appearance of the selected item in the active menu list, hence
that particular module can be called into action.

There may be another list of secondary commands within the
selected module, in which case a new list of menu items may
replace the preceding menu and further commands can then be
called into action accordingly.   Secondary commands may spawn
tertiary commands, and on and on.   A CAD system may have
any number of layers of menu, at least in theory.   Thus the flow
of an interactive design session is a direct result of how the user
drives the system with selected *menu* items.

There are 17 items in the VIEW module's menu list, including
a heading, VIEW, used to indicate the current menu level.   The
first action taken within VIEW is to activate module DMENU to
remove the previous menu listing and display the active one.
An essential ingredient of an interactive design system is the
provision of a mechanism for acknowledging the user's actions.
The SMENU module, also listed below, does this by underlining
the selected menu item (see Fig. 3.5).   With the underlining
always performed in an XOR mode, a second call to SMENU will
remove the underline and restore any prior image.

The VIEW module allows the user to specify a viewing system
by supplying the model space coordinates of an E point.   The
origin of the model space and the E point define the viewing
direction of the desired orthographic projection.   The E point
can be any arbitrary point in the model space, or an existing

point selected with the Mouse Cursor, or determined from a selected line specifying the direction of OE. Other often used viewing systems, such as the X-Y, Y-Z, or Z-X plane views or isometric views, may be prepackaged so the user can select any of them with a simple click on the mouse. These user amenities have been incorporated in the VIEW module. Options for zooming and panning are also included.

Another useful feature in a CAD viewing environment that may be added to the VIEW module is an option for displaying rotated views of a product model about a selected axis of rotation. We will delineate a procedure for producing rotated views of 3-D models about the X, Y or Z axis in Section 4.1. As an illustration here, Figure 3.6 shows rotated views about the Y axis by 30° from the two views given in Figure 3.5. Note that in such a rotated view the maintain-the-vertical condition no longer applies.

The VIEW module is the communicator of the CAD-PS system. It presents the data base of designed product models in the form of line drawings as seen from whatever orientation the user specifies. Module VIEW may be attached to the MAIN module presented in Section 2.1.4 to provide an interface for visualizing the design space (also see Sec. 3.5). A number of supporting modules are needed to provide a simple user interface as well as ease of programming. Among them two supporting I/O modules, PROMPT and INPSTR, play important roles in the passage of information between the user and the CAD-PS system.

As mentioned earlier, the bottom part of the PC's screen is reserved for displaying system-supplied prompts. Module PROMPT is designed to first clean up the prompt area and then display a message specified by a text string. It also places the inherent text cursor at the end of the message, so user's keyboard input can be properly echoed back to the screen. As a counterpart of PROMPT, module INPSTR reads and echoes a string of characters from the keyboard and stores them in an internal file called BUFFER. Such a text input routine is not supported by the GGI graphics system. Module INPSTR, listed below, is written in Microsoft's MASM assembly language making use of two operating system level I/O service routines. Specific functions of other supporting modules are documented in the comment lines of the programs.

```
SUBROUTINE VIEW
CHARACTER*40 BUFFER
CHARACTER*8 MENUV(17)
COMMON /POINTS/ NPTS,XT(300),YT(300),ZT(300),IPTDEF(300)
COMMON /XVYVZV/ XV(300),YV(300),ZV(300)
```

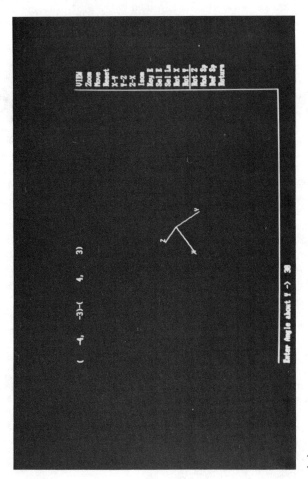

(a)

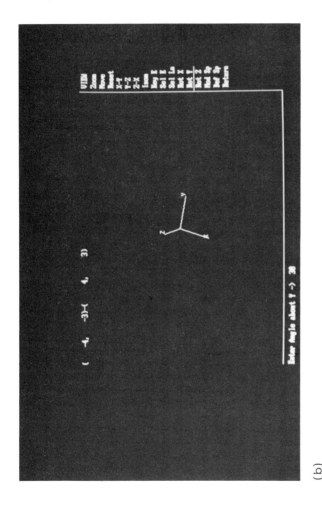

(b)

Figure 3.6   Rotated views from the views in Figure 3.5.

```
      COMMON /LINES/ NLNS,IDPT1(400),IDPT2(400),LNFONT(400)
      COMMON /WINDOW/ XW1,YW1,XW2,YW2
      COMMON /MATRIX/ NMAT,R(3,3,50),T(3,50),IDEF
      DATA MENUV/'\VIEW  \','\Zoom  \','\Move  \','\Reset \',
     &  '\X-Y   \','\Y-Z   \','\Z-X   \','\Isom  \','\Key E \',
     &  '\Sel E \','\Sel Ln\','\Rot X \','\Rot Y \','\Rot Z \',
     &  '\Mod Sp\','\Def Sp\','\Return\'/
      DATA IC2/2/
      RADDEG=3.141593/180.0
      ITEMV=17
10    CALL DMENU(ITEMV,MENUV)
30    CALL USELOC(X,Y,IBUTT)
      IF(IBUTT.EQ.1 .OR. IBUTT.GE.128) GOTO 30
      IF(IBUTT.GE.ITEMV) RETURN
      ITEM=IBUTT-1
      CALL SMENU(ITEM)
      GOTO(100,200,300,400,500,600,700,800,900,1000,1100,1200,
     &  1300,1400,1500),ITEM
*
*  Zoom in or out by changing the size of Window
*
100   CALL RESET
      CALL PROMPT('\Enter Zoom-In factor ->  \')
      CALL INPSTR(BUFFER)
      CALL PROMPT('\ \')
      IF(BUFFER .EQ. ' ') GOTO 9000
      READ(BUFFER,*,ERR=100) ZOOM
      CALL SCAWIN(ZOOM)
      GOTO 9000
*
*  Re-center Window with Cursor
*
200   CALL PROMPT('\Indicate New window center\')
      CALL USELOC(X,Y,IBUTT)
      CALL PROMPT('\ \')
      IF(IBUTT.NE.132) GOTO 9000
      CALL MOVWIN(X,Y)
      GOTO 9000
300   CALL SCAWIN(0.0)
      GOTO 9000
*
*  Set up X-Y View
*
400   CALL PROJTR(0.,0.,1.)
410   CALL VSPACE
      CALL REDRAW
      GOTO 9000
*
*  Set up Y-Z View
*
500   CALL PROJTR(1.,0.,0.)
      GOTO 410
*
*  Set up Z-X View
*
```

```
600   CALL PROJTR(0.,-1.,0.)
      GOTO 410
*
*   Set up Isometric View
*
700   CALL RESET
      CALL PROMPT('\Enter Octant (1-8) ->  \')
      CALL INPSTR(BUFFER)
      CALL PROMPT('\ \')
      IF(BUFFER .EQ. ' ') GOTO 9000
      READ(BUFFER,*,ERR=700) I
      EX=1.0
      EY=1.0
      EZ=1.0
      IF(I.GT.4) EZ=-1.0
      IF(MOD(I,4) .EQ. 2) EX=-1.0
      IF(MOD(I,4) .EQ. 3) THEN
        EX=-1.0
        EY=-1.0
      ENDIF
      IF(MOD(I,4) .EQ. 0) EY=-1.0
      CALL PROJTR(EX,EY,EZ)
      GOTO 410
*
*   Change Viewing Direction
*
800   CALL RESET
      CALL PROMPT('\Enter EX, EY, EZ ->  \')
      CALL INPSTR(BUFFER)
      CALL PROMPT('\ \')
      IF(BUFFER .EQ. ' ') GOTO 9000
      READ(BUFFER,*,ERR=800) EX,EY,EZ
810   CALL PROJTR(EX,EY,EZ)
      GOTO 410
*
*   Define new Viewing Direction by Selecting an E point
*
900   CALL PROMPT('\Select New E Point <L>\')
      CALL USELOC(X,Y,IBUTT)
      CALL PROMPT('\ \')
      IF(IBUTT.NE.132) GOTO 9000

*
*   Identification of Points is discussed in Sec. 3.2.2
*
      CALL SRCHPT(NPT,X,Y)
      IF(NPT.EQ.0) GOTO 900
      CALL MARKPT(NPT,IC2)
      CALL PROMPT('\Confirm Selected Point with <L>\')
      CALL USELOC(X,Y,IBUTT)
      CALL PROMPT('\ \')
      IF(IBUTT.NE.132) THEN
        CALL MARKPT(NPT,IC2)
        GOTO 900
      ENDIF
      CALL DTOM(XT(NPT),YT(NPT),ZT(NPT),EX,EY,EZ,IPTDEF(NPT))
      GOTO 810
```

```
*
*   Define new Viewing Direction by Selecting a refernece Line
*
1000 CALL PROMPT('\Select View Line <L>\')
     CALL USELOC(X,Y,IBUTT)
     CALL PROMPT('\ \')
     IF(IBUTT.NE.132) GOTO 9000
*
*   Identification of Lines is discussed in Sec. 3.3.3
*
     CALL SRCHLN(NLN,X,Y)
     IF(NLN.EQ.0) GOTO 1000
     CALL MARKLN(NLN,IC2)
     CALL PROMPT('\Confirm Selected Line with <L>\')
     CALL USELOC(X,Y,IBUTT)
     CALL PROMPT('\ \')
     IF(IBUTT.NE.132) THEN
       CALL MARKLN(NLN,IC2)
       GOTO 1000
     ENDIF
     CALL DTOM(XT(IDPT2(NLN)),YT(IDPT2(NLN)),ZT(IDPT2(NLN)),
    & XM2,YM2,ZM2,IPTDEF(IDPT2(NLN)))
     CALL DTOM(XT(IDPT1(NLN)),YT(IDPT1(NLN)),ZT(IDPT1(NLN)),
    & XM1,YM1,ZM1,IPTDEF(IDPT1(NLN)))
     EX=XM2-XM1
     EY=YM2-YM1
     EZ=ZM2-ZM1
     GOTO 810
*
*   Display Rotated View about the X axis (see Sec. 4.1)
*
1100 IAXIS=1
     CALL PROMPT('\Enter Angle about X -> \')
1110 CALL INPSTR(BUFFER)
     CALL PROMPT('\ \')
     IF(BUFFER .EQ. ' ') GOTO 9000
     READ(BUFFER,*,ERR=9010) THETA
*
*   Subroutine ROTXYZ is presented in Sec. 4.1
*
1120 CALL ROTXYZ(IAXIS,THETA*RADDEG)
     CALL VSPACE
     CALL REDRAW
     CALL PROMPT('\Continue Rotation with <L>\')
     CALL USELOC(X,Y,IBUTT)
     CALL PROMPT('\ \')
     IF(IBUTT.NE.132) GOTO 9000
     GOTO 1120
*
*   Display Rotated View about the Y axis
*
1200 IAXIS=2
     CALL PROMPT('\Enter Angle about Y -> \')
     GOTO 1110
*
*   Display Rotated View about the Z axis
```

```
*
1300 IAXIS=3
     CALL PROMPT('\Enter Angle about Z -> \')
     GOTO 1110
*
*  Display the X, Y, Z axes of the Model Space in XOR mode
*
1400 CALL SHOXYZ
     GOTO 9000
*
*  Display the XT, YT, ZT axes of current Definition Space
*  in XOR mode (see Sec. 4.2)
*
1500 CALL SHODEF
     GOTO 9000
9010 CALL RESET
9000 CALL SMENU(ITEM)
     GOTO 30
     END


*
*  Display Menu Items in the Menu Area
*
     SUBROUTINE DMENU(ITEM,MENU)
     CHARACTER*8 MENU(ITEM)
     CHARACTER*8 BLANK
     COMMON /DEVICE/ IDPC,IDSCRN,IDLOCA,IDPORT
     DATA IC3/3/,BLANK /'\        \'/
     CALL GCOLOR(IC3)
     ICHR=74
*
*  ICHR=34 for IBM PC's 320*200 screen mode
*
     IF(IDPC.EQ.1 .AND. (IDSCRN.EQ.4 .OR. IDSCRN.EQ.13)) ICHR=34
     DO 10 I=1,23
       CALL GTTCSR(I,ICHR)
       CALL GTTEXT(BLANK)
10   CONTINUE
     DO 20 I=1,ITEM
       CALL GTTCSR(I,ICHR)
       CALL GTTEXT(MENU(I))
20   CONTINUE
     RETURN
     END


*
*  Underline Menu Item selected with Mouse Cursor
*
     SUBROUTINE SMENU(ITEM)
     COMMON /SCRN/ RATIOX,RATIOY,IXD,IYD,IXMAX,MENUDY
     COMMON /WINDOW/ XW1,YW1,XW2,YW2
     CALL GNVIEW(0.,0.,1.,1.)
     CALL GXOR(1)
     LNMENU=(ITEM+1)*MENUDY-1
```

```
      CALL GDGCSR(IXD+3,LNMENU)
      CALL GDLINE(IXMAX-7,LNMENU)
      CALL GXOR(0)
      CALL GNVIEW(0.,RATIOY,RATIOX,1.0)
      RETURN
      END


*
*   Display Message in the Dialog Area (Bottom of Screen);
*   STR is a text string up to 40-character long and
*   bounded by the delimiter "\"
*
      SUBROUTINE PROMPT(STR)
      CHARACTER STR(1)
      CHARACTER*42 BLANK
      COMMON /DEVICE/ IDPC,IDSCRN,IDLOCA,IDPORT
      DATA BLANK/'\                                        \'/
      IF(STR(1).NE.'\') RETURN
      DO 10 I=2,42
        IF(STR(I).EQ.'\') GOTO 20
10    CONTINUE
      RETURN
20    CALL GTTCSR(24,1)
      CALL GTTEXT(BLANK)
*
*   One more BLANK for 80-column mode
*
      IF(IDSCRN.NE.4 .AND. IDSCRN.NE.13) CALL GTTEXT(BLANK)
      CALL GTTCSR(24,1)
      CALL GTTEXT(STR)
      RETURN
      END



*
*    Set Window size and location
*
      SUBROUTINE SCAWIN(ZOOMIN)
      COMMON /UNITS/ IUNIT
      COMMON /MSPACE/ XMIN,YMIN,ZMIN,XMAX,YMAX,ZMAX
      COMMON /WINDOW/ XW1,YW1,XW2,YW2
      COMMON /SCRN/ RATIOX,RATIOY,IXD,IYD,IXMAX,MENUDY
      DATA WINMIN/0.5/,WINMAX/20000.0/
      IF(ZOOMIN .EQ. 0.0) THEN
*
*   Default Window centered at Origin
*
        XCTR=0.0
        YCTR=0.0
*
*   Set default Window size to be identical to Viewport size
*   (see subroutine SETUP)
*
        WIDWIN=RATIOX*9.0
        HEIWIN=(1.0-RATIOY)*7.0
        IF(IUNIT.EQ.2) THEN
          WIDWIN=WIDWIN*25.4
          HEIWIN=HEIWIN*25.4
        ENDIF
```

```
      ELSE
100      IF(ZOOMIN .LT. 0.1) ZOOMIN=0.1
         IF(ZOOMIN .GT. 10.0) ZOOMIN=10.0
         XCTR=(XW1+XW2)/2.0
         YCTR=(YW1+YW2)/2.0
         WIDWIN=(XW2-XW1)/ZOOMIN
         HEIWIN=(YW2-YW1)/ZOOMIN
         IF(ABS(WIDWIN).LT.WINMIN) THEN
            ZOOMIN=(XW2-XW1)/WINMIN
            GOTO 100
         ENDIF
         IF(ABS(WIDWIN).GT.WINMAX) THEN
            ZOOMIN=(XW2-XW1)/WINMAX
            GOTO 100
         ENDIF
      ENDIF
      XW1=XCTR-WIDWIN/2.0
      YW1=YCTR-HEIWIN/2.0
      XW2=XW1+WIDWIN
      YW2=YW1+HEIWIN
*
*  Limit Window size to (XMIN,YMIN)-(XMAX,YMAX)
*
      IF(XW1.LT.XMIN) THEN
         XW1=XMIN
         XM2=XMIN+WIDWIN
      ELSE IF(XW2.GT.XMAX) THEN
         XW2=XMAX
         XW1=XMAX-WIDWIN
      ENDIF
      IF(YW1.LT.YMIN) THEN
         YW1=YMIN
         YW2=YMIN+HEIWIN
      ELSE IF(YW2.GT.YMAX) THEN
         YW2=YMAX
         YW1=YMAX-HEIWIN
      ENDIF
*
*  Reset Window and display model and Window dimension
*
      CALL GWINDO(XW1,YW1,XW2,YW2)
      CALL REDRAW
      RETURN
      END




*
*  Re-center Window
*
      SUBROUTINE MOVWIN(X,Y)
      COMMON /MSPACE/ XMIN,YMIN,ZMIN,XMAX,YMAX,ZMAX
      COMMON /WINDOW/ XW1,YW1,XW2,YW2
      DELX=XW2-XW1
      DELY=YW2-YW1
      XW1=X-DELX/2.0
```

```
      YW1=Y-DELY/2.0
      XW2=XW1+DELX
      YW2=YW1+DELY
      IF(XW1.LT.XMIN) THEN
        XW1=XMIN
        XW2=XMIN+DELX
      ELSE IF(XW2.GT.XMAX) THEN
        XW2=XMAX
        XW1=XMAX-DELX
      ENDIF
      IF(YW1.LT.YMIN) THEN
        YW1=YMIN
        YW2=YMIN+DELY
      ELSE IF(YW2.GT.YMAX) THEN
        YW2=YMAX
        YW1=YMAX-DELY
      ENDIF
      CALL GWINDO(XW1,YW1,XW2,YW2)
      CALL REDRAW
      RETURN
      END


*
*   Compute Viewing Matrix for Given E Point
*
      SUBROUTINE PROJTR(EX,EY,EZ)
      REAL MAT1(4,4),MAT2(4,4),MAT3(4,4)
      COMMON /MATRIX/ NMAT,R(3,3,50),T(3,50),IDEF
      DATA PI/3.141593/,EPS/1.0E-6/
      IF(ABS(EX) .LT. EPS .AND. ABS(EY) .LT. EPS) THEN
        ALPHA=0.0
        BETA=0.0
      ELSE
        ALPHA=ATAN2(EY,EX)+PI/2.0
        BETA=ATAN2(SQRT(EX*EX+EY*EY),EZ)
      ENDIF
      CALL ROTATE(3,ALPHA,MAT1)
      CALL ROTATE(1,BETA,MAT2)
      CALL MULT(MAT2,MAT1,MAT3)
      DO 20 I=1,3
        DO 10 J=1,3
          R(J,I,1)=MAT3(I,J)
10      CONTINUE
        T(I,1)=0.0
20    CONTINUE
      RETURN
      END


*
*   Compute New Viewing Coordinates of all Points
*
      SUBROUTINE VSPACE
      COMMON /POINTS/ NPTS,XT(300),YT(300),ZT(300),IPTDEF(300)
      COMMON /XVYVZV/ XV(300),YV(300),ZV(300)
      COMMON /MATRIX/ NMAT,R(3,3,50),T(3,50),IDEF
```

```
      COMMON /LINES/ NLNS,IDPT1(400),IDPT2(400),LNFONT(400)
      IF(NPTS .EQ. 0) RETURN
      DO 10 I=1,NPTS
        CALL DTOV(XT(I),YT(I),ZT(I),XV(I),YV(I),ZV(I),IPTDEF(I))
10    CONTINUE
      RETURN
      END


*
*   Redraw Model Entities
*
      SUBROUTINE REDRAW
      COMMON /SCRN/ RATIOX,RATIOY,IXD,IYD,IXMAX,MENUDY
      COMMON /POINTS/ NPTS,XT(300),YT(300),ZT(300),IPTDEF(300)
      COMMON /XVYVZV/ XV(300),YV(300),ZV(300)
      COMMON /LINES/ NLNS,IDPT1(400),IDPT2(400),LNFONT(400)
      COMMON /MATRIX/ NMAT,R(3,3,50),T(3,50),IDEF
      DATA IC0/0/,IC1/1/,IC3/3/
      CALL GDBOXF(0,0,IXD,IYD,IC0)
      CALL GCOLOR(IC3)
      DO 10 I=1,NPTS
        CALL GWPSET(XV(I),YV(I))
10    CONTINUE
      DO 20 I=1,NLNS
        IF(LNFONT(I).EQ.0) GOTO 20
        IF(LNFONT(I).EQ.99) CALL GLNTYP(3)
        CALL GWGCSR(XV(IDPT1(I)),YV(IDPT1(I)))
        CALL GWLINE(XV(IDPT2(I)),YV(IDPT2(I)))
        IF(LNFONT(I).EQ.99) CALL GLNTYP(1)
20    CONTINUE
      CALL WSIZE
      IF(IDEF.EQ.0) THEN
        CALL SHOXYZ
      ELSE
        CALL SHODEF
      ENDIF
      RETURN
      END


*
*   Display Window Coordinates at Top of Viewport
*   (The coordinates are rounded to integers to fit
*   the viewport of IBM PC's 320*200 screen mode)
*
      SUBROUTINE WSIZE
      COMMON /WINDOW/ XW1,YW1,XW2,YW2
50    FORMAT('+                                           ')
100   FORMAT('+(',I6,',',I6,')-(',I6,',',I6,')')
      CALL GTTCSR(1,1)
      WRITE(*,50)
      WRITE(*,100) NINT(XW1),NINT(YW1),NINT(XW2),NINT(YW2)
      RETURN
      END
```

```
*
*    Display Model Space Axes in XOR mode
*
      SUBROUTINE SHOXYZ
      CHARACTER*3 AX(3)
      REAL AXL(3,3),TEMP(3,3)
      COMMON /MATRIX/ NMAT,R(3,3,50),T(3,50),IDEF
      COMMON /WINDOW/ XW1,YW1,XW2,YW2
      DATA AX/'\X\','\Y\','\Z\'/,IC2/2/,IC3/3/
      CALL GCOLOR(IC2)
      CALL GXOR(1)
      REF=(XW2-XW1)/8.
      DO 20 I=1,3
        DO 10 J=1,3
          AXL(I,J)=0.
10      CONTINUE
        AXL(I,I)=REF
20    CONTINUE
      DO 50 I=1,3
        DO 40 J=1,3
          TEMP(I,J)=0.0
          DO 30 K=1,3
            TEMP(I,J)=TEMP(I,J)+R(K,I,1)*(AXL(K,J)-T(K,1))
30        CONTINUE
40      CONTINUE
50    CONTINUE
      DO 60 I=1,3
        CALL GWGCSR(0.,0.)
        CALL GWLINE(TEMP(1,I),TEMP(2,I))
        CALL GWTEXT(AX(I))
60    CONTINUE
      CALL GXOR(0)
      CALL GCOLOR(IC3)
      RETURN
      END



*
*    Transform Model Coordinates to Definition Coordinates
*
      SUBROUTINE MTOD(XM,YM,ZM,XD,YD,ZD,ID)
      COMMON /MATRIX/ NMAT,R(3,3,50),T(3,50),IDEF
      XD=XM
      YD=YM
      ZD=ZM
      IF(ID.NE.0) THEN
        XD=R(1,1,ID)*(XM-T(1,ID))+R(2,1,ID)*(YM-T(2,ID))
     &   +R(3,1,ID)*(ZM-T(3,ID))
        YD=R(1,2,ID)*(XM-T(1,ID))+R(2,2,ID)*(YM-T(2,ID))
     &   +R(3,2,ID)*(ZM-T(3,ID))
        ZD=R(1,3,ID)*(XM-T(1,ID))+R(2,3,ID)*(YM-T(2,ID))
     &   +R(3,3,ID)*(ZM-T(3,ID))
      ENDIF
      RETURN
      END
```

```
*
*   Transform Definition Coordinates to Model Coordinates
*
     SUBROUTINE DTOM(XD,YD,ZD,XM,YM,ZM,ID)
     COMMON /MATRIX/ NMAT,R(3,3,50),T(3,50),IDEF
     XM=XD
     YM=YD
     ZM=ZD
     IF(ID.NE.0) THEN
       XM=R(1,1,ID)*XD+R(1,2,ID)*YD+R(1,3,ID)*ZD+T(1,ID)
       YM=R(2,1,ID)*XD+R(2,2,ID)*YD+R(2,3,ID)*ZD+T(2,ID)
       ZM=R(3,1,ID)*XD+R(3,2,ID)*YD+R(3,3,ID)*ZD+T(3,ID)
     ENDIF
     RETURN
     END


*
*   Transform Model Coordinates to Viewing Coordinates
*   (Viewing Space is a special Definition Space with ID=1)
*
     SUBROUTINE MTOV(XM,YM,ZM,XV,YV,ZV,ID)
     CALL MTOD(XM,YM,ZM,XV,YV,ZV,1)
     RETURN
     END


*
*   Transform Viewing Coordinates to Model Coordinates
*
     SUBROUTINE VTOM(XV,YV,ZV,XM,YM,ZM,ID)
*
*   Current Viewing Matrix is stored in R(I,J,1) and T(K,1)
*   (ID is not used)
*
     CALL DTOM(XV,YV,ZV,XM,YM,ZM,1)
     RETURN
     END


*
*   Transform Viewing Coordinates to Definition Coordinates
*
     SUBROUTINE VTOD(XV,YV,ZV,XD,YD,ZD,ID)
     CALL VTOM(XV,YV,ZV,XTEMP,YTEMP,ZTEMP,ID)
     CALL MTOD(XTEMP,YTEMP,ZTEMP,XD,YD,ZD,ID)
     RETURN
     END


*
*   Transform Definition Coordinates to Viewing Coordinates
*
     SUBROUTINE DTOV(XD,YD,ZD,XV,YV,ZV,ID)
```

```
    CALL DTOM(XD,YD,ZD,XTEMP,YTEMP,ZTEMP,ID)
    CALL MTOV(XTEMP,YTEMP,ZTEMP,XV,YV,ZV,ID)
    RETURN
    END



*
*   Reset READ error caused by missing items
*
    SUBROUTINE RESET
    WRITE(*,100)
100 FORMAT('+')
    RETURN
    END



;
;   FORTRAN -> CALL INPSTR(BUFFER)
;   This Assembly Procedure reads an up to 40-character string
;   from keyboard and stores the string in BUFFER;  <CR> termi-
;   nates the string and <BS> deletes the preceding character
;
CODE_SEG  SEGMENT
          ASSUME    CS:CODE_SEG
          PUBLIC    INPSTR
;
INPSTR    PROC      FAR
          PUSH      BP                        ;Save BP
          MOV       BP,SP
          PUSH      ES                        ;Save ES
          LES       DI,DWORD PTR [BP+6]  ;Get Address of BUFFER
          PUSH      DI
          MOV       CX,28H                    ;Clear BUFFER
CLEAR:    MOV       BYTE PTR ES:[DI],20H ;by filling it with ' '
          INC       DI
          LOOP      CLEAR
          XOR       CX,CX                     ;Clear CX
COUNT:    INC       CX
          CMP       CX,28H                    ;CX > 40?
          JZ        EXIT
IDLE:     MOV       DL,0FFH                   ;Set up for Console Input
          MOV       AH,06H
          INT       21H
          TEST      AL,AL
          JZ        IDLE
          CMP       AL,08H          ;BS?
          JNZ       NOTBS
          DEC       CX
          CMP       CX,0H
          JZ        COUNT           ;Ignore First BS
          POP       DI              ;Decrement Pointer
          DEC       DI
          PUSH      DI
          MOV       BYTE PTR ES:[DI],20H   ;Delete entry in BUFFER
          MOV       DL,AL
          MOV       AH,06H
```

```
            INT      21H                    ;Echo BS
            MOV      DL,20H                 ;Send ' ' (SP) to delete
            MOV      AH,06H
            INT      21H
            MOV      DL,08H                 ;Send BS to revert Cursor
            MOV      AH,06H
            INT      21H
            JMP      COUNT
NOTBS:      CMP      AL,0DH                      ;'CR'?
            JZ       EXIT
            POP      DI
            MOV      BYTE PTR ES:[DI],AL
            INC      DI                     ;Next Character
            PUSH     DI
            MOV      DL,AL
            MOV      AH,06H                 ;Set up for Function 06H
            INT      21H                    ;MS-DOS Function Request (Echo)
            JMP      COUNT                  ;Read Next Character
EXIT:       POP      DI
            POP      ES                     ;Restore ES
            POP      BP                     ;Restore BP
            RET      4
INPSTR      ENDP
;
CODE_SEG    ENDS
            END
```

3.2 CREATION OF POINT ENTITIES

A point in a Cartesian definition space can be represented by a set of XT, YT, ZT coordinate values. Although the viewing system devised in the preceding section maintains a viewing matrix for the active view from which the viewing coordinates for any object point can be evaluated when needed, it is often worthwhile to maintain separately a set of active viewing coordinates for all the object points created so entities can be quickly identified or displayed in the viewport.

The following COMMON blocks may be declared to allocate a data area for both the definition and viewing coordinates of up to 300 geometry points:

```
COMMON /POINTS/ NPTS,XT(300),YT(300),ZT(300),IPTDEF(300)

COMMON /XVYVZV/ XV(300),YV(300),ZV(300)
```

The IPTDEF array is to store the integer identifier for the particular definition space associated with each object point. The definition space identifier for points defined directly within the default definition space, which is identical to the model space, has a value of zero.

3.2.1 The POINT Module

In the POINT subprogram module, as listed below along with
three secondary submodules, the user is provided with options to
create a point in the model or design space by either entering
its definition coordinates in the active definition space from the
keyboard or projecting the Mouse Cursor on to a selected XT-YT
plane.

In the current discussion of planar entities, the X-Y, XT-YT,
and XV-YV planes are all identical. However, the reader should
note that the POINT module presented here is directly applicable
to construction of general 3-D points in other user-specified definition spaces, since any plane in the model space can be converted
into an XT-YT plane (see Sec. 4.2). Module POINT may be incorporated in the MAIN program presented in Section 2.1.4 to provide
basic facilities for constructing point entities (see Sec. 3.5).

```
      SUBROUTINE POINT
      CHARACTER*40 BUFFER
      CHARACTER*8 MENUP(4)
      COMMON /POINTS/ NPTS,XT(300),YT(300),ZT(300),IPTDEF(300)
      COMMON /XVYVZV/ XV(300),YV(300),ZV(300)
      COMMON /MATRIX/ NMAT,R(3,3,50),T(3,50),IDEF
      COMMON /GRIDPT/ XTCTR,YTCTR,DELXT,DELYT,ZTGRID
      DATA MENUP/'\POINT \','\Ind Pt\','\Key Pt\','\Return\'/
      DATA IC0/0/,IC1/1/,IC2/2/,IC3/3/
      ITEMP=4
      CALL DMENU(ITEMP,MENUP)
30    CALL USELOC(X,Y,IBUTT)
      IF(IBUTT.EQ.1 .OR. IBUTT.GE.128) GOTO 30
      IF(IBUTT.GE.ITEMP) RETURN
      ITEM=IBUTT-1
      CALL SMENU(ITEM)
      GOTO(200,300),ITEM
*
*  Define Points by projecting Mouse-Cursor onto an XT-YT plane
*
200   IUNDO=0
205   CALL RESET
      CALL PROMPT('\Enter ZT-Plane -> \')
      CALL INPSTR(BUFFER)
      CALL PROMPT('\ \')
      IF(BUFFER.EQ.' ') GOTO 9000
      READ(BUFFER,*,ERR=205) ZTGRID
210   CALL PROMPT('\Ind Pt: <L>-Ind; <M>-End; <R>-Undo\')
      CALL USELOC(X,Y,IBUTT)
      CALL PROMPT('\ \')
      IF(IBUTT.EQ.130 .OR. IBUTT.LT.128) GOTO 9000
      IF(IBUTT.EQ.132) THEN
        CALL VPROJD(X,Y,XTEMP,YTEMP,IDEF,IERR)
        IF(IERR.NE.0) GOTO 210
        CALL ADDPT(XTEMP,YTEMP,ZTGRID,IDEF,IERR)
```

```
          IF(IERR.NE.0) GOTO 210
          CALL MARKPT(NPTS,IC3)
          IUNDO=1
      ELSE
          IF(IUNDO.EQ.0) GOTO 210
          CALL MARKPT(NPTS,IC3)
          NPTS=NPTS-1
          IUNDO=0
      ENDIF
      GOTO 210
*
*   Define Points by entering their (XT,YT,ZT) coordinates
*
300   CALL RESET
      CALL PROMPT('\Enter XT,YT,ZT -> \')
      CALL INPSTR(BUFFER)
      CALL PROMPT('\ \')
      IF(BUFFER.EQ.' ') GOTO 9000
      READ(BUFFER,*,ERR=300) XTEMP,YTEMP,ZTEMP
      CALL ADDPT(XTEMP,YTEMP,ZTEMP,IDEF,IERR)
      IF(IERR.NE.0) GOTO 300
      CALL MARKPT(NPTS,IC3)
      GOTO 300
9000  CALL SMENU(ITEM)
      GOTO 30
      END



*
*   Project a Point in XV-YV Plane onto Plane ZT=ZTGRID
*
      SUBROUTINE VPROJD(XVIEW,YVIEW,XDEF,YDEF,ID,IERR)
      COMMON /GRIDPT/ XTCTR,YTCTR,DELXT,DELYT,ZTGRID
      IERR=1
      CALL VTOD(XVIEW,YVIEW,0.,X1,Y1,Z1,ID)
      CALL VTOD(XVIEW,YVIEW,10.,X2,Y2,Z2,ID)
      IF(ABS(Z2-Z1).LT.1.0E-6) RETURN
      XDEF=(ZTGRID-Z1)*(X2-X1)/(Z2-Z1)+X1
      YDEF=(ZTGRID-Z1)*(Y2-Y1)/(Z2-Z1)+Y1
      IERR=0
      RETURN
      END



*
*   Add a Point Entity to Current Data Base
*
      SUBROUTINE ADDPT(X,Y,Z,ID,IERR)
      COMMON /POINTS/ NPTS,XT(300),YT(300),ZT(300),IPTDEF(300)
      COMMON /XVYVZV/ XV(300),YV(300),ZV(300)
      COMMON /MSPACE/ XMIN,YMIN,ZMIN,XMAX,YMAX,ZMAX
      DATA MAXPTS/300/
      IERR=1
      IF(NPTS.GE.MAXPTS) THEN
        CALL MESSAG('\Number of Points overflows!\')
        RETURN
```

```
      END
      CALL DTOM(X,Y,Z,XM,YM,ZM,ID)
      IF(XM.LT.XMIN .OR. XM.GT.XMAX .OR.
   &     YM.LT.YMIN .OR. YM.GT.YMAX .OR.
   &     ZM.LT.ZMIN .OR. ZM.GT.ZMAX) THEN
         CALL MESSAG('\Point Not in Design Space!\')
         RETURN
      ENDIF
      IERR=0
      NPTS=NPTS+1
      IPTDEF(NPTS)=ID
      XT(NPTS)=X
      YT(NPTS)=Y
      ZT(NPTS)=Z
      CALL DTOV(X,Y,Z,XV(NPTS),YV(NPTS),ZV(NPTS),ID)
      RETURN
      END


*
*   Display text in the Message Area (Top of Viewport)
*
      SUBROUTINE MESSAG(STR)
      CHARACTER STR(1)
      CHARACTER*35 BLANK
      DATA BLANK/'\                                 \'/
      IF(STR(1).NE.'\') RETURN
      DO 10 I=2,35
         IF(STR(I).EQ.'\') GOTO 20
10    CONTINUE
      RETURN
20    CALL GTTCSR(1,1)
      CALL GTTEXT(BLANK)
      CALL GTTCSR(1,1)
      CALL GTTEXT(STR)
      RETURN
      END
```

3.2.2 Identification of Point Entities

In an interactive computer-aided design session, the user is
frequently prompted to identify existing points or lines from the
graphic display using a tracking symbol like the Mouse Cursor.
The SRCHPT submodule listed below is to search, in a small
neighborhood around the cursor location, for the point entity
that is nearest to the cursor location. Also listed below is a
submodule whose function is to highlight an existing point entity
by drawing a small box around it. Both these submodules were
used in the VIEW module to provide the user with an option to
define a specific viewing direction by selecting an E point.

```
*
*   Search for the Nearest Point in the Window
*
      SUBROUTINE SRCHPT(N,X,Y)
      COMMON /POINTS/ NPTS,XT(300),YT(300),ZT(300),IPTDEF(300)
      COMMON /XVYVZV/ XV(300),YV(300),ZV(300)
      COMMON /WINDOW/ XW1,YW1,XW2,YW2
      N=0
      IF(NPTS.EQ.0) RETURN
      DST1=(XW2-XW1)/20
      DO 100 I=1,NPTS
        IF(XV(I).LT.XW1 .OR. XV(I).GT.XW2) GOTO 100
        IF(YV(I).LT.YW1 .OR. YV(I).GT.YW2) GOTO 100
        DST2=(X-XV(I))**2+(Y-YV(I))**2
        IF(DST2.GT.DST1) GOTO 100
        DST1=DST2
        N=I
100   CONTINUE
      RETURN
      END


*
*   Mark a Point Entity on the Screen
*
      SUBROUTINE MARKPT(N,IC)
      COMMON /POINTS/ NPTS,XT(300),YT(300),ZT(300),IPTDEF(300)
      COMMON /XVYVZV/ XV(300),YV(300),ZV(300)
      COMMON /WINDOW/ XW1,YW1,XW2,YW2
      DATA IC3/3/
50    FORMAT('+                                        ')
100   FORMAT('+',I3,'->',F8.1,',',F8.1,',',F8.1)
*
*   The Point is highlighted in XOR mode when IC > 0
*
      ICT=IC
      IF(IC.LT.0) ICT=-IC
      CALL GCOLOR(ICT)
      IF(IC.GT.0) CALL GXOR(1)
      DEL=(XW2-XW1)/200.0
      CALL GWBOX(XV(N)-DEL,YV(N)-DEL,XV(N)+DEL,YV(N)+DEL)
      CALL GCOLOR(IC3)
      IF(IC.GT.0) THEN
        CALL GXOR(0)
        CALL GTTCSR(1,1)
        WRITE(*,50)
        WRITE(*,100) N,XT(N),YT(N),ZT(N)
      ENDIF
      RETURN
      END
```

3.2.3   Other Point Definitions

The POINT module described earlier provides only a minimum set
of design options for adding point entities to the model data base.

Points can also be defined as intersections between lines (see Sec. 3.3.6), as results of translation or rotation of existing points, as projections of existing points on to selected planes, or as divisions on selected line segments.

Knowing how basic design modules can be incorporated in CAD-PS, as illustrated in the first two sections of the chapter, the reader is free to add these and other point-defining facilities to the POINT module.

3.3 CREATION OF LINE ENTITIES

An infinite line can be defined in a plane by a point (P_1) and a slope (m) or by two points (P_1 and P_2). It can be expressed in the form of an explicit equation, an implicit equation, or a set of parametric equations. In general, a finite line segment in a 3-D space can be represented by its two end points. In CAD-PS, all line entities will be finite and represented by two end points, which are represented in the form of three coordinate values associated with specific definition spaces. A line can be defined between two point entities with different definition space identifiers, since their coordinates in the global model space can be readily obtained through their definition space transformation matrices as described in Section 2.2.4.

This section discusses the implementation of several interactive editing utilities for creating line entities in an XT-YT plane. Generalization of these design tools to 3-D applications will also be delineated.

3.3.1 Representation of Lines in an XT-YT Plane

We shall assume the ZT coordinates of all point and line entities discussed in this section to be zero, unless otherwise specified. An explicit equation for the line passing through P_1 with a slope m, m = tan (α) with α being the angle between the line and the positive XT axis, may be written as:

$$y = m \cdot (x_2 - x_1) + y_1 \tag{3.1}$$

with (x, y) denoting all points on the line. This simple form is rather limited because it cannot represent lines that are perpendicular to the XT axis for which the slope value approaches infinity. The form is called *explicit* because the YT-value of any point on the line is expressed as an explicit function of its XT-value.

A line passing through two points P_1 and P_2 can be represented by the following implicit form:

$$(y - y_1) \cdot (x_2 - x_1) - (x - x_1) \cdot (y_2 - y_1) = 0 \qquad (3.2)$$

where a perpendicular line to the XT axis can be expressed as

$$x = x_1 \qquad (3.3)$$

Another way of describing a line in the XT-YT plane is to define both XT and YT coordinates of all the points on the line as independent functions of a common parameter. Thus one can depict any part of the line by tracing out points corresponding to a certain range of the parameter value.

An example of a set of two parametric equations for the line passing through two given points takes the following form:

$$x = (1 - t) \cdot x_1 + t \cdot x_2$$
$$y = (1 - t) \cdot y_1 + t \cdot y_2 \qquad (3.4)$$

where t is a real value parameter and $- \infty < t < + \infty$. The physical implication of the parameter t in its present form may be made clear by reducing the two parametric equations into:

$$t = (x - x_1)/(x_2 - x_1) = (y - y_1)/(y_2 - y_1) \qquad (3.5)$$

which states that any t value represents the ratio of the distance between its geometry point on the line, (x, y), and the beginning point P_1 and that between points P_1 and P_2. Therefore the point set described by $- \infty < t < + \infty$ is equivalent to the whole infinite line, while the point set described by $0 \leqslant t \leqslant 1$ is equivalent to the finite line segment $P_1 P_2$.

Equations 3.4 may be expressed in a vector form as:

$$r(t) = b_1 + t \cdot d_1 \qquad (3.6)$$

where r represents the position vector, from the origin of the coordinate axes to the geometry point, specified by the parameter value t; b_1 is the base position vector (x_1, y_1); and d_1 the directional vector $(x_2 - x_1, y_2 - y_1)$.

The parametric form of lines is particularly useful in representing 3-D lines whose end points may not be in the same XT-
YT plane. Instead of describing a line segment as a particular
part of the intersection of two non-parallel planes in the 3-D
design space, we may describe it as the line segment bounded
by two specific points. The vector equation for such a line
entity is identical to that of a line in the XT-YT plane, but
the base vector b_1 is now (x_1, y_1, z_1) and the directional vector d_1 is now $(x_2 - x_1, y_2 - y_1, z_2 - z_1)$.

The length of the directional vector may be denoted by d_1,
and

$$d_1^2 = (x_2 - x_1)^2 + (y_2 - y_1)^2 + (z_2 - z_1)^2 \qquad (3.7)$$

A vector is a unit vector if it is one unit long. The three
Cartesian components of vector d_1 can be used to compute the
directional angles the vector makes with the positive X, Y and
Z axes. Denoting these angles as Θ_x, Θ_y and Θ_z, we have

$$\cos \Theta_x = (x_2 - x_1) / d_1$$

$$\cos \Theta_y = (y_2 - y_1) / d_1$$

and

$$\cos \Theta_z = (z_2 - z_1) / d_1 \qquad (3.8)$$

The above cosine values are known as the directional cosines of
line $r(t)$.

In CAD-PS, line entities are represented by two end-point
identifiers which point to the memory locations storing the
coordinates of each end point. The COMMON block /LINES/
described in Section 2.2.6 is used to register up to 400 line
segments. We shall utilize only two types of line entities in
developing CAD-PS. The type or *font* number of regular solid
lines is one. The other type of line entities will be needed when
we discuss the formation of polygonal faces in Chapter 4.

3.3.2 The LINE Module

Although only lines with finite lengths are of practical importance,
very often specific lengths of some constructing lines cannot be
pre-determined during the design process. Most CAD systems

provide options to create so-called *infinite* lines which are in
fact long lines having system-provided lengths. In the CAD-PS
system, *long* lines can be created as *angled, parallel*, or *perpendicular* lines with respect to selected reference lines. The length
of a long line is always assigned to be about five times the size
of the active window defined in the XV-YV plane.

The auxiliary modules for creating connected line segments
(module PTPT), long horizontal lines in XT direction (module
HORLN), and long vertical lines in YT direction (module VERLN),
are coordinated by a major module, LINE, which maintains a
second-layer design menu of 19 items. The LINE module itself
is incorporated in the CAD-PS system to provide basic line-
editing facilities (see Sec. 3.5).

Other design options will be discussed in other subsections
as indicated in the LINE module given below. Since lines can
be constructed between points defined in various definition
spaces, calculations requiring coordinates of points are always
performed on converted coordinates measured in the same space.
Listings of modules LINE, PTPT, HORLN, VERLN, MKLN1, and
ADDLN are given as follows.

```
      SUBROUTINE LINE
      CHARACTER*8 MENUL(19)
      DATA MENUL/'\LINE  \','\Grid  \','\Pt-Pt \','\Chain \',
     & '\Hor Ln\','\Ver Ln\','\Ang Ln\','\// Ln \','\_|_ Ln\',
     & '\Corner\','\Round \','\Trim  \','\Circle\','\Arc   \',
     & '\Break \','\Delete\','\Redraw\','\Switch\','\Return\'/
      ITEML=19
      CALL DMENU(ITEML,MENUL)
30    CALL USELOC(X,Y,IBUTT)
      IF(IBUTT.EQ.1 .OR. IBUTT.GE.128) GOTO 30
      IF(IBUTT.GE.ITEML) RETURN
      ITEM=IBUTT-1
      CALL SMENU(ITEM)
      GOTO(100,200,300,400,500,600,700,800,900,1000,1100,
     & 1200,1300,1400,1500,1600,1700),ITEM
*
*     Define Lines from a Grid of template points
*     (see Sec. 3.4)
*
100   CALL GRID(2)
      GOTO 9000
*
*     Define Line segments between point pairs
*
200   CALL PTPT(1)
      GOTO 9000
*
*     Define chained Line segments
*
```

```
300   CALL PTPT(2)
      GOTO 9000
*
*   Define Long horizontal Lines (in XT-direction)
*
400   CALL HORLN
      GOTO 9000
*
*   Define Long vertical Lines (in YT-direction)
*
500   CALL VERLN
      GOTO 9000
*
*   Define Long angled Lines in an XT-YT plane
*   (see Sec. 3.3.4)
*
600   CALL ANGLN
      GOTO 9000
*
*   Define parallel Lines to selected reference Lines
*   (see Sec. 3.3.4)
*
700   CALL PARALN
      GOTO 9000
*
*   Define perpendicular Lines to selected reference Lines
*   (see Sec. 3.3.4)
*
800   CALL PERPLN
      GOTO 9000
*
*   Cornering (see Sec. 3.3.6)
*
900   CALL CORNER(2)
      GOTO 9000
*
*   Rounding (see Sec. 3.3.7)
*
1000 CALL ROUND
      GOTO 9000
*
*   Trimming (see Sec. 3.3.6)
*
1100 CALL CORNER(1)
      GOTO 9000
*
*   Create polygonal circles (see Sec. 3.3.7)
*
1200 CALL ARC(1)
      GOTO 9000
*
*   Create polygonal arcs (see Sec. 3.3.7)
*
1300 CALL ARC(2)
      GOTO 9000
*
```

```
*   Break a Line into two parts (see Sec. 3.3.6)
*
1400 CALL BRKLN
     GOTO 9000
*
*   Delele Line entities (see Sec. 3.3.5)
*
1500 CALL DELELN
     GOTO 9000
*
*   Redraw all entities
*
1600 CALL REDRAW
     GOTO 9000
*
*   Define new Definition Space (see Sec. 4.2)
*
1700 CALL SWITCH
9000 CALL SMENU(ITEM)
     GOTO 30
     END

*
*   Define line segments from existing points
*   (MODE=1 -> Point Pairs; MODE=2 -> Chained Points)
*
     SUBROUTINE PTPT(MODE)
     COMMON /POINTS/ NPTS,XT(300),YT(300),ZT(300),IPTDEF(300)
     COMMON /XVYVZV/ XV(300),YV(300),ZV(300)
     COMMON /LINES/ NLNS,IDPT1(400),IDPT2(400),LNFONT(400)
     DATA IC1/1/,IC3/3/
     NPT1=0
     IUNDO=0
100  CALL PROMPT('\Pt: <L>-Sel; <M>-End; <R>-Undo\')
     CALL USELOC(X,Y,IBUTT)
     CALL PROMPT('\ \')
     IF(IBUTT.EQ.130 .OR. IBUTT.LT.128) RETURN
     IF(IBUTT.EQ.132) THEN
       CALL SRCHPT(NPT2,X,Y)
       IF(NPT2.EQ.0) GOTO 100
       IF(NPT1.EQ.0) THEN
         NPT1=NPT2
         CALL MARKPT(NPT1,IC1)
         IUNDO=0
         GOTO 100
       ENDIF
       CALL MARKPT(NPT2,IC1)
       CALL ADDLN(NPT1,NPT2,1,IERR)
       IF(IERR.NE.0) GOTO 100
       CALL MARKLN(NLNS,IC3)
       NPTEMP=NPT1
       IF(MODE.EQ.1) THEN
         NPT1=0
       ELSE IF(MODE.EQ.2) THEN
         NPT1=NPT2
       ENDIF
       IUNDO=1
```

```
*
*    Undo the Connecting Function
*
      ELSE
        IF(IUNDO.EQ.0) GOTO 100
        CALL MARKLN(NLNS,IC3)
        NLNS=NLNS-1
        NPT1=NPTEMP
        IUNDO=0
      ENDIF
      GOTO 100
      END


*
*    Construct Long horizontal lines in XT-direction
*
      SUBROUTINE HORLN
      CHARACTER*40 BUFFER
      COMMON /POINTS/ NPTS,XT(300),YT(300),ZT(300),IPTDEF(300)
      COMMON /XVYVZV/ XV(300),YV(300),ZV(300)
      COMMON /LINES/ NLNS,IDPT1(400),IDPT2(400),LNFONT(400)
      COMMON /GRIDPT/ XTCTR,YTCTR,DELXT,DELYT,ZTGRID
      COMMON /MATRIX/ NMAT,R(3,3,50),T(3,50),IDEF
      DATA IC1/1/,IC3/3/
100   CALL PROMPT('\<L>-Sel Pt; <M>-End; <R>-Key YT\')
      CALL USELOC(X,Y,IBUTT)
      CALL PROMPT('\ \')
      IF(IBUTT.EQ.130 .OR. IBUTT.LT.128) RETURN
      IF(IBUTT.EQ.132) THEN
        CALL SRCHPT(NPT1,X,Y)
        IF(NPT1.EQ.0) GOTO 100
        CALL MARKPT(NPT1,IC1)
        CALL DTOM(XT(NPT1),YT(NPT1),ZT(NPT1),XM1,YM1,ZM1,
     &       IPTDEF(NPT1))
        CALL MTOD(XM1,YM1,ZM1,XT1,YT1,ZT1,IDEF)
        ZTGRID=ZT1
        CALL MKLN1(XT1,YT1,0.0,IERR)
        IF(IERR.NE.0) GOTO 100
        CALL MARKLN(NLNS,IC3)
      ELSE
50      CALL RESET
        CALL PROMPT('\Enter ZT-Plane -> \')
        CALL INPSTR(BUFFER)
        CALL PROMPT('\ \')
        IF(BUFFER.EQ.' ') GOTO 100
        READ(BUFFER,*,ERR=50) ZTGRID
110     CALL RESET
        CALL PROMPT('\Enter YT -> \')
        CALL INPSTR(BUFFER)
        CALL PROMPT('\ \')
        IF(BUFFER.EQ.' ') GOTO 100
        READ(BUFFER,*,ERR=110) YTEMP
        CALL MKLN1(0.,YTEMP,0.0,IERR)
        IF(IERR.NE.0) GOTO 110
```

```
        CALL MARKLN(NLNS,IC3)
        GOTO 110
      ENDIF
      GOTO 100
      END

*
*   Construct Long vertical lines in YT-direction
*
      SUBROUTINE VERLN
      CHARACTER*40 BUFFER
      COMMON /POINTS/ NPTS,XT(300),YT(300),ZT(300),IPTDEF(300)
      COMMON /XVYVZV/ XV(300),YV(300),ZV(300)
      COMMON /LINES/ NLNS,IDPT1(400),IDPT2(400),LNFONT(400)
      COMMON /GRIDPT/ XTCTR,YTCTR,DELXT,DELYT,ZTGRID
      COMMON /MATRIX/ NMAT,R(3,3,50),T(3,50),IDEF
      DATA IC1/1/,IC3/3/,PI/3.141593/
400   CALL PROMPT('\<L>-Sel Pt; <M>-End; <R>-Key XT\')
      CALL USELOC(X,Y,IBUTT)
      CALL PROMPT('\ \')
      IF(IBUTT.EQ.130 .OR. IBUTT.LT.128) RETURN
      IF(IBUTT.EQ.132) THEN
        CALL SRCHPT(NPT1,X,Y)
        IF(NPT1.EQ.0) GOTO 400
        CALL MARKPT(NPT1,IC1)
        CALL DTOM(XT(NPT1),YT(NPT1),ZT(NPT1),XM1,YM1,ZM1,
     &       IPTDEF(NPT1))
        CALL MTOD(XM1,YM1,ZM1,XT1,YT1,ZT1,IDEF)
        ZTGRID=ZT1
        CALL MKLN1(XT1,YT1,PI/2.0,IERR)
        IF(IERR.NE.0) GOTO 400
        CALL MARKLN(NLNS,IC3)
      ELSE
50      CALL RESET
        CALL PROMPT('\Enter ZT-Plane ->  \')
        CALL INPSTR(BUFFER)
        CALL PROMPT('\ \')
        IF(BUFFER.EQ.' ') GOTO 400
        READ(BUFFER,*,ERR=50) ZTGRID
410     CALL RESET
        CALL PROMPT('\Enter XT -> \')
        CALL INPSTR(BUFFER)
        CALL PROMPT('\ \')
        IF(BUFFER.EQ.' ') GOTO 400
        READ(BUFFER,*,ERR=410) XTEMP
        CALL MKLN1(XTEMP,0.,PI/2.0,IERR)
        IF(IERR.NE.0) GOTO 410
        CALL MARKLN(NLNS,IC3)
        GOTO 410
      ENDIF
      GOTO 400
      END


*
*   Create a Long line with given (XT,YT) and ANGLE
*
```

```
      SUBROUTINE MKLN1(X,Y,ANGLE,IERR)
      COMMON /POINTS/ NPTS,XT(300),YT(300),ZT(300),IPTDEF(300)
      COMMON /XVYVZV/ XV(300),YV(300),ZV(300)
      COMMON /LINES/ NLNS,IDPT1(400),IDPT2(400),LNFONT(400)
      COMMON /MATRIX/ NMAT,R(3,3,50),T(3,50),IDEF
      COMMON /WINDOW/ XW1,YW1,XW2,YW2
      COMMON /GRIDPT/ XTCTR,YTCTR,DELXT,DELYT,ZTGRID
      DATA PI/3.141593/,EPS/0.018/
*
*  Length of Long line equals five times the size of Window
*
      IERR=1
      IF(ANGLE.LT.(-PI*2.0) .OR. ANGLE.GT.(PI*2.0)) RETURN
      IERR=0
      XLEFT=XW1-2.0*(XW2-XW1)
      XRIGHT=XW2+2.0*(XW2-XW1)
      YLOW=YW1-2.0*(YW2-YW1)
      YHIGH=YW2+2.0*(YW2-YW1)
      IF(ABS(ABS(ANGLE)-PI/2.0).LT.EPS .OR.
     &     ABS(ABS(ANGLE)-PI/2.0*3.0).LT.EPS) THEN
        X1=X
        Y1=YLOW
        X2=X
        Y2=YHIGH
      ELSE
*
*  Left end of Long line
*
        SLOPE=TAN(ANGLE)
        X1=XLEFT
        Y1=Y+SLOPE*(X1-X)
        IF(Y1.LT.YLOW) THEN
          Y1=YLOW
          X1=X+(Y1-Y)/SLOPE
        ENDIF
*
*  Right end of Long line
*
        X2=XRIGHT
        Y2=Y+SLOPE*(X2-X)
        IF(Y2.GT.YHIGH) THEN
          Y2=YHIGH
          X2=X+(Y2-Y)/SLOPE
        ENDIF
      ENDIF
      CALL ADDPT(X1,Y1,ZTGRID,IDEF,IERR)
      IF(IERR.NE.0) RETURN
      CALL ADDPT(X2,Y2,ZTGRID,IDEF,IERR)
      IF(IERR.NE.0) RETURN
      CALL ADDLN(NPTS-1,NPTS,1,IERR)
      IF(IERR.NE.0) RETURN
      RETURN
      END


*
*  Add a Line Entity to Current Data Base
*
```

```
      SUBROUTINE ADDLN(I1,I2,IFONT,IERR)
      COMMON /LINES/ NLNS,IDPT1(400),IDPT2(400),LNFONT(400)
      DATA MAXLNS/400/
      IERR=1
      IF(NLNS.GE.MAXLNS) THEN
        CALL MESSAG('\Number of Lines overflows!\')
        RETURN
      ENDIF
      IERR=0
      NLNS=NLNS+1
      LNFONT(NLNS)=IFONT
      IDPT1(NLNS)=I1
      IDPT2(NLNS)=I2
      RETURN
      END
```

3.3.3   Identification of Line Entities

An interactive CAD system must provide a facility for the user
to identify an existing line entity from the graphic display using
a mouse-like device.   This subsection presents two submodules
for identifying and highlighting an existing line entity.   The
functions of SRCHLN and MARKLN, listed below, are similar to
those of SRCHPT and MARKPT discussed in Section 3.2.2.

SRCHLN identifies the nearest line, within a specific neighborhood around the Crosshair Cursor, by comparing the perpendicular distances between the cursor location and the lines near
the cursor.   MARKLN highlights an existing line by redrawing
the line in a different color.   Both SRCHLN and MARKLN were
used in the VIEW module to provide the user with an option to
define a specific viewing direction by selecting an existing line.

```
*
*   Search for the Nearest Line
*
      SUBROUTINE SRCHLN(N,X,Y)
      COMMON /XVYVZV/ XV(300),YV(300),ZV(300)
      COMMON /LINES/ NLNS,IDPT1(400),IDPT2(400),LNFONT(400)
      COMMON /WINDOW/ XW1,YW1,XW2,YW2
      DATA EPS/1.0E-6/
      G(A,B,I1,I2)=(B-YV(I1))*(YV(I2)-YV(I1))+(A-XV(I1))*
     & (XV(I2)-XV(I1))
      H(A,B,I1,I2)=(B-YV(I2))*(YV(I2)-YV(I1))+(A-XV(I2))*
     & (XV(I2)-XV(I1))
      DST(A,B,I1,I2)=ABS((YV(I2)-YV(I1))*A-(XV(I2)-XV(I1))*B
     & +(XV(I2)*YV(I1)-XV(I1)*YV(I2)))/SQRT((XV(I2)-XV(I1))**2
     & +(YV(I2)-YV(I1))**2)
      N=0
      DST1=(XW2-XW1)/20
      DO 100 I=1,NLNS
```

```
      IF(LNFONT(I).EQ.0) GOTO 100
      I1=IDPT1(I)
      I2=IDPT2(I)
      IF(G(X,Y,I1,I2)*G(XV(I2),YV(I2),I1,I2) .LT. 0. .OR.
     &   H(X,Y,I1,I2)*H(XV(I1),YV(I1),I1,I2) .LT. 0.) GOTO 100
      IF((XV(I2)-XV(I1))**2+(YV(I2)-YV(I1))**2 .LT. EPS)
     &   GOTO 100
      DST2=DST(X,Y,I1,I2)
      IF(DST2.GT.DST1) GOTO 100
      DST1=DST2
      N=I
100   CONTINUE
      RETURN
      END


*
*   Mark a Line Entity on the Screen
*
      SUBROUTINE MARKLN(N,IC)
      COMMON /POINTS/ NPTS,XT(300),YT(300),ZT(300),IPTDEF(300)
      COMMON /XVYVZV/ XV(300),YV(300),ZV(300)
      COMMON /LINES/ NLNS,IDPT1(400),IDPT2(400),LNFONT(400)
      COMMON /WINDOW/ XW1,YW1,XW2,YW2
      DATA IC3/3/
50    FORMAT('+                                              ')
100   FORMAT('+',I3,'->',I3,',',I3)
*
*   The Line is highlighted in XOR mode when IC > 0
*
      ICT=IC
      IF(IC.LT.0) ICT=-IC
      CALL GCOLOR(ICT)
      IF(IC.GT.0) CALL GXOR(1)
      IF(LNFONT(N).EQ.99) CALL GLNTYP(3)
      CALL GWGCSR(XV(IDPT1(N)),YV(IDPT1(N)))
      CALL GWLINE(XV(IDPT2(N)),YV(IDPT2(N)))
      IF(LNFONT(N).EQ.99) CALL GLNTYP(1)
      CALL GCOLOR(IC3)
      IF(IC.GT.0) THEN
        CALL GXOR(0)
        CALL GTTCSR(1,1)
        WRITE(*,50)
        WRITE(*,100) N,IDPT1(N),IDPT2(N)
      ENDIF
      RETURN
      END
```

3.3.4 Angled, Parallel and Perpendicular Lines

A line in the XT-YT plane making a specific angle with the XT
axis can be defined by a point and an angle value as described
in Section 3.3.1.   However, as illustrated in module ANGLN below and module MKLN1 in Section 3.3.2, an angled line can always
be represented and stored as if it were defined by two end points.

```
*
*   Construct Long angled lines in selected XT-YT planes
*
      SUBROUTINE ANGLN
      CHARACTER*40 BUFFER
      COMMON /POINTS/ NPTS,XT(300),YT(300),ZT(300),IPTDEF(300)
      COMMON /XVYVZV/ XV(300),YV(300),ZV(300)
      COMMON /LINES/ NLNS,IDPT1(400),IDPT2(400),LNFONT(400)
      COMMON /GRIDPT/ XTCTR,YTCTR,DELXT,DELYT,ZTGRID
      COMMON /MATRIX/ NMAT,R(3,3,50),T(3,50),IDEF
      DATA IC1/1/,IC3/3/,PI/3.141593/
      RADDEG=PI/180.0
500   CALL PROMPT('\<L>-Sel Pt; <M>-End; <R>-Use Origin\')
      CALL USELOC(X,Y,IBUTT)
      CALL PROMPT('\ \')
      IF(IBUTT.EQ.130 .OR. IBUTT.LT.128) RETURN
      IF(IBUTT.EQ.132) THEN
         CALL SRCHPT(NPT1,X,Y)
         IF(NPT1.EQ.0) GOTO 500
         CALL MARKPT(NPT1,IC1)
         CALL DTOM(XT(NPT1),YT(NPT1),ZT(NPT1),XM1,YM1,ZM1,
     &        IPTDEF(NPT1))
         CALL MTOD(XM1,YM1,ZM1,XTEMP,YTEMP,ZTGRID,IDEF)
      ELSE
         XTEMP=0.0
         YTEMP=0.0
         ZTGRID=0.0
      ENDIF
510   CALL RESET
      CALL PROMPT('\Enter Angle (Degree) -> \')
      CALL INPSTR(BUFFER)
      CALL PROMPT('\ \')
      IF(BUFFER.EQ.' ') GOTO 500
      READ(BUFFER,*,ERR=510) ANGLE
      ANGLE=ANGLE*RADDEG
      CALL MKLN1(XTEMP,YTEMP,ANGLE,IERR)
      IF(IERR.NE.0) GOTO 500
      CALL MARKLN(NLNS,IC3)
      GOTO 500
      END
```

Options for constructing parallel and perpendicular lines from selected reference lines and base points can be added to the LINE module. The reader is asked to design his or her own modules, which may be called PARALN and PERPLN, for these two options.

A parallel or perpendicular line (in 2-D XT-YT plane or 3-D X-Y-Z space) to a reference line can be defined by selecting a reference line followed by selecting a base point through which the desired line is to be constructed.

To construct a parallel line, the PARALN module may prompt the user to first select a reference line and then select any number of base points from which *long* lines having the direction-

al vector of the reference line as their own and the selected
points as their mid-points can be created. The new end points
of these parallel lines may be calculated from the mid-points, the
unit directional vector, and a length five times the size of the
current window. Before returning, the PARALN module should
invoke both ADDPT and ADDLN modules to add the new line
entities to the current data base.

If limited to an XT-YT plane, lines perpendicular to a reference line and passing through selected base points can be found
by simply evaluating the slope of the reference line and using
the procedure given in subroutine ANGLN. Constructing a
perpendicular line to a reference line in an X-Y-Z space through
a base point is more involved in that there is no unique solution
when the base point is on the reference line. A general 3-D
PERPLN module should include a filtering procedure to sift out
such undesirable cases.

In the PERPLN module, the line perpendicular to a reference
line represented by

$$r(t) = b_1 + t \cdot d_1 \tag{3.9}$$

and passing through a base point P_3 can be obtained by solving
the following equation for the parameter value t of a point P_4
on the reference line which, together with P_3, defines the perpendicular line:

$$(b_1 + t_4 \cdot d_1 - P_3) \cdot d_1 = 0 \tag{3.10}$$

which yields

$$t_4 = [\ (P_3 - b_1) \cdot d_1]\ /\ (d_1 \cdot d_1) \tag{3.11}$$

and

$$P_4 = r(t_4) \tag{3.12}$$

In the above equations, P_3 and P_4 denote the position vectors
of points P_3 and P_4.

With P_3 and P_4 defined, the PERPLN module can construct a
long line having P_3P_4 as its directional vector and P_3 as its
mid-point. Since the above algorithms are not limited to the 2-D
case, the PARALN and PERPLN modules should be directly applicable to 3-D cases. Figure 3.7 shows several parallel and per-

pendicular lines created from a single reference line and several base points.

3.3.5   The DELELN and PACKIN Submodules

Two more editing utilities are incorporated in the LINE module. Module DELELN provides the user with an option to delete lines from the data base.   As illustrated in the listing below, the system first deletes a selected line from the screen and then fills its LNFONT identifier with zero.   A zero identifier will in-hibit the line from showing up on the screen or engaging in the line selection process (see modules REDRAW and SRCHLN).

When deletion of such unwanted lines from the data base is desired, another module, PACKIN, can be called to perform a garbage-collection task to throw out unwanted lines and reorder the remaining ones.   Note that PACKIN also removes unattached point entities from the data base.   A listing of PACKIN is also given below.

```
*
*   Delete selected line entities
*
      SUBROUTINE DELELN
      COMMON /POINTS/ NPTS,XT(300),YT(300),ZT(300),IPTDEF(300)
      COMMON /XVYVZV/ XV(300),YV(300),ZV(300)
      COMMON /LINES/ NLNS,IDPT1(400),IDPT2(400),LNFONT(400)
      DATA IC0/0/,IC1/1/,IC3/3/
      IUNDO=0
100   CALL PROMPT('\Sel Line: <L>-Del; <M>-End; <R>-Undo\')
      CALL USELOC(X,Y,IBUTT)
      CALL PROMPT('\ \')
      IF(IBUTT.EQ.130 .OR. IBUTT.LT.128) RETURN
      IF(IBUTT.EQ.132) THEN
        CALL SRCHLN(NLN,X,Y)
        IF(NLN.EQ.0) GOTO 100
        CALL FACEDG(NLN,IYES)
        IF(IYES.NE.0) THEN
          CALL MESSAG('\Edge belongs to a Face!\')
          GOTO 100
        ENDIF
        LNF0=LNFONT(NLN)
        IUNDO=1
        CALL MARKLN(NLN,IC0)
        LNFONT(NLN)=0
      ELSE
        IF(IUNDO.EQ.0) GOTO 100
        LNFONT(NLN)=LNF0
        CALL MARKLN(NLN,IC3)
        IUNDO=0
      ENDIF
      GOTO 100
      END
```

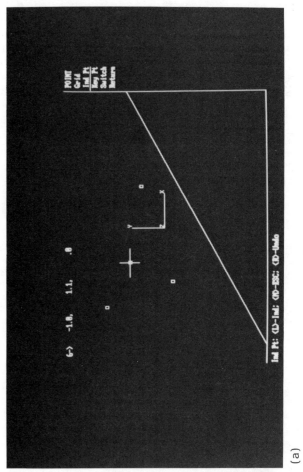

(a)

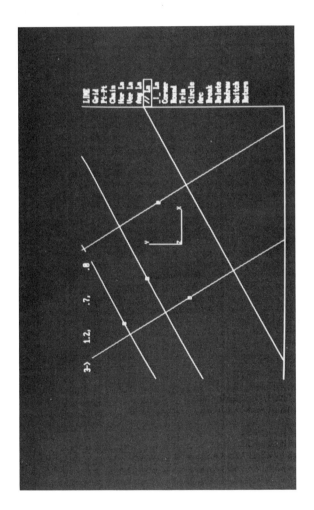

(b)

Figure 3.7   Parallel and perpendicular lines from selected reference line and base points.

```
*
*    Check whether NLN is an edge of a Face entity
*    (definition of Face is given in Sec. 4.5)
*
      SUBROUTINE FACEDG(NLN,IYES)
      COMMON /FACET1/ NFAS,NEDGE(100),IDEDGE(30,100)
      IYES=0
      DO 150 I=1,NFAS
      DO 150 J=1,NEDGE(I)
        IF(NLN.EQ.IDEDGE(J,I)) THEN
          IYES=1
          RETURN
        ENDIF
150   CONTINUE
      RETURN
      END




*
*    Remove lines with zero LNFONT from /LINES/,
*    and remove unattached points from /POINTS/
*
      SUBROUTINE PACKIN
      INTEGER NDEL(50)
      COMMON /POINTS/ NPTS,XT(300),YT(300),ZT(300),IPTDEF(300)
      COMMON /XVYVZV/ XV(300),YV(300),ZV(300)
      COMMON /LINES/ NLNS,IDPT1(400),IDPT2(400),LNFONT(400)
      COMMON /FACET1/ NFAS,NEDGE(100),IDEDGE(30,100)
      COMMON /LNGRP/ NLNGP,LNGP(50)
      DATA EPS/1.0E-6/
      IF(NPTS.EQ.0 .OR. NLNS.EQ.0) RETURN
      NPTS0=NPTS
      NLNS0=NLNS
      I1=1
10    DO 50 I=I1,NLNS
        IF(LNFONT(I).NE.0) GOTO 50
        DO 30 J=I,NLNS-1
          IDPT1(J)=IDPT1(J+1)
          IDPT2(J)=IDPT2(J+1)
          LNFONT(J)=LNFONT(J+1)
30      CONTINUE
        DO 20 K=1,NFAS
        DO 20 L=1,NEDGE(K)
          IF(IDEDGE(L,K).LT.I) GOTO 20
          IDEDGE(L,K)=IDEDGE(L,K)-1
20      CONTINUE
        GOTO 60
50    CONTINUE
      GOTO 70
60    I1=I
      NLNS=NLNS-1
      GOTO 10
70    NPT=0
      DO 200 I=1,NPTS
       DO 100 J=1,NLNS
```

```
            IF(I.EQ.IDPT1(J) .OR. I.EQ.IDPT2(J)) GOTO 200
100     CONTINUE
        IF(NPT.GE.50) GOTO 300
        NPT=NPT+1
        NDEL(NPT)=I
200     CONTINUE
300     IF(NPT.EQ.0) RETURN
        DO 400 I=NPT,1,-1
          DO 460 J=NDEL(I),NPTS-1
            IPTDEF(J)=IPTDEF(J+1)
            XT(J)=XT(J+1)
            YT(J)=YT(J+1)
            ZT(J)=ZT(J+1)
            XV(J)=XV(J+1)
            YV(J)=YV(J+1)
            ZV(J)=ZV(J+1)
460       CONTINUE
          DO 440 K=1,NLNS
            IF(IDPT1(K).GT.NDEL(I)) IDPT1(K)=IDPT1(K)-1
            IF(IDPT2(K).GT.NDEL(I)) IDPT2(K)=IDPT2(K)-1
440       CONTINUE
          NPTS=NPTS-1
400     CONTINUE
        IF(NPTS.EQ.NPTS0 .AND. NLNS.EQ.NLNS0) RETURN
*
*   Clear Group buffer; Group is defined in Sec. 4.3.1
*
        NLNGP=0
        CALL REDRAW
        RETURN
        END
```

3.3.6   Intersection, Cornering, Trimming, and Breaking of Lines

Consider two line segments P_1P_2 and P_3P_4, as shown in Figure 3.8, whose parametric representations are:

$$x = x_1 + t_1 \cdot (x_2 - x_1)$$
$$y = y_1 + t_1 \cdot (y_2 - y_1) \qquad\qquad (3.13)$$

and

$$x = x_3 + t_2 \cdot (x_4 - x_3)$$
$$y = y_3 + t_2 \cdot (y_4 - y_3) \qquad\qquad (3.14)$$

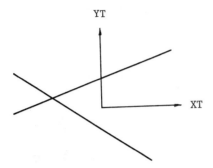

Figure 3.8   Two intersecting lines in an XT-YT plane.

Finding the intersection of these two lines requires solution for a certain set of t_1 and t_2 values which satisfies the following equations:

$$t_1 \cdot (x_2 - x_1) - t_2 \cdot (x_4 - x_3) = - x_1 + x_3$$

and

$$t_1 \cdot (y_2 - y_1) - t_2 \cdot (y_4 - y_3) = - y_1 + y_3 \qquad (3.15)$$

Thus there will be no solution for the case that

$$(x_2 - x_1) \cdot (y_4 - y_3) - (x_4 - x_3) \cdot (y_2 - y_1) = 0 \qquad (3.16)$$

which indicates that the two planar lines are either parallel or coincident. The analysis can be easily extended to 3-D cases because for two intersecting lines the intersection point must exist in all three principal projections in the X-Y, Y-Z, and Z-X planes.

In laying out a 2-D shape on a plane, we often start by constructing a sketchy outline of the product model with critical base lines, which are then edited for an exact description of the model. Two useful editing tools, *cornering* and *trimming*, are provided in CAD-PS for relimiting 2-D and 3-D lines.

The two intersecting lines as shown in Figure 3.8 can be reduced to any one of the four possible *corners* illustrated in Figure 3.9. The procedure presented here for *cornering* involves two interactive steps: selection of the intersecting lines followed

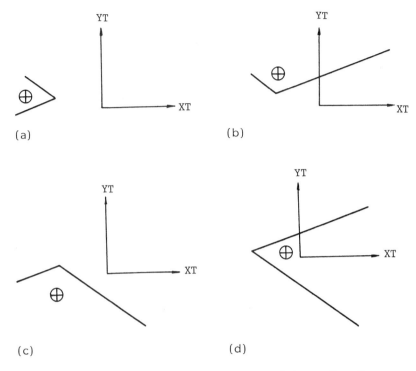

Figure 3.9   Four possible corners at two intersecting lines.

by indication of a desired corner as denoted by the circled plus sign in Figure 3.9.

The second mode of module CORNER, listed below, performs the cornering function. In order to make the same procedure applicable to general 3-D cases, CORNER uses the XV and YV coordinates of the intersecting lines to determine the indicated corner. Also given below is an accompanying module LNLN for computing the intersection of two selected lines by first finding the intersection (parameters t_1 and t_2) of the projected images of the two lines in any of the X-Y, Y-Z, and Z-X planes and then checking whether this solution also produces an intersection point along the direction of the remaining axis.

```
*
*    Cornering or Trimming two intersecting lines
*    (MODE=1 -> Trimming; MODE=2 -> Cornering)
```

```
*
      SUBROUTINE CORNER(MODE)
      COMMON /POINTS/ NPTS,XT(300),YT(300),ZT(300),IPTDEF(300)
      COMMON /XVYVZV/ XV(300),YV(300),ZV(300)
      COMMON /LINES/ NLNS,IDPT1(400),IDPT2(400),LNFONT(400)
      COMMON /WINDOW/ XW1,YW1,XW2,YW2
      COMMON /MATRIX/ NMAT,R(3,3,50),T(3,50),IDEF
      DATA IC0/0/,IC2/2/,IC3/3/,EPS/1.0E-6/
*
*   F(X,Y)=(X-X1)*(Y1-Y2)-(Y-Y1)*(X1-X2)
*
      FLINE(AA,BB,CC,DD,EE,FF)=(AA-CC)*(DD-FF)-(BB-DD)*(CC-EE)
10    DO 100 I=1,2
110   IF(I.EQ.1) CALL PROMPT('\1st Ln: <L>-Sel; <M,R>-End\')
      IF(I.EQ.2) CALL PROMPT('\2nd Ln: <L>-Sel; <M,R>-End\')
      CALL USELOC(X,Y,IBUTT)
      CALL PROMPT('\ \')
      IF(IBUTT.NE.132) RETURN
      IF(I.EQ.1) THEN
        CALL SRCHLN(NLN1,X,Y)
        IF(NLN1.EQ.0) GOTO 110
        CALL FACEDG(NLN1,IYES)
        IF(IYES.NE.0) THEN
          CALL MESSAG('\Edge belongs to a Face!\')
          GOTO 10
        ENDIF
        NLN=NLN1
      ELSE
        CALL SRCHLN(NLN2,X,Y)
        IF(NLN2.EQ.0) GOTO 110
        IF(MODE.NE.1) THEN
          CALL FACEDG(NLN2,IYES)
          IF(IYES.NE.0) THEN
            CALL MESSAG('\Edge belongs to a Face!\')
            GOTO 10
          ENDIF
        ENDIF
        NLN=NLN2
      ENDIF
      CALL MARKLN(NLN,IC2)
100   CONTINUE
      CALL LNLN(NLN1,NLN2,XX,YY,ZZ,IERR)
      CALL MTOD(XX,YY,ZZ,XT1,YT1,ZT1,IDEF)
      IF(IERR.NE.0) THEN
        CALL MARKLN(NLN1,IC2)
        CALL MARKLN(NLN2,IC2)
        CALL MESSAG('\Lines Don''t Intersect!\')
        GOTO 10
      ENDIF
      CALL PROMPT('\Indicate Quadrant\')
      CALL USELOC(X,Y,IBUTT)
      CALL PROMPT('\ \')
      IF(IBUTT.EQ.130 .OR. IBUTT.LT.128) RETURN
*
*   Determine Trimmed corner from Viewing coordinates
*
```

```
      U1=XV(IDPT1(NLN2))
      V1=YV(IDPT1(NLN2))
      U2=XV(IDPT2(NLN2))
      V2=YV(IDPT2(NLN2))
      UT=XV(IDPT1(NLN1))
      VT=YV(IDPT1(NLN1))
      FREF=FLINE(X,Y,U1,V1,U2,V2)
      F1=FLINE(UT,VT,U1,V1,U2,V2)
      UT=XV(IDPT2(NLN1))
      VT=YV(IDPT2(NLN1))
      F2=FLINE(UT,VT,U1,V1,U2,V2)
      IF(F1*F2 .LT. EPS) GOTO 150
130   CALL MARKLN(NLN1,IC2)
      CALL MARKLN(NLN2,IC2)
      CALL MESSAG('\Lines Don''t Cross!\')
      GOTO 10
140   CALL MARKLN(NLN1,IC2)
      CALL MARKLN(NLN2,IC2)
      CALL MESSAG('\Ambiguous Geometry?!\')
      GOTO 10
150   IF(FREF*F1 .GT. EPS) THEN
        I1=IDPT1(NLN1)
        I1T=IDPT2(NLN1)
      ELSE IF(FREF*F1 .LT. -EPS) THEN
        I1=IDPT2(NLN1)
        I1T=IDPT1(NLN1)
      ELSE
        IF(FREF*F2 .GT. EPS) THEN
          I1=IDPT2(NLN1)
          I1T=IDPT1(NLN1)
        ELSE IF(FREF*F2 .LT. -EPS) THEN
          I1=IDPT1(NLN1)
          I1T=IDPT2(NLN1)
        ELSE
          GOTO 140
        ENDIF
      ENDIF
      I2=IDPT1(NLN2)
      I2T=IDPT2(NLN2)
      IF(MODE.EQ.1) GOTO 200
      U1=XV(IDPT1(NLN1))
      V1=YV(IDPT1(NLN1))
      U2=XV(IDPT2(NLN1))
      V2=YV(IDPT2(NLN1))
      UT=XV(IDPT1(NLN2))
      VT=YV(IDPT1(NLN2))
      FREF=FLINE(X,Y,U1,V1,U2,V2)
      F1=FLINE(UT,VT,U1,V1,U2,V2)
      UT=XV(IDPT2(NLN2))
      VT=YV(IDPT2(NLN2))
      F2=FLINE(UT,VT,U1,V1,U2,V2)
      IF(F1*F2 .GE. EPS) GOTO 130
      IF(FREF*F1 .GT. EPS) THEN
        I2=IDPT1(NLN2)
        I2T=IDPT2(NLN2)
```

```
      ELSE IF(FREF*F1 .LT. -EPS) THEN
        I2=IDPT2(NLN2)
        I2T=IDPT1(NLN2)
      ELSE
        IF(FREF*F2 .GT. EPS) THEN
          I2=IDPT2(NLN2)
          I2T=IDPT1(NLN2)
        ELSE IF(FREF*F2 .LT. -EPS) THEN
          I2=IDPT1(NLN2)
          I2T=IDPT2(NLN2)
        ELSE
          GOTO 140
        ENDIF
      ENDIF
200   CALL MARKLN(NLN1,IC0)
      CALL MARKLN(NLN2,IC0)
*   Trimming
      IDPT1(NLN1)=I1
      CALL DTOM(XT(I1T),YT(I1T),ZT(I1T),XM1,YM1,ZM1,IPTDEF(I1T))
      CALL DTOM(XT(I2T),YT(I2T),ZT(I2T),XM2,YM2,ZM2,IPTDEF(I2T))
      IF(MODE.EQ.1) THEN
*   Check if Intersection Point is identical to an End Point
*   to avoid creating duplicate points
        CALL DTOM(XT(I2),YT(I2),ZT(I2),XM3,YM3,ZM3,IPTDEF(I2))
        IF((XX-XM1)**2+(YY-YM1)**2+(ZZ-ZM1)**2 .GT. EPS) THEN
          IF((XX-XM2)**2+(YY-YM2)**2+(ZZ-ZM2)**2 .LE. EPS) THEN
            IDPT2(NLN1)=I2T
          ELSEIF((XX-XM3)**2+(YY-YM3)**2+(ZZ-ZM3)**2.LE.EPS) THEN
            IDPT2(NLN1)=I2
          ELSE
            CALL ADDPT(XT1,YT1,ZT1,IDEF,IERR)
            IF(IERR.NE.0) GOTO 10
            IDPT2(NLN1)=NPTS
          ENDIF
        ELSE
          IDPT2(NLN1)=I1T
        ENDIF
      ELSE
*   Cornering
        IF((XX-XM1)**2+(YY-YM1)**2+(ZZ-ZM1)**2 .GT. EPS) THEN
          IF((XX-XM2)**2+(YY-YM2)**2+(ZZ-ZM2)**2 .LE. EPS) THEN
            IDPT2(NLN1)=I2T
            IDPT1(NLN2)=I2T
          ELSE
            CALL ADDPT(XT1,YT1,ZT1,IDEF,IERR)
            IF(IERR.NE.0) GOTO 10
            IDPT2(NLN1)=NPTS
            IDPT1(NLN2)=NPTS
          ENDIF
        ELSE
          IDPT2(NLN1)=I1T
          IDPT1(NLN2)=I1T
        ENDIF
      ENDIF
      IDPT2(NLN2)=I2
      CALL MARKLN(NLN1,IC3)
      CALL MARKLN(NLN2,IC3)
      GOTO 10
      END
```

```
*
*    Compute the intersection of two selected lines
*
     SUBROUTINE LNLN(LN1,LN2,XX,YY,ZZ,IERR)
     COMMON /POINTS/ NPTS,XT(300),YT(300),ZT(300),IPTDEF(300)
     COMMON /XVYVZV/ XV(300),YV(300),ZV(300)
     COMMON /LINES/ NLNS,IDPT1(400),IDPT2(400),LNFONT(400)
     DATA IC0/0/,IC2/2/,IC3/3/,EPS/1.0E-3/
     DET(AA,BB,CC,DD)=AA*DD-BB*CC
     IERR=1
     CALL DTOM(XT(IDPT1(LN1)),YT(IDPT1(LN1)),ZT(IDPT1(LN1)),
   & XM11,YM11,ZM11,IPTDEF(IDPT1(LN1)))
     CALL DTOM(XT(IDPT2(LN1)),YT(IDPT2(LN1)),ZT(IDPT2(LN1)),
   & XM21,YM21,ZM21,IPTDEF(IDPT2(LN1)))
     CALL DTOM(XT(IDPT1(LN2)),YT(IDPT1(LN2)),ZT(IDPT1(LN2)),
   & XM12,YM12,ZM12,IPTDEF(IDPT1(LN2)))
     CALL DTOM(XT(IDPT2(LN2)),YT(IDPT2(LN2)),ZT(IDPT2(LN2)),
   & XM22,YM22,ZM22,IPTDEF(IDPT2(LN2)))
     A11=XM21-XM11
     A12=-XM22+XM12
     A13=XM12-XM11
     A21=YM21-YM11
     A22=-YM22+YM12
     A23=YM12-YM11
     A31=ZM21-ZM11
     A32=-ZM22+ZM12
     A33=ZM12-ZM11
     DDD=DET(A11,A12,A21,A22)
     IF(ABS(DDD).LT.EPS) GOTO 200
     UU=(A13*A22-A23*A12)/DDD
     VV=(A11*A23-A21*A13)/DDD
     DDD=ABS(A31*UU+A32*VV-A33)
100  IF(DDD.GT.EPS) RETURN
     XX=XM11+UU*A11
     YY=YM11+UU*A21
     ZZ=ZM11+UU*A31
     IERR=0
     RETURN
200  DDD=DET(A21,A22,A31,A32)
     IF(ABS(DDD).LT.EPS) GOTO 300
     UU=(A23*A32-A33*A22)/DDD
     VV=(A21*A33-A31*A23)/DDD
     DDD=ABS(A11*UU+A12*VV-A13)
     GOTO 100
300  DDD=DET(A31,A32,A11,A12)
     IF(ABS(DDD).LT.EPS) RETURN
     UU=(A33*A12-A13*A32)/DDD
     VV=(A31*A13-A11*A33)/DDD
     DDD=ABS(A21*UU+A22*VV-A23)
     GOTO 100
     END
```

The first step in *cornering* two lines or *trimming* one line against another is to activate the Mouse Cursor and prompt the user to maneuver the cursor toward the desired lines and press the left button <L>. The user is then prompted to indicate a desired corner with the Mouse Cursor. Indication of a desire

corner (see Fig. 3.9) can be validated by checking the relative
position of the indicating cursor and the involved end points,
since a line in the XV-YV plane divides the plane into two parts:
one whose points (x, y) satisfy the inequality

$$(x - x_1) (y_2 - y_1) - (y - y_1) (x_2 - x_1) > 0 \qquad (3.17)$$

and the other whose points (x, y) satisfy

$$(x - x_1) (y_2 - y_1) - (y - y_1) (x_2 - x_1) < 0 \qquad (3.18)$$

After prompting and waiting for the user's actions, the CORNER
module first finds the intersection point of the two selected lines,
then identifies the desired corner from the above inequalities,
and finally replaces the unwanted end points of the selected
lines with the intersection point. An extra step is taken in
CORNER to avoid duplication of data by comparing the calculated
intersection point with the involved end points of the two intersecting lines and merging them if they are less than 0.001 units
apart from each other.

Another useful feature for editing lines is *trimming* one line
against another. Trimming is much like cornering because an
intersection point and a specific side of the trimmed line must
be determined from the selected lines and indicated corner. As
documented in the above program listing, the first mode of
CORNER is designed to trim the first line against the second
line according to the side indicator clicked by the user.

All line entities created in the LINE module are represented
by pointers to their two end points. Very often in a CAD design session a line needs to be broken up into two separate line
segments at a desired location so each new segment can be further edited. Module BRKLN listed below allows the breaking of
a selected line entity at a location indicated by the Mouse Cursor.
Like other editing procedures in CAD-PS, BRKLN provides an
"Undo" option to allow the user to reverse the preceding editing
process.

```
*
*    Break a selected line into two parts at indicated location
*
     SUBROUTINE BRKLN
     COMMON /POINTS/ NPTS,XT(300),YT(300),ZT(300),IPTDEF(300)
     COMMON /XVYVZV/ XV(300),YV(300),ZV(300)
     COMMON /LINES/ NLNS,IDPT1(400),IDPT2(400),LNFONT(400)
     COMMON /MATRIX/ NMAT,R(3,3,50),T(3,50),IDEF
```

```
        DATA IC0/0/,IC1/1/,IC2/2/,IC3/3/,EPS/1.0E-6/
        F(X,Y,X1,Y1,X2,Y2)=(Y-Y1)*(Y2-Y1)+(X-X1)*(X2-X1)
        G(X,Y,X1,Y1,X2,Y2)=(Y2-Y)*(Y2-Y1)+(X2-X)*(X2-X1)
        IUNDO=0
100     CALL PROMPT('\Sel Line: <L>-Break; <M>-End; <R>-Undo\')
        CALL USELOC(X,Y,IBUTT)
        CALL PROMPT('\ \')
        IF(IBUTT.EQ.130 .OR. IBUTT.LT.128) RETURN
        IF(IBUTT.EQ.132) THEN
          CALL SRCHLN(NLN,X,Y)
          IF(NLN.EQ.0) GOTO 100
          CALL FACEDG(NLN,IYES)
          IF(IYES.NE.0) THEN
            CALL MESSAG('\Edge belongs to a Face!\')
            GOTO 100
          ENDIF
          LNFO=LNFONT(NLN)
          I1=IDPT1(NLN)
          I2=IDPT2(NLN)
          IF(F(X,Y,XV(I1),YV(I1),XV(I2),YV(I2)).LT.EPS) GOTO 100
          IF(G(X,Y,XV(I1),YV(I1),XV(I2),YV(I2)).LT.EPS) GOTO 100
          RATIO=SQRT(((X-XV(I1))**2+(Y-YV(I1))**2)/
     &           ((XV(I2)-XV(I1))**2+(YV(I2)-YV(I1))**2))
          CALL DTOM(XT(I1),YT(I1),ZT(I1),XM1,YM1,ZM1,IPTDEF(I1))
          CALL DTOM(XT(I2),YT(I2),ZT(I2),XM2,YM2,ZM2,IPTDEF(I2))
          XTEMP=XM1+RATIO*(XM2-XM1)
          YTEMP=YM1+RATIO*(YM2-YM1)
          ZTEMP=ZM1+RATIO*(ZM2-ZM1)
          CALL MTOD(XTEMP,YTEMP,ZTEMP,XT1,YT1,ZT1,IDEF)
          CALL ADDPT(XT1,YT1,ZT1,IDEF,IERR)
          IF(IERR.NE.0) GOTO 100
          CALL MARKLN(NLN,IC0)
          CALL MARKPT(NPTS,IC2)
          IDPT2(NLN)=NPTS
          CALL MARKLN(NLN,IC3)
          CALL ADDLN(NPTS,I2,LNFO,IERR)
          IF(IERR.NE.0) GOTO 100
          CALL MARKLN(NLNS,IC3)
          IUNDO=1
        ELSE
          IF(IUNDO.EQ.0) GOTO 100
          CALL MARKPT(NPTS,IC2)
          CALL MARKLN(NLN,IC3)
          CALL MARKLN(NLNS,IC3)
          NPTS=NPTS-1
          NLNS=NLNS-1
          IDPT2(NLN)=I2
          CALL MARKLN(NLN,IC3)
          IUNDO=0
        ENDIF
        GOTO 100
        END
```

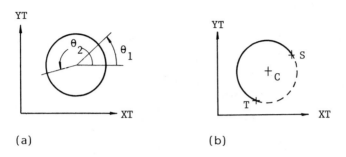

(a)   (b)

Figure 3.10   Circular arcs in an XT-YT plane.

3.3.7   Linear Approximation of Circular Arcs

In an XT-YT plane as depicted in Figure 3.10a, the circle centered at (x_c, y_c) with radius R may be represented in the following parametric form:

$$x = x_c + R \cdot \cos \Theta$$

$$y = y_c + R \cdot \sin \Theta \qquad\qquad (3.19)$$

with parameter Θ measured counterclockwise from the positive
XT axis and varying between Θ_1 and $\Theta_1 + 2\pi$. Thus any point
on a circle may serve as both the start and the terminate points
of the circular loop. The same equations with Θ ranging from
Θ_1 to Θ_2 (see Figure 3.10a) can be used to describe a circular
arc with the same center and radius.

As defined in the Initial Graphics Exchange Specification
(IGES): "A circular arc is a connected portion of a parent circle which consists of more than one point. The definition space
coordinate system is always chosen so that the circular arc lies
in a plane either coincident with or parallel to the XT-YT plane."
Thus we may define circular arcs in a 3-D model space as planar
entities lying in planes parallel to a selected XT-YT plane.

The IGES standard specifies a circular arc through an arc
center, a start point on the parent circle, and a terminate point
on the parent circle. It registers a circular arc in the form of
seven coordinate values: a ZT coordinate value for the underlying plane and three pairs of XT, YT coordinates for the three
reference points. Since two distinct points on a circle will divide

the circle into two circular arcs, as shown in Figure 3.10b, a
specific order must be assigned to the start and the terminate
points in order to specify a circular arc unambiguously.

In IGES, the direction from the start point to the terminate
point is always in the counterclockwise direction while *looking*
from the positive ZT axis *down* upon the XT-YT plane. This
notation applies to all planes parallel to the XT-YT plane. As
depicted in Figure 3.10b, the C (center), S (start), and T
(terminate) points define the solid arc. It is obvious that angles
Θ_1 and Θ_2 for the foregoing parametric equations to represent
the solid arc can be obtained from the XT, YT coordinates of
points S and T. The complementary dashed arc can be specified by switching the roles of points S and T. The IGES registers a full circle as a circular arc whose start and terminate
points coincide.

In CAD-PS, we are interested only in modeling polyhedral
solids with straight edges. However, practical designs often
require circles, arcs, and rounded and filleted corners. In a
polyhedral model, such curved edges and faces are usually approximated with polygonal edges and faces. As an illustration,
subroutine ARC, listed below, is designed to provide the user
with options to create polygonal approximations of circles and
arcs in selected XT-YT planes.

Note that, in module ARC, an approximated circular arc is
defined by the projections of the selected center, start and
terminate points, and that the parametric form of the circle discussed earlier is utilized to generate linear segments between a
number of evenly distributed points on a circle or arc. In the
case of full circles (MODE = 1), the range of the angular coordinate, Θ, is between 0 and 2π. In the case of circular arcs
(MODE = 2), the range of Θ is determined by the XT, YT coordinates of the reference start and terminate points. The range
of Θ for circular arcs is always less than or equal to 2π.

```
*
*   ARC provides the facilities for constructing polygonal
*   circles and arcs in a selected XT-YT plane
*
    SUBROUTINE ARC(MODE)
    CHARACTER*40 BUFFER
    COMMON /POINTS/ NPTS,XT(300),YT(300),ZT(300),IPTDEF(300)
    COMMON /XVYVZV/ XV(300),YV(300),ZV(300)
    COMMON /LINES/ NLNS,IDPT1(400),IDPT2(400),LNFONT(400)
    COMMON /MATRIX/ NMAT,R(3,3,50),T(3,50),IDEF
    COMMON /WINDOW/ XW1,YW1,XW2,YW2
    DATA IC2/2/,IC3/3/,TWOPI/6.283186/,EPS/1.0E-6/
```

```
100    CALL PROMPT('\Center: <L>-Sel; <M>-End; <R>-Key\')
       CALL USELOC(X,Y,IBUTT)
       CALL PROMPT('\ \')
       IF(IBUTT.EQ.130 .OR. IBUTT.LT.128) GOTO 900
       IF(IBUTT.EQ.132) THEN
         CALL SRCHPT(NPT,X,Y)
         IF(NPT.EQ.0) GOTO 100
         CALL MARKPT(NPT,IC2)
         CALL DTOM(XT(NPT),YT(NPT),ZT(NPT),XM,YM,ZM,IPTDEF(NPT))
         CALL MTOD(XM,YM,ZM,XC,YC,ZC,IDEF)
       ELSE
*
*   Specify the working plane (parallel to the XT-YT plane)
*
150      CALL RESET
         CALL PROMPT('\Enter ZT-Plane ->  \')
         CALL INPSTR(BUFFER)
         CALL PROMPT('\ \')
         IF(BUFFER.EQ.' ') GOTO 100
         READ(BUFFER,*,ERR=150) ZC
200      CALL RESET
         CALL PROMPT('\Enter Center: XC,YC ->  \')
         CALL INPSTR(BUFFER)
         CALL PROMPT('\ \')
         IF(BUFFER.EQ.' ') GOTO 100
         READ(BUFFER,*,ERR=200) XC,YC
       ENDIF
300    CALL RESET
       CALL PROMPT('\Enter Radius ->  \')
       CALL INPSTR(BUFFER)
       CALL PROMPT('\ \')
       IF(BUFFER.EQ.' ') GOTO 100
       READ(BUFFER,*,ERR=300) RAD
       IF(RAD .LT. (XW2-XW1)/100) GOTO 300
       IF(MODE.EQ.1) THEN
         ANG=TWOPI
         ANG1=0.0
         X1=XC+RAD
         Y1=YC
       ELSE IF(MODE.EQ.2) THEN
*
*   Projections of selected Start and Terminate Points onto the
*   XT-YT plane are registered in (X1, Y1) and (X2, Y2)
*
320      CALL PROMPT('\Start Pt: <L>-Sel; <M>-End; <R>-Key\')
         CALL USELOC(X,Y,IBUTT)
         CALL PROMPT('\ \')
         IF(IBUTT.EQ.130 .OR. IBUTT.LT.128) GOTO 900
         IF(IBUTT.EQ.132) THEN
           CALL SRCHPT(NPT,X,Y)
           IF(NPT.EQ.0) GOTO 320
           CALL MARKPT(NPT,IC2)
           CALL DTOM(XT(NPT),YT(NPT),ZT(NPT),XM,YM,ZM,IPTDEF(NPT))
           CALL MTOD(XM,YM,ZM,X1,Y1,Z1,IDEF)
         ELSE
```

```
340       CALL RESET
          CALL PROMPT('\Enter Start Pt: X1,Y1 ->  \')
          CALL INPSTR(BUFFER)
          CALL PROMPT('\ \')
          IF(BUFFER.EQ.' ') GOTO 320
          READ(BUFFER,*,ERR=340) X1,Y1
       ENDIF
360    CALL PROMPT('\End Pt: <L>-Sel; <M>-End; <R>-Key\')
       CALL USELOC(X,Y,IBUTT)
       CALL PROMPT('\ \')
       IF(IBUTT.EQ.130 .OR. IBUTT.LT.128) GOTO 900
       IF(IBUTT.EQ.132) THEN
          CALL SRCHPT(NPT,X,Y)
          IF(NPT.EQ.0) GOTO 360
          CALL MARKPT(NPT,IC2)
          CALL DTOM(XT(NPT),YT(NPT),ZT(NPT),XM,YM,ZM,IPTDEF(NPT))
          CALL MTOD(XM,YM,ZM,X2,Y2,Z2,IDEF)
       ELSE
380       CALL RESET
          CALL PROMPT('\Enter End Pt: X2,Y2 ->  \')
          CALL INPSTR(BUFFER)
          CALL PROMPT('\ \')
          IF(BUFFER.EQ.' ') GOTO 360
          READ(BUFFER,*,ERR=380) X2,Y2
       ENDIF
       DIST1=SQRT((X1-XC)**2+(Y1-YC)**2)
       DIST2=SQRT((X2-XC)**2+(Y2-YC)**2)
*
*   Projection of reference points coincides with Center
*
       IF(DIST1.LT.EPS .OR. DIST2.LT.EPS) THEN
          CALL MESSAG('\Impossible Geometry\')
          GOTO 100
       ENDIF
       ANG1=ATAN2(Y1-YC,X1-XC)
       ANG2=ATAN2(Y2-YC,X2-XC)
       IF(ABS(ANG1-ANG2).LT.EPS) THEN
          ANG=TWOPI
       ELSE IF(ANG2.GT.ANG1) THEN
          ANG=ANG2-ANG1
       ELSE
          ANG=ANG2-ANG1+TWOPI
       ENDIF
       X1=XC+(X1-XC)/DIST1*RAD
       Y1=YC+(Y1-YC)/DIST1*RAD
       X2=XC+(X2-XC)/DIST2*RAD
       Y2=YC+(Y2-YC)/DIST2*RAD
    ENDIF
*
*   Specify the number of linear segments
*
400    CALL RESET
       CALL PROMPT('\Enter #Edges -> [12] \')
       CALL INPSTR(BUFFER)
       CALL PROMPT('\ \')
       IF(BUFFER.EQ.' ') THEN
          NSEG=12
```

```
        ELSE
           READ(BUFFER,*,ERR=400) NSEG
        ENDIF
        IF(NSEG.LE.0 .OR. NSEG.GT.24) GOTO 100
        THETA=ANG/NSEG
        CALL ADDPT(X1,Y1,ZC,IDEF,IERR)
        IF(IERR.NE.0) GOTO 900
        NPT1=NPTS
        DO 500 I=1,NSEG-1
           X1=XC+RAD*COS(ANG1+I*THETA)
           Y1=YC+RAD*SIN(ANG1+I*THETA)
           CALL ADDPT(X1,Y1,ZC,IDEF,IERR)
           IF(IERR.NE.0) GOTO 900
           CALL ADDLN(NPTS-1,NPTS,1,IERR)
           IF(IERR.NE.0) GOTO 900
           CALL MARKLN(NLNS,IC3)
500     CONTINUE
        IF(MODE.EQ.1) THEN
           CALL ADDLN(NPTS,NPT1,1,IERR)
        ELSE IF(MODE.EQ.2) THEN
           CALL ADDPT(X2,Y2,ZC,IDEF,IERR)
           IF(IERR.NE.0) GOTO 900
           CALL ADDLN(NPTS-1,NPTS,1,IERR)
        ENDIF
        IF(IERR.NE.0) GOTO 900
        CALL MARKLN(NLNS,IC3)
        GOTO 100
900     RETURN
        END
```

The procedure adopted in module ARC may be used to enhance the CORNER module in Section 3.3.6 to provide a facility for constructing rounded or filleted corners between two intersecting lines. Consider the two intersecting lines and the required round corner of radius R as shown in Figure 3.11. The tangent points of the round corner are equivalent to the start and terminate points of the arc forming the corner. They can be obtained from the specified radius and the angle between the intersecting lines.

If we let u_1 and u_2 be the unit vectors from P_1 to P_2 and from P_1 to P_3, the angle ϕ between the two intersecting lines will be

$$\phi = \cos^{-1} (u_1 \cdot u_2) \tag{3.20}$$

Thus point S can be identified as the point on P_1P_2 whose distance from P_1 is $R \cdot \tan (\phi/2)$. Point T can be obtained similarly. The radial angle of the arc forming the round corner is $\pi - \phi$.

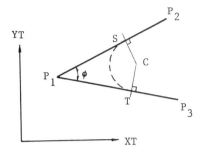

Figure 3.11   Round corner between two intersecting lines.

The center of the arc forming the round corner, point C, can be obtained as the intersection of the two radial lines passing through S and T and perpendicular to P_1P_2 and P_1P_3 respectively. With the coordinates of points C, S and T in the XT-YT plane determined, the round corner can be approximated by a specific number of line segments as described in the ARC module above.

Figure 3.12 shows several circular arcs and round corners constructed with the ARC module and an enhanced CORNER module called ROUND. Implementation of module ROUND is left to the reader as a programming exercise.

3.4 GRID OF TEMPLATE POINTS IN XT-YT PLANES

To facilitate creation of points located at regular spacings in an XT-YT plane or line segments joining such points, an option for displaying regularly spaced template points on a selected XT-YT plane (with its ZT value specified by the user) may be added to the POINT and LINE modules. Implementation of such a GRID module is left to the reader as another programming exercise.

The matrix of template points may be displayed on the specified XT-YT plane with its center point and spacings in the XT and YT directions also specified by the user. With the grid points displayed, the user can easily pick and construct point entities located at desired spacings (in POINT), or line entities joining these points (in LINE).

As illustrations, Figure 3.13 shows a grid of points displayed on the screen along with several selected points which are

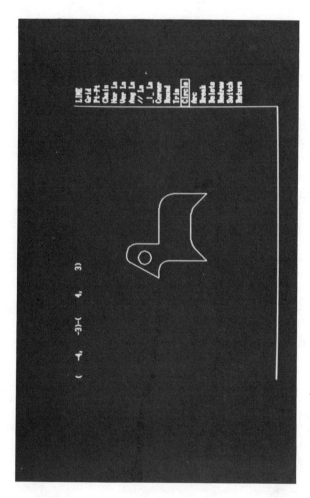

Figure 3.12   Circular arcs and rounded corners.

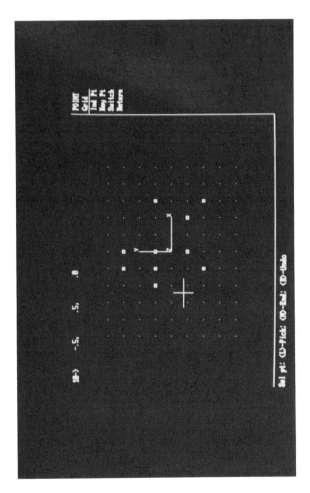

Figure 3.13   Creating points from XT-YT grid points.

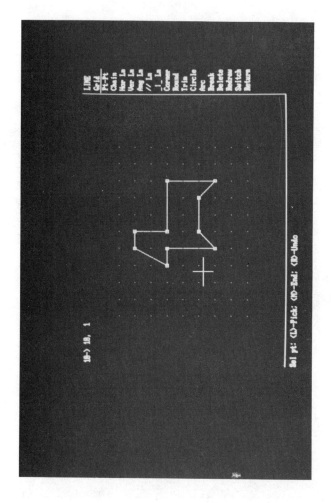

Figure 3.14   Creating polylines from XT-YT grid points.

highlighted (by small boxes) as a reaction to the user's picking action, and Figure 3.14 shows a series of connected line segments joining selected grid points. The temporary grid points may be erased from the screen when the GRID option is terminated. The reader may utilize the COMMON block /GRIDPT/ declared in the POINT and VPROJD modules to store the grid center, the grid spacings, and a user specified ZT-value for use in the GRID module.

3.5   DESIGN OF POLYGONAL SHAPES IN AN XT-YT PLANE

The building-block modules presented thus far can be organized into a practical CAD system for designing 2-D polygonal shapes in an XT-YT plane. Although most of the modules already have the ability to handle 3-D designs, their 3-D features will not be discussed until the next chapter. The MAIN module which builds the current version of CAD-PS with these block modules is listed as follows.

```
      PROGRAM MAIN
      CHARACTER*8 MENU0(11)
      CHARACTER*14 FNAME
      COMMON /DEVICE/ IDPC,IDSCRN,IDLOCA,IDPORT
      COMMON /MSPACE/ XMIN,YMIN,ZMIN,XMAX,YMAX,ZMAX
      COMMON /UNITS/ IUNIT
      COMMON /POINTS/ NPTS,XT(300),YT(300),ZT(300),IPTDEF(300)
      COMMON /XVYVZV/ XV(300),YV(300),ZV(300)
      COMMON /MATRIX/ NMAT,R(3,3,50),T(3,50),IDEF
      COMMON /LINES/ NLNS,IDPT1(400),IDPT2(400),LNFONT(400)
      COMMON /WINDOW/ XW1,YW1,XW2,YW2
      COMMON /SCRN/ RATIOX,RATIOY,IXD,IYD,IXMAX,MENUDY
      COMMON /GRIDPT/ XTCTR,YTCTR,DELXT,DELYT,ZTGRID
      COMMON /FILE/ FNAME
      DATA MENU0/'\CAD-PS\','\View  \','\Point \','\Line  \',
     & '\Mod Sp\','\Def Sp\','\Pack  \','\Redraw\','\File  \',
     & '\New   \','\Exit  \'/
*     IDPC=1     -> IBM PC
*     IDPC=2     -> TI PC
*     IDSCRN=3   -> IBM PC alphanumeric mode
*     IDSCRN=4   -> IBM PC resolution: 320*200 (4 colors)
*     IDSCRN=13 ·-> IBM PC resolution: 320*200 (16 colors)
*     IDSCRN=16 -> IBM PC resolution: 640*350 (16 colors)
*     IDLOCA=2   -> SummaMouse of Summagraphics Corp.
*     IUNIT=1    -> Inch
*
      IDPC=1
      IDSCRN=16
      IDLOCA=2
```

```
        IDPORT=1
        IUNIT=1
        CALL SETUP(IERR)
        IF(IERR.NE.0) THEN
          WRITE(*,*) 'Workstation initiation fails...'
          WRITE(*,*) '  IDPC   -> ',IDPC
          WRITE(*,*) '  IDSCRN -> ',IDSCRN
          WRITE(*,*) '  IDLOCA -> ',IDLOCA
          WRITE(*,*) '  IDPORT -> ',IDPORT
          STOP
        ENDIF
        CALL GTBCSR(0)
        ITEM0=11
10      NLNGP=0
        NPTS=0
        NLNS=0
        FNAME='XXXXXXXX.NNN'
*
*   Reserve first matrix entity for viewing space coordinate
*   system and define default X-Y view and Definition space
*
        NMAT=1
        IDEF=0
        CALL PROJTR(0.,0.,1.)
*
*   Set default Window
*
        CALL SCAWIN(0.0)
*
*   Display Menu items and prompt the user for Locator input
*
20      CALL DMENU(ITEM0,MENU0)
30      CALL USELOC(X,Y,IBUTT)
        IF(IBUTT.EQ.1 .OR. IBUTT.GT.ITEM0) GOTO 30
        GOTO(100,200,300,400,500,600,700,800,900,1000),IBUTT-1
*
*   Activate Viewing options
*
100     CALL VIEW
        GOTO 20
*
*   Activate Point options
*
200     CALL POINT
        GOTO 20
*
*   Activate Line options
*
300     CALL LINE
        GOTO 20
*
*   Display Model Space axes
*
```

```
400  CALL SHOXYZ
     GOTO 30
*
*  Display active Definition Space axes (Sec. 4.2)
*
500  CALL SHODEF
     GOTO 30
*
*  Remove unwanted points and lines from data base (Sec. 3.3.5)
*
600  CALL PACKIN
     GOTO 30
*
*  Re-display current data base
*
700  CALL REDRAW
     GOTO 30
*
*  Activate Filing options (see Sec. 3.6)
*
800  CALL FILEIO
     GOTO 20
900  CALL PROMPT('\Press <L> Button to restart\')
     CALL USELOC(X,Y,IBUTT)
     CALL PROMPT('\ \')
     IF(IBUTT.EQ.132) GOTO 10
     GOTO 20
1000 CALL PROMPT('\Press <L> Button to exit from CAD-PS\')
     CALL USELOC(X,Y,IBUTT)
     CALL PROMPT('\ \')
     IF(IBUTT.NE.132) GOTO 20
     CALL GGCLS
     CALL GTCLS
     CALL GTBCSR(1)
     CALL GLDTCH
     IF(IDPC .EQ. 1) CALL GSCRN(3)
     STOP
     END
```

Figures 3.15 through 3.17 illustrate the use of CAD-PS in designing polygonal shapes in the X-Y plane, which is also the default XT-YT plane. The sketchy outline of a cross section of a product model shown in Figure 3.15 is produced by constructing four vertical lines, four horizontal lines, and two angled lines, using the menu items "Ver Ln," "Hor Ln," and "Ang Ln" in the LINE module.

The "Corner" and "Trim" features can then be used to edit the constructing lines, results of which are shown in Figure 3.16. To complete the cross section as shown in Figure 3.17, the "Break" option is activated to break the shoulder and base lines before applying the "Trim" Option.

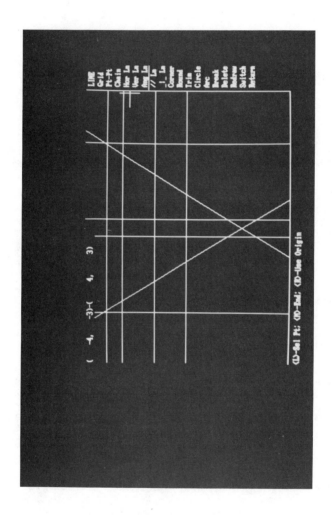

Figure 3.15   A sketchy outline in the X-Y plane.

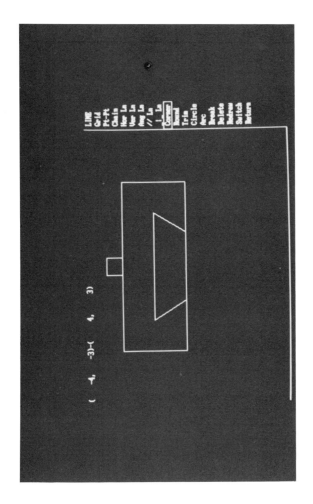

Figure 3.16   Editing with "Corner" and "Trim" options.

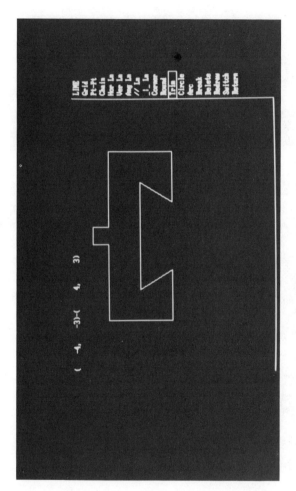

Figure 3.17   A completed cross section of a product model.

3.6 DOCUMENTATION OF GEOMETRIC MODELS

To store geometric models as concise text files for later retrievals or specific post-processing such as plotting, IGES conversion, or data preparation for finite element analysis, this section presents module FILEIO for registering the geometric data base and information on the current viewing system. Module FILEIO allows models to be filed and later revised with minimum disruption.

The model file produced is IGES-compatible in that it can be processed by an IGES translation module into a complete IGES file. The model file for the cross section shown in Figure 3.17 is listed below, followed by a listing of the FILEIO module. The format of the model file is described in the listing of FILEIO. Since all the point and line entities in Figure 3.17 are constructed in the default XT-YT plane, all the definition space identifiers are zero and the ZT coordinates of all point entities are also zero. The data-compact feature of CORNER can be seen from the data file which records only the 12 vertices and 12 edges needed to form the cross section.

It ought to be noted that coordinate values of point entities can be rounded to required design accuracies, and that the filing facilities provided by FILEIO are only exemplary. In addition to just saving and retrieving geometry files, the FILEIO module can be expanded to provide options for saving and retrieving parts of the current geometric model, for detecting oversized models that would overflow the data base, and for merging one geometry file with another.

```
FIG3_17.001
 -.40500E+01  -.31500E+01   .40500E+01   .31500E+01
      1     0
  .10000E+01   .00000E+00   .00000E+00
  .00000E+00   .10000E+01   .00000E+00
  .00000E+00   .00000E+00   .10000E+01
  .00000E+00   .00000E+00   .00000E+00
     12    12
      0       .25000E+01   .20000E+01   .00000E+00
      0       .25000E+01   .37253E-07   .00000E+00
      0       .15772E+01   .10000E+01   .00000E+00
      0      -.15773E+01   .10000E+01   .00000E+00
      0      -.25000E+01   .20000E+01   .00000E+00
      0      -.25000E+01   .29065E-07   .00000E+00
      0      -.25000E+00   .25000E+01   .00000E+00
      0       .25000E+00   .25000E+01   .00000E+00
      0       .99985E+00  -.16391E-06   .00000E+00
      0      -.99997E+00   .24574E-07   .00000E+00
      0      -.25000E+00   .20000E+01   .00000E+00
      0       .25000E+00   .20000E+01   .00000E+00
```

```
1    3    4
1    7    8
1    6    5
1    1    2
1    7   11
1    8   12
1    3    9
1    4   10
1    1   12
1    5   11
1    2    9
1    6   10
```

```
*
*   Read or Write current Data Base from or to a Disk file
*
      SUBROUTINE FILEIO
      LOGICAL OK
      CHARACTER*8 MENUF(4)
      CHARACTER*14 FNAME,FTEMP
      CHARACTER CURFIL(16)
      CHARACTER*40 BUFFER
      EQUIVALENCE (CURFIL(2),FTEMP)
      COMMON /POINTS/ NPTS,XT(300),YT(300),ZT(300),IPTDEF(300)
      COMMON /XVYVZV/ XV(300),YV(300),ZV(300)
      COMMON /MATRIX/ NMAT,R(3,3,50),T(3,50),IDEF
      COMMON /LINES/ NLNS,IDPT1(400),IDPT2(400),LNFONT(400)
      COMMON /WINDOW/ XW1,YW1,XW2,YW2
      COMMON /FILE/ FNAME
      DATA MENUF/'\FILE  \','\Save  \','\Read  \','\Return\'/
      DATA CURFIL(1)/'\'/,CURFIL(16)/'\'/
110   FORMAT(A)
120   FORMAT(4E12.5)
130   FORMAT(2I5)
160   FORMAT(3E12.5)
180   FORMAT(I5,5X,3E12.5)
210   FORMAT(3I5)
      ITEMF=4
5     FTEMP=FNAME
      CALL MESSAG(CURFIL)
      CALL DMENU(ITEMF,MENUF)
10    CALL USELOC(X,Y,IBUTT)
      IF(IBUTT.EQ.1 .OR. IBUTT.GE.128) GOTO 10
      IF(IBUTT.GE.ITEMF) RETURN
      ITEM=IBUTT-1
      CALL SMENU(ITEM)
      GOTO(100,300),ITEM
100   CALL RESET
      CALL PROMPT('\Enter PARTNAME.NNN: \')
      CALL INPSTR(BUFFER)
      CALL PROMPT('\ \')
      IF(BUFFER.EQ.' ') GOTO 9010
      READ(BUFFER,'(A)',ERR=100) FNAME
      INQUIRE(FILE=FNAME,EXIST=OK)
      IF(OK) THEN
```

```
      CALL PROMPT('\Overwrite Existing File? <L>-Yes\')
      CALL USELOC(X,Y,IBUTT)
      CALL PROMPT('\ \')
      IF(IBUTT.NE.132) GOTO 9010
      ENDIF
      OPEN(6,FILE=FNAME,STATUS='NEW',IOSTAT=IOCHK)
      IF(IOCHK.NE.0) THEN
        FNAME=FTEMP
        GOTO 100
      ENDIF
      WRITE(6,110) FNAME
      WRITE(6,120) XW1,YW1,XW2,YW2
      WRITE(6,130) NMAT,IDEF
      DO 150 I=1,NMAT
        DO 140 J=1,3
          WRITE(6,160) (R(J,K,I),K=1,3)
140     CONTINUE
        WRITE(6,160) (T(K,I),K=1,3)
150   CONTINUE
      WRITE(6,130) NPTS,NLNS
      DO 170 I=1,NPTS
        WRITE(6,180) IPTDEF(I),XT(I),YT(I),ZT(I)
170   CONTINUE
      DO 200 I=1,NLNS
        WRITE(6,210) LNFONT(I),IDPT1(I),IDPT2(I)
200   CONTINUE
      CLOSE(6)
      GOTO 9000
300   CALL RESET
      CALL PROMPT('\Enter PARTNAME.NNN: \')
      CALL INPSTR(BUFFER)
      CALL PROMPT('\ \')
      IF(BUFFER.EQ.' ') GOTO 9010
      READ(BUFFER,'(A)',ERR=300) FNAME
      INQUIRE(FILE=FNAME,EXIST=OK)
      IF(.NOT. OK) THEN
        CALL MESSAG('\File Not on Disk\')
        GOTO 9010
      ENDIF
      OPEN(5,FILE=FNAME,STATUS='OLD',IOSTAT=IOCHK)
      IF(IOCHK.NE.0) THEN
        FNAME=FTEMP
        GOTO 300
      ENDIF
      READ(5,110,ERR=9005) FNAME
      READ(5,120,ERR=9005) XW1,YW1,XW2,YW2
      READ(5,130,ERR=9005) NMAT,IDEF
      DO 350 I=1,NMAT
        DO 340 J=1,3
          READ(5,160,ERR=9005) (R(J,K,I),K=1,3)
340     CONTINUE
        READ(5,160,ERR=9005) (T(K,I),K=1,3)
350   CONTINUE
      READ(5,130,ERR=9005) NPTS,NLNS
      DO 370 I=1,NPTS
        READ(5,180,ERR=9005) IPTDEF(I),XT(I),YT(I),ZT(I)
```

```
        CALL DTOV(XT(I),YT(I),ZT(I),XV(I),YV(I),ZV(I),IPTDEF(I))
 370    CONTINUE
        DO 400 I=1,NLNS
          READ(5,210,ERR=9005) LNFONT(I),IDPT1(I),IDPT2(I)
 400    CONTINUE
        CLOSE(5)
        CALL GWINDO(XW1,YW1,XW2,YW2)
        CALL REDRAW
9000    CALL SMENU(ITEM)
        GOTO 5
9005    CALL MESSAG('\Input File Format Error!\')
9010    CALL SMENU(ITEM)
        GOTO 10
        END
```

3.7   SUMMARY

In this chapter we have presented four major building blocks for
the CAD-PS system: VIEW, POINT, LINE, and FILEIO, along
with a number of supporting submodules. Each of the four
modules maintains a separate, second-layer menu. The MAIN
module, which maintains the first-layer menu, is responsible for
the coordination of all the building blocks. The CAD-PS system
in its present form supports only two layers of design menu.

   In the next chapter we shall extend the use of the CAD-PS
system to the design of 3-D wire-frames. Facilities for relocating and duplicating a group of line entities in the design space,
and for forming polygonal faces will also be added to the open
system.

Chapter 4

Geometric Modeling
in 3-D Design Space

In the preceding chapter CAD-PS, a microcomputer-aided design
system, started to take shape from three major design modules:
VIEW, POINT, and LINE. The examples given at the end of the
preceding chapter have proven CAD-PS, in its present form, a
useful 2-D drafting tool.

We shall begin this chapter by revealing the 3-D design features of the three major design modules. These 3-D drafting
functions alone would not make CAD-PS a practical CAD system,
however. An objective of CAD-PS is to provide the designer
with an easy-to-use geometric modeler capable of constructing
wire-frames, polygonal surfaces and polyhedral solids, and, ulti-
mately, designing complex shapes by combining solid primitives
with Boolean set-operations. Modeling of polyhedral solids is
the concern of the next chapter.

After revealing the 3-D design features already incorporated
in the VIEW module, we will present a submodule which allows
CAD-PS to display rotated views of a model space. Then a mechanism for defining new definition spaces will be implemented.
This will turn the 2-D editing tools implemented earlier into 3-D
facilities. To add to the 3-D drafting toolbox, another major design module will be implemented to provide options for transforming 2-D wire-frames through the design space to form 3-D
wire-frames. This will be followed by a discussion on modeling
of finite-element meshes.

The formation of polygonal faces from interactively constructed
3-D wire-frames will be the next design facility to be implemented.
An extension of the face formation algorithm for generating

surfaces of revolution will be examined. An efficient algorithm for computing the area of polygons will then be presented. We shall conclude this chapter with a pair of algorithms for displaying surfaced models with their hidden lines or edges removed.

4.1 DISPLAY OF 3-D MODELS

A single orthographic view of a model space, such as those X-Y plane views shown in the preceding chapter, is apparently insufficient in a 3-D CAD environment. In Section 3.1 we established that an orthographic projection of a 3-D model can be specified by a viewing direction, and that *isometric* views are specially oriented orthographic projections commonly used in engineering drawings. The VIEW module presented in that section provides menu options for selecting commonly used viewing systems, such as the three principal plane views and any of the eight isometric views, and a menu option for specifying any other orthographic views. Figures 4.1 and 4.2 show a first-octant isometric view and a plain orthographic view of the cross section in Figure 3.17.

Changes of the viewing system will result in different projectional views of the model or design space, actions of such may be compared to adjustments of the location and angle of an *orthographic* video camera suspended in the computer generated 3-D design space and transmitting images to the computer display. The creation and editing of product models in the design space is apparently independent of the selected viewing system.

An essential feature in a powerful user interface for computer-aided design is the ability afforded the user to adjust his or her viewing angle into the design space, since the optimum viewing angle changes frequently during a design session. For such fine-tuning of the viewing system, CAD-PS provides options to relocate the suspended orthographic camera such that the design space would appear to rotate about its X, Y or Z axis at increments of a specified angle. Algorithmically, this can be achieved by reshaping the active viewing transformation matrix.

Consider an active viewing system as shown in Figure 4.3a and a modified viewing system as shown in Figure 4.3b where the image of the model space shows a rotation about the Z axis by angle Θ. As discussed earlier, the transformation matrix from the viewing to the model space coordinates is registered as the first transformation matrix in the COMMON block /MATRIX/.

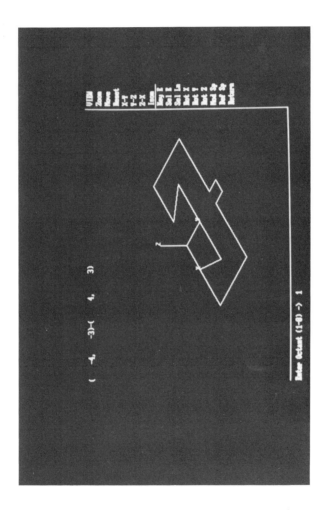

Figure 4.1 An isometric view of a cross section.

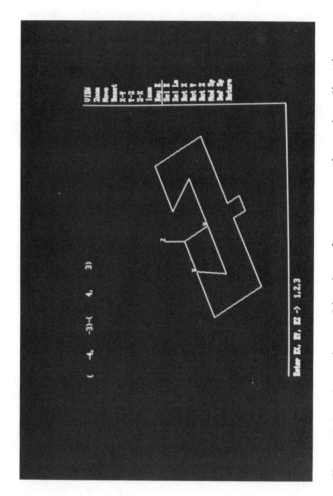

Figure 4.2   An orthographic view of a cross section; view direction:
(1, 2, 3).

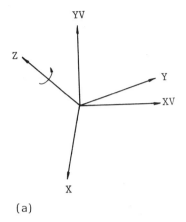

(a)

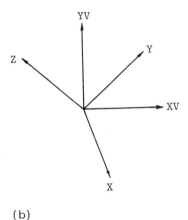

(b)

Figure 4.3   Display of rotation of model space.

In order to obtain a new viewing transformation matrix that
would correspond to a rotation of the model space about its Z
axis, as depicted in Figure 4.3, all we need to do is pre-mul-
tiply the current viewing matrix by a matrix representing the
desired rotation.

Let P be a reference point with model space coordinates (x_1, y_1, z_1) and viewing space coordinates (x_1^V, y_1^V, z_1^V), and T_1^V
the current viewing matrix, then we have

$$
\begin{bmatrix} x_1 \\ y_1 \\ z_1 \\ 1 \end{bmatrix} = T_1^V \cdot \begin{bmatrix} x_1^V \\ y_1^V \\ z_1^V \\ 1 \end{bmatrix}
\tag{4.1}
$$

The new viewing coordinates of P are those that will produce, under the current viewing transformation, a point in the model space that is equivalent to P being rotated about the Z axis. Thus if we denote the desired rotation of the model space by R_Z (Θ), the new viewing matrix by T_2^V, and the new viewing coordinates of P by (x_2^V, y_2^V, z_2^V), then the model space and the new viewing space coordinates of P may be related by

$$
R_Z(-\Theta) \cdot \begin{bmatrix} x_1 \\ y_1 \\ z_1 \\ 1 \end{bmatrix} = T_1^V \cdot \begin{bmatrix} x_2^V \\ y_2^V \\ z_2^V \\ 1 \end{bmatrix}
\tag{4.2}
$$

Note that the sign of the rotational angle is reversed in the above equation to achieve the required object transformation. Thus the formula for this particular viewing operation may be obtained by pre-multiplying both sides of the above equation by $R_Z(\Theta)$, and

$$
T_2^V = R_Z(\Theta) \cdot T_1^V
\tag{4.3}
$$

The above analysis is implemented in subroutine ROTXYZ, listed below, which will adjust the current viewing matrix according to the axis and angle of rotation given to the subroutine.

```
*
*    Compute Viewing Matrix for Rotated View about Model Space Axes
*
     SUBROUTINE ROTXYZ(IAXIS,THETA)
     REAL T1(4,4),T2(3,3),T3(3)
     COMMON /MATRIX/ NMAT,R(3,3,50),T(3,50),IDEF
     CALL ROTATE(IAXIS,THETA,T1)
     DO 20 I=1,3
        DO 10 J=1,3
```

```
            T2(I,J)=R(I,J,1)
10      CONTINUE
            T3(1)=T(1,1)
20      CONTINUE
        DO 60 I=1,3
            DO 40 J=1,3
            R(I,J,1)=0.0
                DO 30 K=1,3
                R(I,J,1)=R(I,J,1)+T1(I,K)*T2(K,J)
30          CONTINUE
40      CONTINUE
            T(I,1)=0.0
            DO 50 K=1,3
                T(I,1)=T(I,1)+T1(I,K)*T3(K)
50      CONTINUE
60      CONTINUE
        RETURN
        END
```

Figure 4.4 shows two orthographic views resulting from rotating the model space shown in Figures 4.1 and 4.2 about the
X axis by 30°.

4.2   3-D DESIGN IN SWITCHABLE DEFINITION SPACES

Vertex (point) and edge (line segment) entities are the backbone
of a polyhedral solid.   The drafting front-end of CAD-PS is to
provide design tools for constructing 3-D wire-frames, consisting
of vertices and edges, from which polyhedral solids may be built.
    There are many approaches to specifying a geometry point.
The POINT module presented in Section 3.2 provided only two
definition modes: keyboard entry of definition space coordinates
and digitizing on selected XT-YT planes via the Mouse Cursor.
However, most of the editing options in the LINE module also
create point entities, for there are always two end points on a
line segment.
    The 3-D characteristics of most of the design features in LINE
are limited to selected XT-YT planes that are parallel to the X-Y
plane, since only a default definition space, which is identical to
the model space, is allowed thus far.   To broaden the utility of
these design tools, we now devise a definition space-switching
scheme that will allow the user to establish arbitrarily oriented
definition spaces.
    To define a new definition space is to establish a particular
transformation matrix for relating the coordinates of point entities
in that definition space to those in the model space.   The default
definition space in CAD-PS is the model space itself, for which

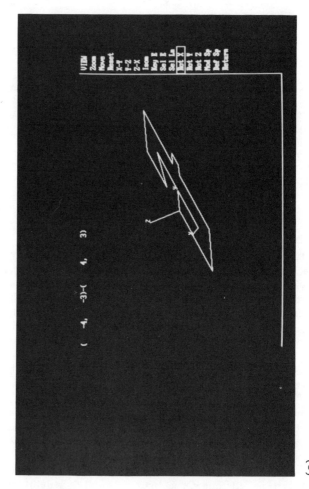

(a)

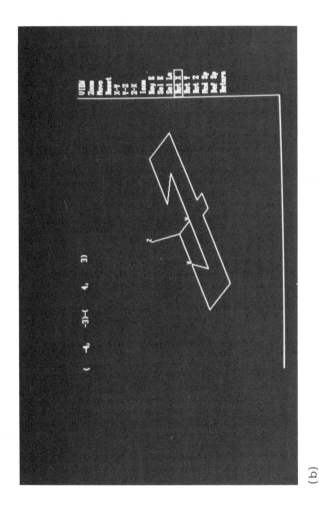

(b)

Figure 4.4   Rotation of model spaces in Figures 4.1 and 4.2 about the X axis.

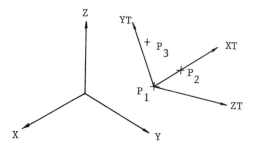

Figure 4.5   A three-point definition space.

the transformation matrix is an identity matrix. A set of XT,
YT and ZT axes may be placed at any point along any desired
orientation in the model space to establish a *local* coordinate reference system to facilitate the design of specifically oriented
geometric entities.

As discussed in Section 2.2.4, the location and orientation of
the XT, YT and ZT axes are directly responsible for the twelve
elements (R_{ij} and T_i) defining the transformation matrix between
a definition space and the model space. Using this relationship,
a local definition space may be established by a three-point approach. Consider three non-collinear points P_1, P_2 and P_3 as
shown in Figure 4.5. If the origin of a new definition space is
to be put at P_1, with its XT axis lying along the P_1P_2 direction,
and its YT axis lying in the plane containing the three points
and located on the same side of P_1P_2 with P_3, then the model
space coordinates of these three points may be used to derive
the desired transformation relation.

The procedure involves four steps: (1) taking the cross product of vector P_1P_2 and vector P_1P_3 to obtain a vector in the
new ZT direction; (2) normalizing this vector and vector P_1P_2
to obtain the unit vectors in the new ZT and XT directions which
would provide the elements at the first and third columns of the
R matrix described in Section 2.2.4; (3) taking the cross product of the new ZT and XT unit vectors to produce the unit vector in the new YT axis which would fill the second column of the
R matrix; and (4) filling the T vector with the model space coordinates of P_1. This process is implemented in module SWITCH
listed below, with the three points being specified either by
Mouse Cursor selection or direct keyboard input. Also listed below is a module for displaying the XT, YT and ZT axes of the
active definition space.

```
*
*   Defining a new Definition Space via the Three-Point Approach
*
      SUBROUTINE SWITCH
      REAL MAT1(4,4),MAT2(4,4),MAT3(4,4)
      CHARACTER*40 BUFFER
      COMMON /POINTS/ NPTS,XT(300),YT(300),ZT(300),IPTDEF(300)
      COMMON /XVYVZV/ XV(300),YV(300),ZV(300)
      COMMON /MATRIX/ NMAT,R(3,3,50),T(3,50),IDEF
      DATA EPS/1.0E-6/,IC2/2/,IC1/1/,MAXMAT/50/
      IF(NMAT.GE.MAXMAT) RETURN
100   CALL PROMPT('\Switch: <L>-Global; <M>-End; <R>-New\')
      CALL USELOC(X,Y,IBUTT)
      CALL PROMPT('\ \')
      IF(IBUTT.EQ.130 .OR. IBUTT.LT.128) RETURN
      IF(IBUTT.EQ.129) GOTO 500
      IF(IDEF.NE.0) THEN
        CALL SHODEF
        CALL SHOXYZ
      ENDIF
      IDEF=0
      RETURN
500   CALL SCALE(1.0,1.0,1.0,MAT1)
      CALL SCALE(1.0,1.0,1.0,MAT2)
520   CALL PROMPT('\Origin: <L>-Sel; <M>-End; <R>-Key\')
      CALL USELOC(X,Y,IBUTT)
      CALL PROMPT('\ \')
      IF(IBUTT.EQ.130 .OR. IBUTT.LT.128) GOTO 100
      IF(IBUTT.EQ.132) THEN
        CALL SRCHPT(NPT1,X,Y)
        IF(NPT1.EQ.0) GOTO 520
        CALL MARKPT(NPT1,IC2)
        CALL DTOM(XT(NPT1),YT(NPT1),ZT(NPT1),XPP,YPP,ZPP,
     &      IPTDEF(NPT1))
        CALL MTOD(XPP,YPP,ZPP,XP,YP,ZP,IDEF)
      ELSE
530     CALL RESET
        CALL PROMPT('\Enter Origin -> [0,0,0]  \')
        CALL INPSTR(BUFFER)
        CALL PROMPT('\ \')
        IF(BUFFER.EQ.' ') THEN
          XP=0.0
          YP=0.0
          ZP=0.0
        ELSE
          READ(BUFFER,*,ERR=530) XP,YP,ZP
        ENDIF
      ENDIF
540   CALL PROMPT('\XT-Axis Pt: <L>-Sel; <M>-End; <R>-Key\')
      CALL USELOC(X,Y,IBUTT)
      CALL PROMPT('\ \')
      IF(IBUTT.EQ.130 .OR. IBUTT.LT.128) GOTO 100
      IF(IBUTT.EQ.132) THEN
        CALL SRCHPT(NPT2,X,Y)
        IF(NPT2.EQ.0 .OR. NPT2.EQ.NPT1) GOTO 540
        CALL MARKPT(NPT2,IC2)
        CALL DTOM(XT(NPT2),YT(NPT2),ZT(NPT2),XPP,YPP,ZPP,
```

```
   &      IPTDEF(NPT2))
          CALL MTOD(XPP,YPP,ZPP,XP1,YP1,ZP1,IDEF)
        ELSE
550       CALL RESET
          CALL PROMPT('\Enter XT-Axis Pt -> [Same]  \')
          CALL INPSTR(BUFFER)
          CALL PROMPT('\ \')
          IF(BUFFER.EQ.' ') GOTO 560
          READ(BUFFER,*,ERR=550) XP1,YP1,ZP1
        ENDIF
        DENOM=SQRT((XP1-XP)**2+(YP1-YP)**2+(ZP1-ZP)**2)
        IF(DENOM.LT.EPS) GOTO 100
        MAT1(1,1)=(XP1-XP)/DENOM
        MAT1(2,1)=(YP1-YP)/DENOM
        MAT1(3,1)=(ZP1-ZP)/DENOM
560     CALL PROMPT('\YT-Axis Pt: <L>-Sel; <M>-End; <R>-Key\')
        CALL USELOC(X,Y,IBUTT)
        CALL PROMPT('\ \')
        IF(IBUTT.EQ.130 .OR. IBUTT.LT.128) GOTO 100
        IF(IBUTT.EQ.132) THEN
          CALL SRCHPT(NPT3,X,Y)
          IF(NPT3.EQ.0 .OR. NPT3.EQ.NPT1 .OR. NPT3.EQ.NPT2) GOTO 560
          CALL MARKPT(NPT3,IC1)
          CALL DTOM(XT(NPT3),YT(NPT3),ZT(NPT3),XPP,YPP,ZPP,
   &        IPTDEF(NPT3))
          CALL MTOD(XPP,YPP,ZPP,XP2,YP2,ZP2,IDEF)
        ELSE
570       CALL RESET
          CALL PROMPT('\Enter YT-Axis Pt -> [Same]  \')
          CALL INPSTR(BUFFER)
          CALL PROMPT('\ \')
          IF(BUFFER.EQ.' ') GOTO 580
          READ(BUFFER,*,ERR=570) XP2,YP2,ZP2
        ENDIF
        DENOM=SQRT((XP2-XP)**2+(YP2-YP)**2+(ZP2-ZP)**2)
        IF(DENOM.LT.EPS) GOTO 100
        MAT1(1,2)=(XP2-XP)/DENOM
        MAT1(2,2)=(YP2-YP)/DENOM
        MAT1(3,2)=(ZP2-ZP)/DENOM
580     MAT1(1,3)=MAT1(2,1)*MAT1(3,2)-MAT1(3,1)*MAT1(2,2)
        MAT1(2,3)=MAT1(1,2)*MAT1(3,1)-MAT1(1,1)*MAT1(3,2)
        MAT1(3,3)=MAT1(1,1)*MAT1(2,2)-MAT1(1,2)*MAT1(2,1)
        DENOM=SQRT(MAT1(1,3)**2+MAT1(2,3)**2+MAT1(3,3)**2)
        IF(DENOM.LT.EPS) GOTO 100
        MAT1(1,3)=MAT1(1,3)/DENOM
        MAT1(2,3)=MAT1(2,3)/DENOM
        MAT1(3,3)=MAT1(3,3)/DENOM
        MAT1(1,2)=MAT1(2,3)*MAT1(3,1)-MAT1(2,1)*MAT1(3,3)
        MAT1(2,2)=MAT1(1,1)*MAT1(3,3)-MAT1(1,3)*MAT1(3,1)
        MAT1(3,2)=MAT1(1,3)*MAT1(2,1)-MAT1(1,1)*MAT1(2,3)
        CALL TRANSL(-XP,-YP,-ZP,MAT2)
        CALL MULT(MAT2,MAT1,MAT3)
        IF(IDEF.NE.0) THEN
          DO 610 J=1,3
            DO 600 K=1,3
              MAT1(J,K)=R(J,K,IDEF)
```

```
            MAT2(J,K)=MAT3(J,K)
600       CONTINUE
          MAT1(J,4)=T(J,IDEF)
          MAT2(J,4)=MAT3(J,4)
610     CONTINUE
        CALL MULT(MAT1,MAT2,MAT3)
      ENDIF
      IF(IDEF.EQ.0) THEN
        CALL SHOXYZ
      ELSE
        CALL SHODEF
      ENDIF
      NMAT=NMAT+1
      IDEF=NMAT
      DO 660 J=1,3
        DO 650 K=1,3
          R(J,K,IDEF)=MAT3(J,K)
650     CONTINUE
        T(J,IDEF)=MAT3(J,4)
660   CONTINUE
      CALL SHODEF
      RETURN
      END




*
*   Display active Definition Space axes
*
      SUBROUTINE SHODEF
      CHARACTER*4 AX(3)
      REAL AXL(3,3),TEMP(3,3)
      COMMON /MATRIX/ NMAT,R(3,3,50),T(3,50),IDEF
      COMMON /WINDOW/ XW1,YW1,XW2,YW2
      DATA AX/'\XT\','\YT\','\ZT\'/,IC0/0/,IC2/2/,IC3/3/
      IF(IDEF.EQ.0) RETURN
      CALL GCOLOR(IC2)
      CALL GXOR(1)
      CALL DTOV(0.,0.,0.,XV0,YV0,ZV0,IDEF)
      REF=(XW2-XW1)/8.
      DO 20 I=1,3
        DO 10 J=1,3
          AXL(I,J)=0.
10      CONTINUE
        AXL(I,I)=REF
20      CONTINUE
      DO 30 I=1,3
        CALL DTOV(AXL(1,I),AXL(2,I),AXL(3,I),TEMP(1,I),TEMP(2,I),
     &    TEMP(3,I),IDEF)
30    CONTINUE
      DO 60 I=1,3
        CALL GWGCSR(XV0,YV0)
        CALL GWLINE(TEMP(1,I),TEMP(2,I))
        CALL GWTEXT(AX(I))
60    CONTINUE
      CALL GXOR(0)
```

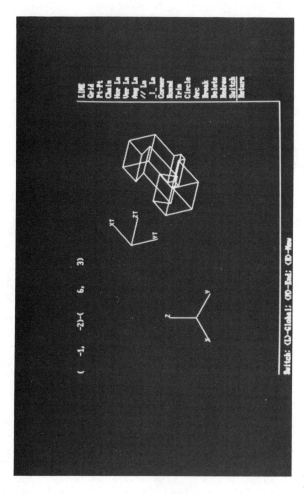

(a)

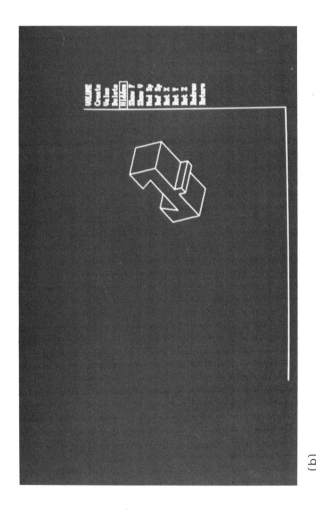

(b)

Figure 4.6   Designing in a definition space: (a) wire-frame;
(b) solid model.

```
CALL GCOLOR(IC3)
RETURN
END
```

The SWITCH module may be included in the major design
modules POINT and LINE. As an example, it will be incorporated
in the TRANSF module to be implemented in the next section.
Figure 4.6 illustrates a wire-frame design within the definition
space defined by points (0, 3, 4), (−1, 5, 7), and (1, 4, 3) in
the model space, along with a hidden lines removed image of a
polyhedral solid based on the wire-frame.

4.3 TRANSFORMATION OF POLYGONAL EDGES

Geometric symmetry seems to be an invariant in all shapes, natural or manmade. In computer-aided geometric design, symmetry
can be given to a shape by transforming a basis geometry
through the design space in linear or rotary paths. In this
section we will add six subroutine modules to CAD-PS to provide the user with facilities to group existing line or edge entities and to transform them in the model space in linear or rotary paths.

The TRANSF module given below may be incorporated in the
root menu of the MAIN module presented in Section 3.5 to provide basic transformation utilities. The individual transformation
modules incorporated in TRANSF will be presented in the following subsections. The reader should note that other transformation functions can easily be added to the menu list of the
TRANSF module. For instance, the reflection or mirroring of
the grouped edge entities with respect to the active XT-YT
plane can be obtained by multiplying the XT, YT, ZT coordinates of the underlying vertices with the scaling matrix S (1,
1, −1).

The TRANSF module given here works only on line entities.
The reader may extend it to provide the same transformation
utilities for relocating or copying other geometric entities, such
as the face and volume entities to be defined later in this chapter and in Chapter 5.

```
*
*    Module for transformation of Polygonal Edges
*
     SUBROUTINE TRANSF
     CHARACTER*8 MENUT(7)
```

```
      DATA MENUT/'\TRANSF\','\Group \','\Transl\','\Rotate\',
    & '\Redraw\','\Switch\','\Return\'/
      ITEMT=7
      CALL DMENU(ITEMT,MENUT)
30    CALL USELOC(X,Y,IBUTT)
      IF(IBUTT.EQ.1 .OR. IBUTT.GE.128) GOTO 30
      IF(IBUTT.GE.ITEMT) RETURN
      ITEM=IBUTT-1
      CALL SMENU(ITEM)
      GOTO(100,200,300,400,500),ITEM
100   CALL DEFGRP
      GOTO 9000
200   CALL EDTRAL
      GOTO 9000
300   CALL EDROTA
      GOTO 9000
400   CALL REDRAW
      GOTO 9000
500   CALL SWITCH
9000  CALL SMENU(ITEM)
      GOTO 30
      END
```

4.3.1 Group of Line Entities

In building 3-D wire-frames, oftentimes it is necessary to move a group of line entities across the design space or duplicate them at specific locations as a whole. The frame in Figure 4.6a was constructed by lifting a plane polygon defined in an XT-YT plane into the ZT direction. First the edges of the base polygon were formed into a *group* using the "Group" option offered by module DEFGRP, which prompts the user to select group members with the Mouse Cursor. A listing of module DEFGRP is given below, followed by module MARKGR which highlights the line entities in the active group.

```
*
*   DEFGRP defines a Group consisting of selected line entities
*
      SUBROUTINE DEFGRP
      COMMON /LINES/ NLNS,IDPT1(400),IDPT2(400),LNFONT(400)
      COMMON /LNGRP/ NLNGP,LNGP(50)
      DATA IC2/2/,MAXGLN/50/
      NLNGP=0
100   CALL PROMPT('\Group: <L>-Sel; <M>-End; <R>-Undo\')
      CALL USELOC(X,Y,IBUTT)
      CALL PROMPT('\ \')
      IF(IBUTT.EQ.130 .OR. IBUTT.LT.128) GOTO 200
      IF(IBUTT.EQ.132) THEN
        CALL SRCHLN(NLN,X,Y)
```

```
      IF(NLN.EQ.0) GOTO 100
      IF(NLNGP.EQ.MAXGLN) THEN
        CALL MESSAG('\Group buffer full!\')
        GOTO 100
      ENDIF
      CALL FACEDG(NLN,IYES)
      IF(IYES.NE.0) THEN
        CALL MESSAG('\Edge of Face not allowed!\')
        GOTO 100
      ENDIF
      CALL MARKLN(NLN,IC2)
      NLNGP=NLNGP+1
      LNGP(NLNGP)=NLN
    ELSE
      IF(NLNGP.EQ.0) GOTO 100
      CALL MARKLN(LNGP(NLNGP),IC2)
      NLNGP=NLNGP-1
    ENDIF
    GOTO 100
200 CALL MARKGR
    RETURN
    END



*
*   Mark current Group menbers
*
    SUBROUTINE MARKGR
    COMMON /XVYVZV/ XV(300),YV(300),ZV(300)
    COMMON /LINES/ NLNS,IDPT1(400),IDPT2(400),LNFONT(400)
    COMMON /LNGRP/ NLNGP,LNGP(50)
    DATA IC2/2/,IC3/3/
    IF(NLNGP.EQ.0) RETURN
    CALL GCOLOR(IC2)
    CALL GXOR(1)
    DO 100 I=1,NLNGP
      I1=IDPT1((LNGP(I)))
      I2=IDPT2((LNGP(I)))
      CALL GWGCSR(XV(I1),YV(I1))
      CALL GWLINE(XV(I2),YV(I2))
100 CONTINUE
    CALL GXOR(0)
    CALL GCOLOR(IC3)
    RETURN
    END
```

4.3.2   Translation and Rotation of Grouped
Line Entities

Two editing options for a non-empty group are presented here:
translation by a given displacement vector in the active definition

space and rotation about the XT, YT or ZT axis. It should again
be emphasized that, due to varied definition spaces utilized in constructing geometric entities and a data base registering only definition space coordinates, all calculations involving non-viewing
coordinates will be performed on corresponding model space coordinates, or on coordinates in the same definition space.

CAD-PS offers three variations in each editing option. The
grouped lines may be simply relocated to a different location in
the design space, or copied to specific locations with the original group retained, or copied to specific locations with linking
lines joining the new and the old grouped entities. The last
version is particularly useful for sweeping plane cross sections
into wire-frames. Figure 4.7 shows the three functions of the
translation option, performed through the following EDTRAL
module. It ought to be noted that an "Undo" option is provided
to allow the user to retract from an unwanted transformation.

```
*
*    Translation of the Grouped entities in Definition space
*    with options to duplicate the Group with or without Links
*
      SUBROUTINE EDTRAL
      CHARACTER*40 BUFFER
      INTEGER LNGPT(50)
      COMMON /POINTS/ NPTS,XT(300),YT(300),ZT(300),IPTDEF(300)
      COMMON /XVYVZV/ XV(300),YV(300),ZV(300)
      COMMON /LINES/ NLNS,IDPT1(400),IDPT2(400),LNFONT(400)
      COMMON /LNGRP/ NLNGP,LNGP(50)
      COMMON /MATRIX/ NMAT,R(3,3,50),T(3,50),IDEF
      DATA IC0/0/,IC3/3/
      IF(NLNGP.EQ.0) THEN
        CALL MESSAG('\Empty Group!\')
        RETURN
      ENDIF
      NPTST=NPTS
      NLNST=NLNS
      DO 2 I=1,NLNGP
        LNGPT(I)=LNGP(I)
2     CONTINUE
5     CALL MARKGR
900   CALL PROMPT('\Translate: <L>-Yes; <M>-End; <R>-Undo\')
      CALL USELOC(X,Y,IBUTT)
      CALL PROMPT('\ \')
      IF(IBUTT.EQ.130 .OR. IBUTT.LT.128) THEN
        CALL MARKGR
        RETURN
      ENDIF
      IF(IBUTT.EQ.129) THEN
        NPTS=NPTST
        NLNS=NLNST
        DO 6 I=1,NLNGP
          LNGP(I)=LNGPT(I)
```

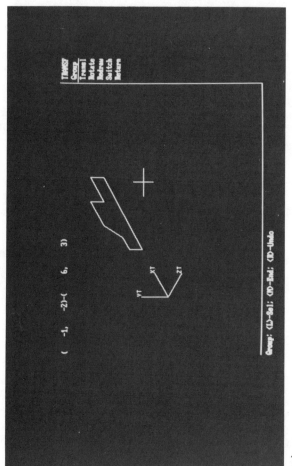

(a)

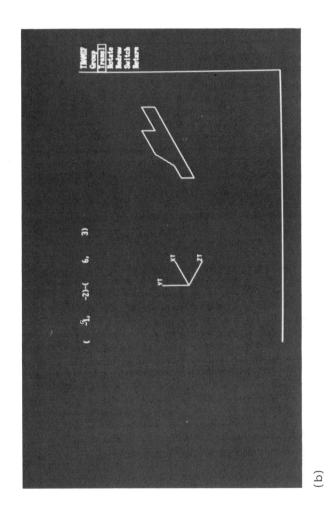

(b)

Figure 4.7   Translation of grouped line entities: (a) cross section;
(b) move Group; (c) copy Group; (d) copy Group with links.

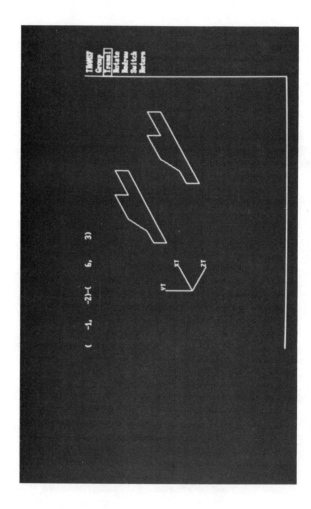

(c)

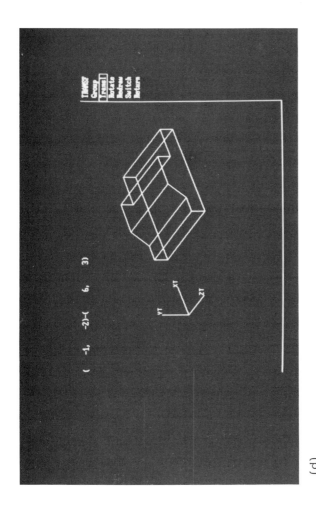

(d)

Figure 4.7   (Continued)

```
6       CONTINUE
        CALL REDRAW
        GOTO 5
      ENDIF
      NPTST=NPTS
      NLNST=NLNS
      DO 8 I=1,NLNGP
        LNGPT(I)=LNGP(I)
8     CONTINUE
10    ICOPY=0
      ILINK=0
      CALL PROMPT('\Action: <L>-Copy; <M>-End; <R>-Move\')
      CALL USELOC(X,Y,IBUTT)
      CALL PROMPT('\ \')
      IF(IBUTT.EQ.130 .OR. IBUTT.LT.128) GOTO 900
      IF(IBUTT.EQ.132) THEN
        ICOPY=1
        CALL PROMPT('\Link Option: <L>-Yes; <M>-End; <R>-No\')
        CALL USELOC(X,Y,IBUTT)
        CALL PROMPT('\ \')
        IF(IBUTT.EQ.130 .OR. IBUTT.LT.128) GOTO 900
        IF(IBUTT.EQ.132) ILINK=1
      ENDIF
20    CALL RESET
      CALL PROMPT('\Enter DX,DY,DZ ->  \')
      CALL INPSTR(BUFFER)
      CALL PROMPT('\ \')
      IF(BUFFER.EQ.' ') GOTO 10
      READ(BUFFER,*,ERR=20) DX,DY,DZ
30    IF(ICOPY.EQ.0) THEN
*
*   Erase Line entities in current Group
*
        DO 100 I=1,NLNGP
          CALL MARKLN(LNGP(I),IC0)
          LNFONT(LNGP(I))=0
100     CONTINUE
      ELSE
        CALL MARKGR
      ENDIF
*
*   Construct new Group
*
      NPTS0=NPTS
      NLNS0=NLNS
      DO 260 I=1,NLNGP
        I1=IDPT1(LNGP(I))
        I2=IDPT2(LNGP(I))
        DO 220 J=1,I-1
          J1=IDPT1(LNGP(J))
          J2=IDPT2(LNGP(J))
          IF(I1.NE.J1 .AND. I1.NE.J2) GOTO 220
          IF(I1.EQ.J1) I1=IDPT1(NLNS0+J)
          IF(I1.EQ.J2) I1=IDPT2(NLNS0+J)
          GOTO 230
220     CONTINUE
        IF(IPTDEF(I1).EQ.IDEF) THEN
```

```
                XTEMP=XT(I1)+DX
                YTEMP=YT(I1)+DY
                ZTEMP=ZT(I1)+DZ
              ELSE
               CALL VECTRA(IDEF,DX,DY,DZ,IPTDEF(I1),XT1,YT1,ZT1)
                XTEMP=XT(I1)+XT1
                YTEMP=YT(I1)+YT1
                ZTEMP=ZT(I1)+ZT1
              ENDIF
              CALL ADDPT(XTEMP,YTEMP,ZTEMP,IPTDEF(I1),IERR)
              IF(IERR.NE.0) RETURN
              I1=NPTS
230           DO 240 J=1,I-1
                J1=IDPT1(LNGP(J))
                J2=IDPT2(LNGP(J))
                IF(I2.NE.J1 .AND. I2.NE.J2) GOTO 240
                IF(I2.EQ.J1) I2=IDPT1(NLNS0+J)
                IF(I2.EQ.J2) I2=IDPT2(NLNS0+J)
                GOTO 250
240           CONTINUE
              IF(IPTDEF(I2).EQ.IDEF) THEN
                XTEMP=XT(I2)+DX
                YTEMP=YT(I2)+DY
                ZTEMP=ZT(I2)+DZ
              ELSE
                CALL VECTRA(IDEF,DX,DY,DZ,IPTDEF(I2),XT1,YT1,ZT1)
                XTEMP=XT(I2)+XT1
                YTEMP=YT(I2)+YT1
                ZTEMP=ZT(I2)+ZT1
              ENDIF
              CALL ADDPT(XTEMP,YTEMP,ZTEMP,IPTDEF(I2),IERR)
              IF(IERR.NE.0) RETURN
              I2=NPTS
250           CALL ADDLN(I1,I2,1,IERR)
              IF(IERR.NE.0) RETURN
260       CONTINUE
*
*    Join new and old Group members if requested
*
          IF(ILINK.NE.0) THEN
            DO 360 I=1,NLNGP
              I1=IDPT1(LNGP(I))
              I2=IDPT2(LNGP(I))
              I3=0
              I4=0
              DO 320 J=1,I-1
                J1=IDPT1(LNGP(J))
                J2=IDPT2(LNGP(J))
                IF(I1.NE.J1 .AND. I1.NE.J2) GOTO 320
                GOTO 330
320           CONTINUE
              I3=IDPT1(NLNS0+I)
330           DO 340 J=1,I-1
                J1=IDPT1(LNGP(J))
                J2=IDPT2(LNGP(J))
                IF(I2.NE.J1 .AND. I2.NE.J2) GOTO 340
                GOTO 350
```

```
340       CONTINUE
          I4=IDPT2(NLNS0+I)
350       IF(I3.NE.0) THEN
             CALL ADDLN(I1,I3,1,IERR)
             IF(IERR.NE.0) RETURN
             CALL MARKLN(NLNS,-IC3)
          ENDIF
          IF(I4.NE.0) THEN
             CALL ADDLN(I2,I4,1,IERR)
             IF(IERR.NE.0) RETURN
             CALL MARKLN(NLNS,-IC3)
          ENDIF
360    CONTINUE
      ENDIF
      DO 380 I=1,NLNGP
        LNGP(I)=NLNS0+I
        CALL MARKLN(LNGP(I),-IC3)
380   CONTINUE
      CALL MARKGR
      GOTO 900
      END


*
*   Transform vector from Def. Space ID1 to Def. Space ID2
*
      SUBROUTINE VECTRA(ID1,DX1,DY1,DZ1,ID2,DX2,DY2,DZ2)
      CALL DTOM(0.,0.,0.,XT1,YT1,ZT1,ID1)
      CALL DTOM(DX1,DY1,DZ1,XT2,YT2,ZT2,ID1)
      CALL MTOD(XT1,YT1,ZT1,XT3,YT3,ZT3,ID2)
      CALL MTOD(XT2,YT2,ZT2,XT4,YT4,ZT4,ID2)
      DX2=XT4-XT3
      DY2=YT4-YT3
      DZ2=ZT4-ZT3
      RETURN
      END
```

As to rotation of grouped line entities with respect to a selected axis of rotation, the system should provide that any line in the model space may be used as an axis of rotation. Here the basic design concept of utilizing definition space coordinate systems as the spine of a design space shows its prowess for ready expansion. With the ability to switch definition space at will, the user needs only options to rotate a group about the current XT, YT or ZT axis in order to perform any desired rotations. Formulas for these basic *object rotations* have been discussed in Section 2.2.3.

Figure 4.8 illustrates four design possibilities. Shown in Figure 4.8a is a cross section constructed in the XT-YT plane of the definition space depicted in Figure 4.6. In Figure 4.8a, a new definition space is created by moving the current definition space by a translation vector (0, 2, 0) defined in that space. The cross section is then rotated about the new XT axis by 60° as shown in Figure 4.8b. Another scenario may have been

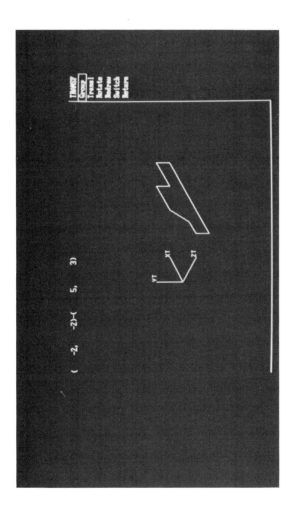

(a)

Figure 4.8   Rotation of grouped line entities: (a) cross section;
(b) rotate Group; (c) copy Group ; (d) copy Group with links.

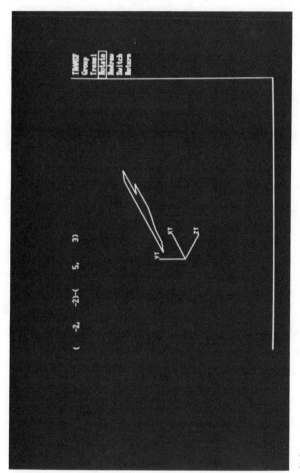

(b)

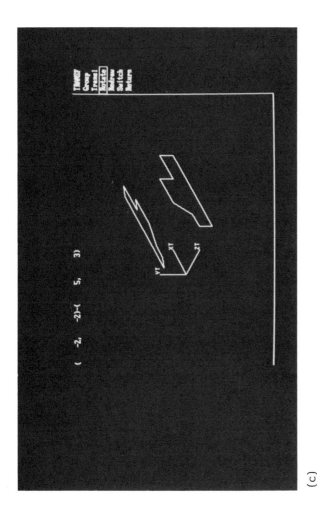

(c)

Figure 4.8   (Continued)

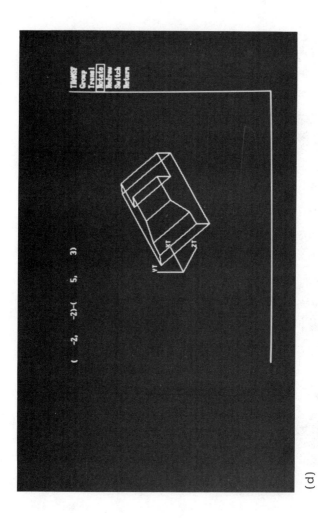

(d)   Figure 4.8   (Continued)

copying the group to its rotated position with the original retained, as illustrated in Figure 4.8c. The copying utility can also
be instructed to connect the new and the old groups with lines
bounded by the corresponding end points. Figure 4.8d shows
the cross section rotated with links to form a 3-D wire-frame.

In the EDROTA module listed below, the definition space pointer
of new group members is inherited from current group members
and is independent of the active definition space providing the
axis of rotation.

```
*
*    Rotation of the Grouped entities in Definition space
*    with options to duplicate the Group with or without Links
*
     SUBROUTINE EDROTA
     INTEGER LNGP0(50),LNGPT(50)
     CHARACTER*40 BUFFER
     REAL T1(4,4)
     COMMON /POINTS/ NPTS,XT(300),YT(300),ZT(300),IPTDEF(300)
     COMMON /XVYVZV/ XV(300),YV(300),ZV(300)
     COMMON /LINES/ NLNS,IDPT1(400),IDPT2(400),LNFONT(400)
     COMMON /LNGRP/ NLNGP,LNGP(50)
     COMMON /MATRIX/ NMAT,R(3,3,50),T(3,50),IDEF
     DATA IC0/0/,IC3/3/,PI/3.141593/,EPS/1.0E-3/
     IF(NLNGP.EQ.0) THEN
       CALL MESSAG('\Empty Group!\')
       RETURN
     ENDIF
     NPTST=NPTS
     NLNST=NLNS
     DO 2 I=1,NLNGP
       LNGPT(I)=LNGP(I)
2    CONTINUE
5    CALL MARKGR
900  CALL PROMPT('\Rotate: <L>-Yes; <M>-End; <R>-Undo\')
     CALL USELOC(X,Y,IBUTT)
     CALL PROMPT('\ \')
     IF(IBUTT.EQ.130 .OR. IBUTT.LT.128) THEN
       CALL MARKGR
       RETURN
     ENDIF
     IF(IBUTT.EQ.129) THEN
       NPTS=NPTST
       NLNS=NLNST
       DO 6 I=1,NLNGP
         LNGP(I)=LNGPT(I)
6      CONTINUE
       CALL REDRAW
       GOTO 5
     ENDIF
     NPTST=NPTS
     NLNST=NLNS
     DO 8 I=1,NLNGP
       LNGPT(I)=LNGP(I)
8    CONTINUE
*
*    Select axis of rotation
```

```
*
      CALL PROMPT('\Axis: <L>-ZT; <M>-YT; <R>-XT\')
      CALL USELOC(X,Y,IBUTT)
      CALL PROMPT('\ \')
      IF(IBUTT.LT.128) RETURN
      IAXIS=IBUTT-128
      IF(IAXIS.GT.3) IAXIS=3
10    ICOPY=0
      ILINK=0
      CALL PROMPT('\Action: <L>-Copy; <M>-End; <R>-Rotate\')
      CALL USELOC(X,Y,IBUTT)
      CALL PROMPT('\ \')
      IF(IBUTT.EQ.130 .OR. IBUTT.LT.128) GOTO 900
      IF(IBUTT.EQ.132) THEN
        ICOPY=1
        CALL PROMPT('\Link Option: <L>-Yes; <M>-End; <R>-No\')
        CALL USELOC(X,Y,IBUTT)
        CALL PROMPT('\ \')
        IF(IBUTT.EQ.130 .OR. IBUTT.LT.128) GOTO 900
        IF(IBUTT.EQ.132) ILINK=1
      ENDIF
20    CALL RESET
*
*   Prompt for angle of rotation and number of rotations
*
      CALL PROMPT('\Enter ANGLE (Degree) ->  \')
      CALL INPSTR(BUFFER)
      CALL PROMPT('\ \')
      IF(BUFFER.EQ.' ') GOTO 10
      READ(BUFFER,*,ERR=20) ANGLE
      IF(ICOPY.NE.0) THEN
22      CALL RESET
        CALL PROMPT('\Enter #Rotations: [1] \')
        CALL INPSTR(BUFFER)
        CALL PROMPT('\ \').
        IF(BUFFER.EQ.' ') THEN
          NCOPY=1
        ELSE
          READ(BUFFER,*,ERR=22) NCOPY
        ENDIF
*
*   Turn on Flag ICLOSE if complete circular rotation
*   is requested
*
        ICLOSE=0
        IF(ABS(NCOPY*ANGLE-360.0).LT.EPS) ICLOSE=1
      ENDIF
      ANGLE=-ANGLE*PI/180.0
      CALL ROTATE(IAXIS,ANGLE,TI)
30    IF(ICOPY.EQ.0) THEN
        DO 100 I=1,NLNGP
          CALL MARKLN(LNGP(I),IC0)
          LNFONT(LNGP(I))=0
100     CONTINUE
        NCOPY=1
        ICLOSE=0
```

```
      ELSE
        CALL MARKGR
      ENDIF
      IF(ICLOSE.NE.0) THEN
        DO 210 I=1,NLNGP
          LNGP0(I)=LNGP(I)
210     CONTINUE
      ENDIF
*
*   Construct new Group(s)
*
      DO 400 N=1,NCOPY
        IF(ICLOSE.NE.0 .AND. N.EQ.NCOPY) GOTO 270
*
*   Merge into original Group to complete circular rotation
*
        NPTS0=NPTS
        NLNS0=NLNS
        DO 260 I=1,NLNGP
          I1=IDPT1(LNGP(I))
          I2=IDPT2(LNGP(I))
          DO 220 J=1,I-1
            J1=IDPT1(LNGP(J))
            J2=IDPT2(LNGP(J))
            IF(I1.NE.J1 .AND. I1.NE.J2) GOTO 220
            IF(I1.EQ.J1) I1=IDPT1(NLNS0+J)
            IF(I1.EQ.J2) I1=IDPT2(NLNS0+J)
            GOTO 230
220       CONTINUE
          IF(IPTDEF(I1).EQ.IDEF) THEN
            XTEMP=T1(1,1)*XT(I1)+T1(1,2)*YT(I1)+T1(1,3)*ZT(I1)
            YTEMP=T1(2,1)*XT(I1)+T1(2,2)*YT(I1)+T1(2,3)*ZT(I1)
            ZTEMP=T1(3,1)*XT(I1)+T1(3,2)*YT(I1)+T1(3,3)*ZT(I1)
          ELSE
            CALL DTOM(XT(I1),YT(I1),ZT(I1),XM1,YM1,ZM1,IPTDEF(I1))
            CALL MTOD(XM1,YM1,ZM1,XT1,YT1,ZT1,IDEF)
            XTEMP=T1(1,1)*XT1+T1(1,2)*YT1+T1(1,3)*ZT1
            YTEMP=T1(2,1)*XT1+T1(2,2)*YT1+T1(2,3)*ZT1
            ZTEMP=T1(3,1)*XT1+T1(3,2)*YT1+T1(3,3)*ZT1
            CALL DTOM(XTEMP,YTEMP,ZTEMP,XM1,YM1,ZM1,IDEF)
            CALL MTOD(XM1,YM1,ZM1,XTEMP,YTEMP,ZTEMP,IPTDEF(I1))
          ENDIF
          CALL ADDPT(XTEMP,YTEMP,ZTEMP,IPTDEF(I1),IERR)
          IF(IERR.NE.0) RETURN
          I1=NPTS
230       DO 240 J=1,I-1
            J1=IDPT1(LNGP(J))
            J2=IDPT2(LNGP(J))
            IF(I2.NE.J1 .AND. I2.NE.J2) GOTO 240
            IF(I2.EQ.J1) I2=IDPT1(NLNS0+J)
            IF(I2.EQ.J2) I2=IDPT2(NLNS0+J)
            GOTO 250
240       CONTINUE
          IF(IPTDEF(I2).EQ.IDEF) THEN
            XTEMP=T1(1,1)*XT(I2)+T1(1,2)*YT(I2)+T1(1,3)*ZT(I2)
            YTEMP=T1(2,1)*XT(I2)+T1(2,2)*YT(I2)+T1(2,3)*ZT(I2)
```

```
              ZTEMP=T1(3,1)*XT(I2)+T1(3,2)*YT(I2)+T1(3,3)*ZT(I2)
          ELSE
            CALL DTOM(XT(I2),YT(I2),ZT(I2),XM1,YM1,ZM1,IPTDEF(I2))
            CALL MTOD(XM1,YM1,ZM1,XT1,YT1,ZT1,IDEF)
            XTEMP=T1(1,1)*XT1+T1(1,2)*YT1+T1(1,3)*ZT1
            YTEMP=T1(2,1)*XT1+T1(2,2)*YT1+T1(2,3)*ZT1
            ZTEMP=T1(3,1)*XT1+T1(3,2)*YT1+T1(3,3)*ZT1
            CALL DTOM(XTEMP,YTEMP,ZTEMP,XM1,YM1,ZM1,IDEF)
            CALL MTOD(XM1,YM1,ZM1,XTEMP,YTEMP,ZTEMP,IPTDEF(I2))
          ENDIF
          CALL ADDPT(XTEMP,YTEMP,ZTEMP,IPTDEF(I2),IERR)
          IF(IERR.NE.0) RETURN
          I2=NPTS
250       CALL ADDLN(I1,I2,1,IERR)
          IF(IERR.NE.0) RETURN
260     CONTINUE
270     IF(ILINK.NE.0) THEN
*
*   Define Links between new and old Group members
*
          DO 360 I=1,NLNGP
            I1=IDPT1(LNGP(I))
            I2=IDPT2(LNGP(I))
            I3=0
            I4=0
            DO 320 J=1,I-1
              J1=IDPT1(LNGP(J))
              J2=IDPT2(LNGP(J))
              IF(I1.NE.J1 .AND. I1.NE.J2) GOTO 320
              GOTO 330
320         CONTINUE
            IF(ICLOSE.NE.0 .AND. N.EQ.NCOPY) THEN
              I3=IDPT1(LNGP0(I))
            ELSE
              I3=IDPT1(NLNS0+I)
            ENDIF
330         DO 340 J=1,I-1
              J1=IDPT1(LNGP(J))
              J2=IDPT2(LNGP(J))
              IF(I2.NE.J1 .AND. I2.NE.J2) GOTO 340
              GOTO 350
340         CONTINUE
            IF(ICLOSE.NE.0 .AND. N.EQ.NCOPY) THEN
              I4=IDPT2(LNGP0(I))
            ELSE
              I4=IDPT2(NLNS0+I)
            ENDIF
350         IF(I3.NE.0) THEN
              CALL ADDLN(I1,I3,1,IERR)
              IF(IERR.NE.0) RETURN
              CALL MARKLN(NLNS,-IC3)
            ENDIF
            IF(I4.NE.0) THEN
              CALL ADDLN(I2,I4,1,IERR)
```

```
                  IF(IERR.NE.0) RETURN
                  CALL MARKLN(NLNS,-IC3)
                ENDIF
360         CONTINUE
          ENDIF
          IF(ICLOSE.NE.0 .AND. N.EQ.NCOPY) THEN
            DO 370 I=1,NLNGP
              LNGP(I)=LNGP0(I)
370         CONTINUE
          ELSE
            DO 380 I=1,NLNGP
              LNGP(I)=NLNS0+I
              CALL MARKLN(LNGP(I),-IC3)
380         CONTINUE
          ENDIF
400     CONTINUE
        CALL MARKGR
        GOTO 900
        END
```

4.4   MODELING OF 3-D FINITE-ELEMENT MESHES

At this point, CAD-PS is empowered to perform basic 3-D
drafting tasks. We shall continue our course of implementing a
polyhedral solid modeling system on the PC in the next section.
Here we take a brief diversion to examine another possible use
of the 3-D drafting capacity of CAD-PS.

In modern design methodology, finite element analysis is essential in providing the designer with a powerful evaluation
tool to put preliminary product models to the test, by simulating
on the computer the performance of designed models subjecting
to any desired functional constraints. Such simulation results
are to serve as criteria for design revisions or acceptance.

To perform finite element analysis, the geometric shape of a
designed model must first be discretized or split into connected
small elements. These well-arranged small finite elements, together with specific material properties and functional constraints,
are then processed by a finite element solver program to produce numerical results for the input system, in the form of
specific physical quantities such as temperature and stress.

A 3-D drafting system such as CAD-PS can be used to generate finite-element meshes required for the numerical simulation. As of now, CAD-PS does not provide specific design
options for creating finite-element meshes. However, special-
purpose modules can be implemented to perform interactive
finite-element mesh generation. Figure 4.9 shows a primitive
finite-element mesh.

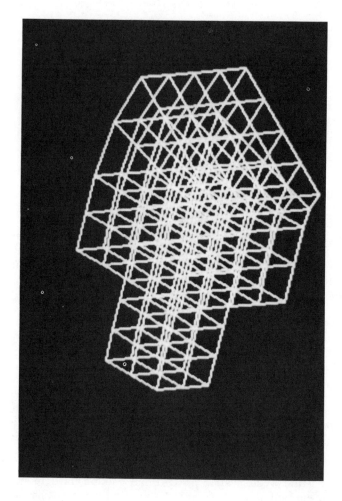

Figure 4.9   A 3-D finite-element mesh.

4.5   REPRESENTATION AND FORMATION OF POLYGONAL FACES

Wire-frame models as shown in Figures 4.6a, 4.7 and 4.8 are precursors of CAD-PS's solid models, they do not represent any realistic product models at this stage. A typical example used to demonstrate the deficiency of wire-frame modeling is a frame made up of two connected cubes, as shown in Figure 4.10a. Without imparting precise surface definitions to the wire-frame, one may mentally relate the frame to any of the three solids shown in Figures 4.10b, 4.10c and 4.10d. Such ambiguities can be eliminated through solid modeling.

The next step toward modeling polyhedral solids is to add to CAD-PS design modules for forming polygonal faces from 3-D wire-frames. In this section we will expand the data base of CAD-PS to accommodate the polygonal face entity, and implement a FACE module which will allow the user to define polygonal faces from selected line segments or edges.

4.5.1   Representation of Polygonal Faces

Until now we have been building wire-frames with point and line entities. In order to impart surface information to a wire-frame, we need to expand the data base of CAD-PS so polygonal face entities can be incorporated in the model file.

A polygonal face, or simply polygon, is a closed plane region bounded by an arrangement of connected, but non-intersecting line segments or edges. Thus only coplanar, properly connected line segments can be used to form a polygon. A polygon is *convex* when it lies entirely on one side of each of its edges. This implies that any line segments joining any two interior points in the polygon will stay wholly inside the polygon.

Polyhedron is the 3-D counterpart of polygon. A polyhedron is *convex* when it lies entirely on one side of each of its polygon faces. In a convex polyhedron any line segments joining any two interior points in the polyhedron will stay wholly inside the polyhedron. The definition and characteristics of the polyhedron entity will be elaborated in Chapter 5.

A consequence of the above analysis is that a non-convex or *concave* polygon or polyhedron would have *reentrant* edges or faces. Figure 4.11 gives examples of these geometric entities.

In establishing data blocks for line entities, we adopted a pointer approach in which a line segment is registered as two

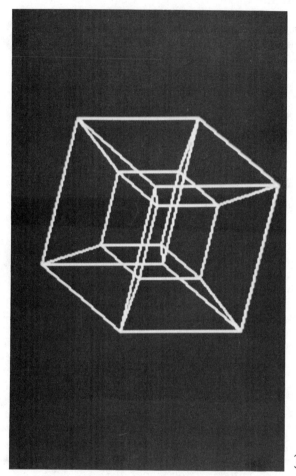

(a)

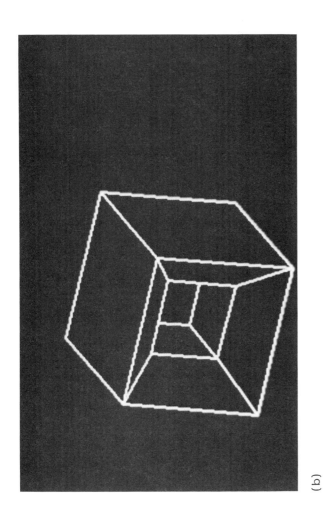

(b)

Figure 4.10   Deficiency of wire-frames in representing solid entities.

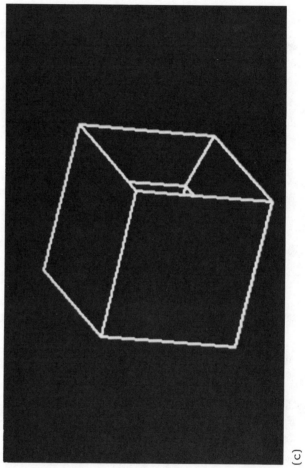

(c)

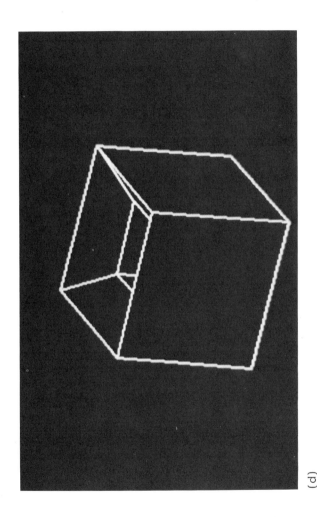

(d)

Figure 4.10   (Continued)

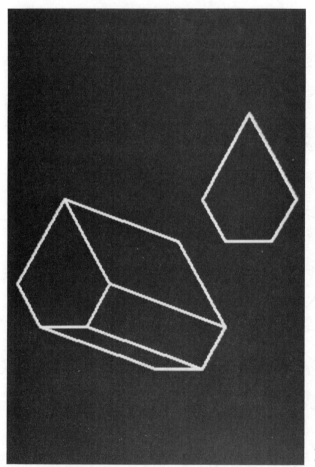

(a)

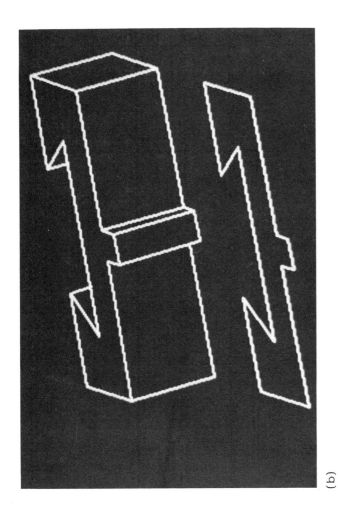

(b)

Figure 4.11   (a) Convex polygon/polyhedron; (b) concave polygon/
polyhedron.

pointers to the locations of the definition space coordinates of
its two end points. Since a polygon is bounded by an arrangement of edges or line segments, we may register a polygon as
a sequence of pointers to its bounding edges.

The COMMON block /FACET1/ listed below is used to register
up to 100 polygonal faces each can have up to 30 edges.

```
COMMON /FACET1/ NFAS,NEDGE(100),IDEDGE(30,100)
```

In order to identify specific faces, we need to attach a label
to each face. We shall use the /FACET2/ block given below to
store the label locations of existing face entities, in model space
coordinates.

```
COMMON /FACET2/ FX(100),FY(100),FZ(100)
```

4.5.2 The FACE Module

In modules FACE and MKFAC given at the end of this subsection, a polygon is defined by the user's selecting its bounding
edges in counterclockwise order when viewed from outside of
the underlying polyhedron. The order in selecting the edges is
important because it allows us to calculate the outer normal vector of each polygonal face, as well as the volume contained in
the underlying polyhedron (see Sec. 5.1.4). This definition
also implies that if one stands upright in the direction of the
outer normal vector and walks along the bounding edges in the
specified order, the *inside* of the polygon is always to the left
of the observer. Figure 4.12 shows the definition of two polygons in this order.

Convex and concave polygons are known as *simple* polygons
because any loops formed inside such a polygon can always be
contracted into a single point without cutting through the boundary of the polygon. A polygon with *holes* in it is *not* a simple
polygon. Such polygons may be defined by their inner and
outer edge-loops through separate data blocks, but this will
inevitably complicate the design of CAD-PS. A practical alterna-
tive to this is to define a special type of edge which connects
the outer and inner loops so that the definition of simple polygons
can still be applied to polygons with holes. Such a connecting
edge has been called a *Bridge* edge or B-edge. Module BEDGE
listed below implements an interactive procedure for constructing
B-edges.

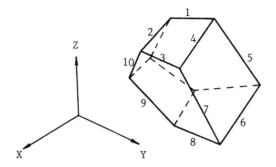

Face 1	Face 2
NEDGE(1)=4	NEDGE(2)=5
IDEDGE(1,1)=1	IDEDGE(1,2)=3
IDEDGE(2,1)=2	IDEDGE(2,2)=10
IDEDGE(3,1)=3	IDEDGE(3,2)=9
IDEDGE(4,1)=4	IDEDGE(4,2)=8
	IDEDGE(5,2)=7

Figure 4.12   Formation of polygonal faces from edges.

Figure 4.13 gives an example of using a B-edge to register a double-loop polygon. Notice that the order of entry of the edges is maintained such that the *inside* of the polygon is always to the left of an observer walking along the edges, and that the dotted B-edge is entered twice to form a closed polygon. In CAD-PS, a B-edge is assigned a font number of 99, while a regular edge has the font number of a solid line, 1.

CAD-PS requires that its user assume the responsibility of designing well-formed edges, and select the edges in proper order while constructing polygon entities. However, it does check for the connectivity of selected edges and retain an equation of the plane calculated from the first two edges so the user may be notified when a selected edge is not in the same plane. In addition, CAD-PS automatically closes a polygon and displays its label, at the mid-point between the first and third vertices, when a selected edge meets the beginning edge at the beginning vertex and the user decides not to add any more edges. (See module MKFAC.)

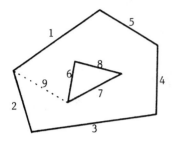

<u>Face N</u>

```
NEDGE(N)=10
IDEDGE(1,N)=1
IDEDGE(2,N)=9
IDEDGE(3,N)=6
IDEDGE(4,N)=8
IDEDGE(5,N)=7
IDEDGE(6,N)=9
IDEDGE(7,N)=2
IDEDGE(8,N)=3
IDEDGE(9,N)=4
IDEDGE(10,N)=5
```

Figure 4.13   Polygonal face with one hole.

An equation of the plane containing a polygon entity can be determined from any three non-collinear vertices associated with the polygon. The problem is equivalent to finding the four real coefficients of the general equation of a plane in 3-D space:

$$a \cdot x + b \cdot y + c \cdot z = d \qquad\qquad (4.4)$$

where (x, y, z) represents a general point in the plane.

It is known that, in a plane equation, the first three coefficients define a normal vector to the plane which may be denoted by (a, b, c). These coefficients can be obtained by taking the cross product of the vector from the first vertex to the second vertex with the vector from the second vertex to the third vertex. The cross product will result in a vector that is normal to the underlying plane. To complete the plane equation, the coordinates of any vertex may be used to evaluate the remaining coefficient d. The listing of CAD modules presented in this subsection includes a module, named PLN, for evaluating a plane equation from two neighboring edge entities.

It is notable that the normal vector of a polygon as obtained above does not always point to the outside of the underlying polyhedron. It does so only when the three vertices do not form a reentrant corner, otherwise an *inner* normal vector will result. However, the outer normal vector of a polygon can always be obtained by dividing the polygon into triangles and using any of the triangles to evaluate the plane equation. The triangulation of polygons will be discussed in Section 4.7.1.

The plane equation of a polygon can be used to identify possible intersections between two polygons. The plane equation may be rewritten as

$$f(x, y, z) = 0$$

where

$$f(x, y, z) = a \cdot x + b \cdot y + c \cdot z - d \qquad (4.5)$$

The f-value of any point in the plane is zero. The f-form provides a quick reference for determining if two points are located on the opposite sides of the plane, for the f-values of points on one side have different signs from those on the other side.

Suppose we need to determine if an edge of a polygon intersects with another polygon occupying the plane specified by $f(x, y, z) = 0$. It is evident that, when both f-values of its two vertices are zero, the edge will share the same plane with the target polygon, thus having an infinite number of intersections with the plane containing the target polygon. When both f-values are of the same sign, then the edge is wholly on one side of the target polygon and will not intersect the target polygon.

Denoting the f-values of the two vertices as f_1 and f_2 and knowing f_1 and f_2 differ in signs, we obtain the following formulas for the coordinates of the intersection point (x_0, y_0, z_0):

$$x_0 = x_1 + [f_1/(f_1 - f_2)] (x_2 - x_1)$$

$$y_0 = y_1 + [f_1/(f_1 - f_2)] (y_2 - y_1)$$

and

$$z_0 = z_1 + [f_1/(f_1 - f_2)] (z_2 - z_1) \qquad (4.6)$$

The edge will intersect the polygon when the above intersection point lies *inside* the target polygon (see Sec. 4.7.1). This procedure for detecting intersecting polygons will be utilized in Section 5.3.

The face formation and editing procedure is carried out by the FACE module, which may be incorporated in the MAIN module in Section 3.5, and several auxiliary modules. They are listed as follows.

```
*
*   Definition and editing of Face entities
*
      SUBROUTINE FACE
      CHARACTER*8 MENUF(10)
      COMMON /LINES/ NLNS,IDPT1(400),IDPT2(400),LNFONT(400)
      DATA MENUF/'\FACE   \','\Create\','\B-Edge\','\Ln Typ\',
     & '\Corner\','\Brk Ln\','\Delete\','\Show F\','\Redraw\',
     & '\Return\'/
      ITEMF=10
      IF(NLNS.LT.3) RETURN
      CALL DMENU(ITEMF,MENUF)
30    CALL USELOC(X,Y,IBUTT)
      IF(IBUTT.EQ.1 .OR. IBUTT.GE.128) GOTO 30
      IF(IBUTT.GE.ITEMF) RETURN
      ITEM=IBUTT-1
      CALL SMENU(ITEM)
      GOTO (100,200,300,400,500,600,700,800),ITEM
100   CALL MKFAC
      GOTO 9000
200   CALL BEDGE
      GOTO 9000
300   CALL LNTYP
      GOTO 9000
400   CALL CORNER(2)
      GOTO 9000
500   CALL BRKLN
      GOTO 9000
600   CALL DELFAC
      GOTO 9000
700   CALL SHOFAC
      GOTO 9000
800   CALL REDRAW
9000  CALL SMENU(ITEM)
      GOTO 30
      END



*
*   Formation of Face entities
*
      SUBROUTINE MKFAC
      COMMON /POINTS/ NPTS,XT(300),YT(300),ZT(300),IPTDEF(300)
```

```
      COMMON /LINES/ NLNS,IDPT1(400),IDPT2(400),LNFONT(400)
      COMMON /FACET1/ NFAS,NEDGE(100),IDEDGE(30,100)
      COMMON /FACET2/ FX(100),FY(100),FZ(100)
      DATA IC0/0/,IC1/1/,IC2/2/,IC3/3/,MAXFAS/100/,MAXEDG/30/
10    IF(NFAS.GE.MAXFAS) THEN
        CALL MESSAG('\Number of Faces overflows!\')
        RETURN
      ENDIF
      IUNDO=0
      NFAS=NFAS+1
      NEDGE(NFAS)=0
100   CALL PROMPT('\Edges: <L>-Sel; <M>-End; <R>-Undo\')
      CALL USELOC(X,Y,IBUTT)
      CALL PROMPT('\ \')
      IF(IBUTT.NE.130 .AND. IBUTT.GE.128) GOTO 130
110   DO 120 I=1,NEDGE(NFAS)
        CALL MARKLN(IDEDGE(I,NFAS),IC2)
120   CONTINUE
      NFAS=NFAS-1
      RETURN
130   IF(IBUTT.EQ.129) THEN
        IF(IUNDO.EQ.0) GOTO 100
        CALL MARKLN(NLN,IC2)
        NEDGE(NFAS)=NEDGE(NFAS)-1
        IFREE=ITEMP
        IUNDO=0
        GOTO 100
      ENDIF
      CALL SRCHLN(NLN,X,Y)
      IF(NLN.EQ.0) GOTO 100
      DO 140 I=1,NEDGE(NFAS)
        IF(NLN.EQ.IDEDGE(I,NFAS) .AND. LNFONT(NLN).NE.99)
     &    GOTO 100
140   CONTINUE
      IF(NEDGE(NFAS).GT.0) THEN
        IF(NEDGE(NFAS).EQ.1) THEN
          IFREE=IDPT1(IDEDGE(1,NFAS))
          CALL JOINT(NLN,IFREE,IYES)
          IF(IYES.EQ.0) THEN
            IFREE=IDPT2(IDEDGE(1,NFAS))
            CALL JOINT(NLN,IFREE,IYES)
            IF(IYES.EQ.0) GOTO 150
            ISTART=IDPT1(IDEDGE(1,NFAS))
          ELSE
            ISTART=IDPT2(IDEDGE(1,NFAS))
          ENDIF
          CALL PLN(IDEDGE(1,NFAS),NLN,A,B,C,D,IERR)
          IF(IERR.NE.0) THEN
            CALL PROMPT('\Edges Not Co-planar! <L>\')
            CALL USELOC(X,Y,IBUTT)
            CALL PROMPT('\ \')
            GOTO 110
          ENDIF
          GOTO 160
        ENDIF
      ENDIF
```

```
        ITEMP=IFREE
        CALL JOINT(NLN,IFREE,IYES)
150     IF(IYES.EQ.0) THEN
          CALL MESSAG('\Edges do Not connect! \')
          IFREE=ITEMP
          GOTO 100
        ENDIF
        CALL COPLN(IFREE,A,B,C,D,IYES)
        IF(IYES.EQ.0) THEN
          CALL MESSAG('\Edge Not on Face! \')
          IFREE=ITEMP
          GOTO 100
        ENDIF
      ENDIF
160   CONTINUE
      IF(NEDGE(NFAS).GE.MAXEDG) THEN
        CALL MESSAG('\Number of Edges overflows!\')
        GOTO 110
      ENDIF
      NEDGE(NFAS)=NEDGE(NFAS)+1
      IDEDGE(NEDGE(NFAS),NFAS)=NLN
      CALL MARKLN(NLN,IC2)
      IUNDO=1
      IF(NEDGE(NFAS).LT.3) GOTO 100
      IF(IFREE.NE.ISTART) GOTO 100
      CALL MESSAG('\Edges Close! \')
      CALL PROMPT('\Loop: <L>-Face; <M>-End; <R>-More\')
      CALL USELOC(X,Y,IBUTT)
      CALL PROMPT('\ \')
      CALL MESSAG('\ \')
      IF(IBUTT.EQ.130 .OR. IBUTT.LT.128) GOTO 110
      IF(IBUTT.EQ.129) GOTO 100
*
*   Label is placed at mid-point between 1st & 3rd vertices
*
      I1=ISTART
      J1=IDPT2(IDEDGE(2,NFAS))
      IF(J1.EQ.IDPT1(IDEDGE(1,NFAS)) .OR.
     & J1.EQ.IDPT2(IDEDGE(1,NFAS))) J1=IDPT1(IDEDGE(2,NFAS))
      CALL DTOM(XT(I1),YT(I1),ZT(I1),XTI1,YTI1,ZTI1,IPTDEF(I1))
      CALL DTOM(XT(J1),YT(J1),ZT(J1),XTJ1,YTJ1,ZTJ1,IPTDEF(J1))
      FX(NFAS)=(XTI1+XTJ1)/2.
      FY(NFAS)=(YTI1+YTJ1)/2.
      FZ(NFAS)=(ZTI1+ZTJ1)/2.
      CALL MARKFA(NFAS,-IC3)
      CALL PROMPT('\Create another Face? <L>-Yes\')
      CALL USELOC(X,Y,IBUTT)
      CALL PROMPT('\ \')
      IF(IBUTT.EQ.132) GOTO 10
      RETURN
      END



*
*   Option for creating B-edges
*
```

```
      SUBROUTINE BEDGE
      COMMON /POINTS/ NPTS,XT(300),YT(300),ZT(300),IPTDEF(300)
      COMMON /LINES/ NLNS,IDPT1(400),IDPT2(400),LNFONT(400)
      COMMON /FACET1/NFAS,NEDGE(100),IDEDGE(30,100)
      COMMON /FACET2/ FX(100),FY(100),FZ(100)
      DATA IC1/1/,IC2/2/,IC3/3/
      IUNDO=0
200   CALL PROMPT('\First Pt: <L>-Sel; <M>-End; <R>-Undo\')
      CALL USELOC(X,Y,IBUTT)
      CALL PROMPT('\ \')
      IF(IBUTT.EQ.130 .OR. IBUTT.LT.128) RETURN
      IF(IBUTT.EQ.132) THEN
        CALL SRCHPT(NPT,X,Y)
        IF(NPT.EQ.0) GOTO 200
        CALL MARKPT(NPT,IC2)
      ELSE
        IF(IUNDO.EQ.0) GOTO 200
        CALL MARKLN(NLNS,IC3)
        NLNS=NLNS-1
        IUNDO=0
        GOTO 200
      ENDIF
210   CALL PROMPT('\Second Pt: <L>-Sel; <M,R>-End\')
      CALL USELOC(X,Y,IBUTT)
      CALL PROMPT('\ \')
      IF(IBUTT.NE.132) RETURN
      CALL SRCHPT(NPT2,X,Y)
      IF(NPT2.EQ.0 .OR. NPT2.EQ.NPT) GOTO 210
      IF(IPTDEF(NPT2).NE.IPTDEF(NPT)) GOTO 210
      CALL ADDLN(NPT,NPT2,99,IERR)
      IF(IERR.NE.0) GOTO 210
      CALL MARKLN(NLNS,IC3)
      IUNDO=1
      GOTO 200
      END


*
*   Option for changing LNFONT of edge entities
*
      SUBROUTINE LNTYP
      COMMON /POINTS/ NPTS,XT(300),YT(300),ZT(300),IPTDEF(300)
      COMMON /LINES/ NLNS,IDPT1(400),IDPT2(400),LNFONT(400)
      COMMON /FACET1/ NFAS,NEDGE(100),IDEDGE(30,100)
      COMMON /FACET2/ FX(100),FY(100),FZ(100)
      DATA IC0/0/,IC2/2/,IC3/3/
100   CALL PROMPT('\Type Change: <L>-Sel; <M,R>-End\')
      CALL USELOC(X,Y,IBUTT)
      CALL PROMPT('\ \')
      IF(IBUTT.NE.132) RETURN
      CALL SRCHLN(NLN,X,Y)
      IF(NLN.EQ.0) GOTO 100
      CALL MARKLN(NLN,IC0)
      LNFONT(NLN)=100-LNFONT(NLN)
      CALL MARKLN(NLN,IC3)
      GOTO 100
      END
```

```
*
*    Option for deleting Face entities
*
      SUBROUTINE DELFAC
      INTEGER IDTEMP(30)
      COMMON /FACET1/ NFAS,NEDGE(100),IDEDGE(30,100)
      COMMON /FACET2/ FX(100),FY(100),FZ(100)
      COMMON /VOL/ NVOS,NFACE(5),IDFACE(50,5),VOLVAL(5),SAREA(5)
      DATA IC0/0/,IC1/1/,IC2/2/,IC3/3/
      IUNDO=0
100   IF(NFAS.EQ.0) RETURN
      CALL PROMPT('\Delete: <L>-Sel; <M>-End; <R>-Undo\')
      CALL USELOC(X,Y,IBUTT)
      CALL PROMPT('\ \')
      IF(IBUTT.EQ.130 .OR. IBUTT.LT.128) RETURN
      IF(IBUTT.EQ.132) THEN
        CALL SRCHFA(NF,X,Y)
        IF(NF.EQ.0) GOTO 100
        DO 150 I=1,NVOS
        DO 150 J=1,NFACE(I)
          IF(NF.EQ.IDFACE(J,I)) THEN
            CALL MESSAG('\Face belongs to a Volume!\')
            GOTO 100
          ENDIF
150     CONTINUE
        DO 155 I=1,NFAS
          CALL MARKFA(I,IC0)
155     CONTINUE
        NFTEMP=NF
        CALL RMVFAC(NF,NED,IDTEMP,FXTEMP,FYTEMP,FZTEMP)
        DO 165 I=1,NFAS
          CALL MARKFA(I,-IC3)
165     CONTINUE
        IUNDO=1
      ELSE
        IF(IUNDO.EQ.0) GOTO 100
        DO 170 I=1,NFAS
          CALL MARKFA(I,IC0)
170     CONTINUE
        CALL INSFAC(NFTEMP,NED,IDTEMP,FXTEMP,FYTEMP,FZTEMP)
        DO 210 I=1,NFAS
          CALL MARKFA(I,-IC3)
210     CONTINUE
        IUNDO=0
      ENDIF
      GOTO 100
      END



*
*    Remove Face NF from data base
*
      SUBROUTINE RMVFAC(N,NED,IDTEMP,FXTEMP,FYTEMP,FZTEMP)
      INTEGER IDTEMP(30)
      COMMON /FACET1/ NFAS,NEDGE(100),IDEDGE(30,100)
```

```
      COMMON /FACET2/ FX(100),FY(100),FZ(100)
      COMMON /VOL/ NVOS,NFACE(5),IDFACE(50,5),VOLVAL(5),SAREA(5)
      IF(NFAS.EQ.0) RETURN
      NED=NEDGE(N)
      DO 10 I=1,NED
      IDTEMP(I)=IDEDGE(I,N)
10    CONTINUE
      FXTEMP=FX(N)
      FYTEMP=FY(N)
      FZTEMP=FZ(N)
      DO 20 I=1,NVOS
      DO 20 J=1,NFACE(I)
        IF(IDFACE(J,I).GT.N) IDFACE(J,I)=IDFACE(J,I)-1
20    CONTINUE
      NFAS=NFAS-1
      IF(N.GT.NFAS) RETURN
      DO 40 I=N,NFAS
        NEDGE(I)=NEDGE(I+1)
        DO 30 J=1,NEDGE(I)
          IDEDGE(J,I)=IDEDGE(J,I+1)
30      CONTINUE
        FX(I)=FX(I+1)
        FY(I)=FY(I+1)
        FZ(I)=FZ(I+1)
40    CONTINUE
      RETURN
      END



*
*   Insert Face NF into data base
*
      SUBROUTINE INSFAC(N,NED,IDTEMP,FXTEMP,FYTEMP,FZTEMP)
      INTEGER IDTEMP(30)
      COMMON /FACET1/ NFAS,NEDGE(100),IDEDGE(30,100)
      COMMON /FACET2/ FX(100),FY(100),FZ(100)
      COMMON /VOL/ NVOS,NFACE(5),IDFACE(50,5),VOLVAL(5),SAREA(5)
      IF(NFAS.EQ.0) RETURN
      DO 10 I=NFAS,N,-1
        NEDGE(I+1)=NEDGE(I)
        FX(I+1)=FX(I)
        FY(I+1)=FY(I)
        FZ(I+1)=FZ(I)
        DO 10 J=1,NEDGE(I+1)
          IDEDGE(J,I+1)=IDEDGE(J,I)
10    CONTINUE
      NEDGE(N)=NED
      DO 20 I=1,NED
        IDEDGE(I,N)=IDTEMP(I)
20    CONTINUE
      FX(N)=FXTEMP
      FY(N)=FYTEMP
      FZ(N)=FZTEMP
      DO 30 I=1,NVOS
      DO 30 J=1,NFACE(I)
```

```
      IF(IDFACE(J,I).GE.N) IDFACE(J,I)=IDFACE(J,I)+1
30    CONTINUE
      NFAS=NFAS+1
      RETURN
      END



*
*   Display labels of all Faces
*
      SUBROUTINE SHOFAC
      COMMON /FACET1/ NFAS,NEDGE(100),IDEDGE(30,100)
      DATA IC0/0/,IC3/3/
      IF(NFAS.EQ.0) RETURN
      DO 100 I=1,NFAS
        CALL MARKFA(I,IC3)
100   CONTINUE
      RETURN
      END



*
*   Calculate Equation of Plane from its first two edges
*
      SUBROUTINE PLN(NLN1,NLN2,A,B,C,D,IERR)
      COMMON /POINTS/ NPTS,XT(300),YT(300),ZT(300),IPTDEF(300)
      COMMON /LINES/ NLNS,IDPT1(400),IDPT2(400),LNFONT(400)
      DATA EPS/1.0E-6/
      IERR=1
      IF(NLN1.EQ.NLN2) RETURN
      I1=IDPT1(NLN1)
      I2=IDPT2(NLN1)
      I3=IDPT1(NLN2)
      I4=IDPT2(NLN2)
      IF(I3.EQ.I1 .OR. I3.EQ.I2) THEN
        I3=I4
      ELSE IF(.NOT. (I4.EQ.I1 .OR. I4.EQ.I2)) THEN
        RETURN
      ENDIF
      CALL DTOM(XT(I1),YT(I1),ZT(I1),XM1,YM1,ZM1,IPTDEF(I1))
      CALL DTOM(XT(I2),YT(I2),ZT(I2),XM2,YM2,ZM2,IPTDEF(I2))
      CALL DTOM(XT(I3),YT(I3),ZT(I3),XM3,YM3,ZM3,IPTDEF(I3))
      XM1=XM1-XM2
      YM1=YM1-YM2
      ZM1=ZM1-ZM2
      XM3=XM3-XM2
      YM3=YM3-YM2
      ZM3=ZM3-ZM2
      A=YM1*ZM3-YM3*ZM1
      B=ZM1*XM3-ZM3*XM1
      C=XM1*YM3-XM3*YM1
      IF(A*A+B*B+C*C .LT. EPS) RETURN
      IERR=0
      D=A*XM2+B*YM2+C*ZM2
      RETURN
      END
```

```
*
*   Determine whether IFREE is in the plane
*
      SUBROUTINE COPLN(IFREE,A,B,C,D,IYES)
      COMMON /POINTS/ NPTS,XT(300),YT(300),ZT(300),IPTDEF(300)
      COMMON /LINES/ NLNS,IDPT1(400),IDPT2(400),LNFONT(400)
      DATA EPS/1.0E-3/
      IYES=0
      CALL DTOM(XT(IFREE),YT(IFREE),ZT(IFREE),XM1,YM1,ZM1,
     &   IPTDEF(IFREE))
      VAL=A*XM1+B*YM1+C*ZM1-D
      IF(ABS(VAL) .LT. EPS) IYES=1
      RETURN
      END




*
*   Check connectivity of consecutive edges
*
      SUBROUTINE JOINT(NLN,IFREE,IYES)
      COMMON /POINTS/ NPTS,XT(300),YT(300),ZT(300),IPTDEF(300)
      COMMON /LINES/ NLNS,IDPT1(400),IDPT2(400),LNFONT(400)
      IYES=1
      IF(IDPT1(NLN).EQ.IFREE) THEN
        IFREE=IDPT2(NLN)
      ELSE IF(IDPT2(NLN).EQ.IFREE) THEN
        IFREE=IDPT1(NLN)
      ELSE
        IYES=0
      ENDIF
      RETURN
      END
```

4.5.3 Identification of Face Entities

To provide facilities for displaying labels of existing polygonal faces and selecting individual face entities via the Mouse Cursor, we add the three submodules given in this subsection to the FACE module.

Module SRCHFA is to search for the face entity whose projected label on the window is nearest to the center of the Mouse or Crosshair Cursor. Module MARKFA highlights an existing face by displaying its label in a specified color. Module FLABEL prepares the label for a specific face in the form of a text string starting with an *F* and followed by an integer indicating the sequence number of the face in the /FACET1/ data block.

```
*
*   Search for Face nearest to (X, Y) in XV-YV plane
*
```

```
      SUBROUTINE SRCHFA(NF,X,Y)
      COMMON /WINDOW/ XW1,YW1,XW2,YW2
      COMMON /FACET1/ NFAS,NEDGE(100),IDEDGE(30,100)
      COMMON /FACET2/ FX(100),FY(100),FZ(100)
      NF=0
      DEL=(XW2-XW1)/20
      DO 100 I=1,NFAS
      CALL MTOV(FX(I),FY(I),FZ(I),FXV,FYV,FZV,0)
      DST=(X-FXV)**2+(Y-FYV)**2
      IF(DST.GE.DEL) GOTO 100
      DEL=DST
      NF=I
100   CONTINUE
      RETURN
      END


*
*   Highlight Face N
*

      SUBROUTINE MARKFA(N,IC)
      CHARACTER*6 FID
      COMMON /FACET2/ FX(100),FY(100),FZ(100)
      DATA IC3/3/
      ICT=IC
      IF(IC.LT.0) ICT=-IC
      CALL GCOLOR(ICT)
      IF(IC.GT.0) CALL GXOR(1)
      CALL MTOV(FX(N),FY(N),FZ(N),FXV,FYV,FZV,0)
      CALL FLABEL(N,FID)
      CALL GWGCSR(FXV,FYV)
      CALL GWTEXT(FID)
      IF(IC.GT.0) CALL GXOR(0)
      CALL GCOLOR(IC3)
      RETURN
      END


*
*   Prepare Label for Face N; N < 1000
*

      SUBROUTINE FLABEL(N,FID)
      CHARACTER*6 DUMMY,FID
      CHARACTER FEQ(6)
      EQUIVALENCE (DUMMY,FEQ(1))
      DATA FEQ(1)/'\'/,FEQ(2)/'F'/,FEQ(6)/'\'/
      I1=MOD(N,10)
      I2=MOD(N,100)/10
      I3=N/100
      IF(I3.NE.0) THEN
        FEQ(3)=CHAR(I3+ICHAR('0'))
        FEQ(4)=CHAR(I2+ICHAR('0'))
        FEQ(5)=CHAR(I1+ICHAR('0'))
      ELSE IF(I2.NE.0) THEN
        FEQ(3)=CHAR(I2+ICHAR('0'))
        FEQ(4)=CHAR(I1+ICHAR('0'))
        FEQ(5)=' '
      ELSE
        FEQ(3)=CHAR(I1+ICHAR('0'))
```

```
FEQ(4)='  '
FEQ(5)='  '
ENDIF
FID=DUMMY
RETURN
END
```

4.5.4   Surface of Revolution

The above FACE module offers facilities for interactively selecting
individual line or edge entities to form closed polygonal face or
polygon entities. In creating face entities, the user has no
option but to select boundary edges and define one face at a
time. The procedure is sufficient in creating irregularly shaped
faces. In creating symmetrical shapes such as surfaces of revolution, the procedure should be simplified.

A surface of revolution is a smooth surface generated by revolving a planar curve, known as the profile curve, around a
reference line, known as the axis of revolution, by a certain
angle of revolution. In general the profile curve shares the
same plane with the axis of rotation but does not intersect with
the axis of rotation. A complete-loop surface can be generated
by revolving the profile curve by 360°.

In a polyhedral surface/solid modeler, surfaces of revolution
may be approximated by polyhedral face patches. The EDROTA
module presented in Section 4.3.2, for rotating the line segments
registered in a *group* buffer about the XT, YT or ZT axis, can
be modified to provide a user option for creating polyhedral surfaces of revolution. With an added mechanism for automatically
forming the wire-frame created in EDROTA into connected faces,
CAD-PS will allow the user to create a polyhedral surface patch
in a single command. Figure 4.14 depicts such a polyhedral
surface.

Many other face-defining facilities may be added to the FACE
module. In Section 5.3.3 we shall examine a procedure for identifying the intersection of two polyhedral solids. The procedure
will involve a method for obtaining the intersection of two polygons. The method can be used to provide design options for
identifying the intersection of two face entities and for dividing
a face into two separate face entities with a cutting plane.

4.6 THE AREA OF A POLYGON

The area contained in a plane polygon can be evaluated with a
determinant approach. The algorithm is based on a simple

Figure 4.14   A polyhedral surface of revolution.

relationship between matrix determinant and plane geometry.
Consider an X-Y plane and a directed line segment **AB** in the
plane, the coordinates of points A and B are shown in Figure
4.15.   The coordinates of A and B can be used to form a two by
two *segment matrix* with the coordinates of B above those of A,
namely

$$\begin{bmatrix} x_B & y_B \\ x_A & y_A \end{bmatrix}$$

The perpendiculars from the end points of the segment to the
X axis define points C and D, while those to the Y axis define
points E and F.   Points G and H are possible intersections of
AB with the X and Y axes respectively.   The perpendiculars also
define two enclosed regions, ABDC and ABFE, in the cases shown

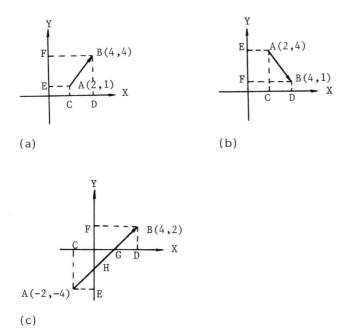

(a)

(b)

(c)

Figure 4.15   Matrix determinant and analytical geometry.

in Figure 4.15a and 4.15b. They define four such regions, AGC, GBD, AHE and HBF, in the case depicted in Figure 4.15c.

An interesting relationship exists between the determinant of the segment matrix and the areas of these enclosed regions which states that the determinant value of the segment matrix, $x_B y_A - x_A y_B$, is equivalent to the algebraic sum of the areas of these enclosed regions, provided that areas to the right of the directed segment (with observer standing at A and facing B) are assigned positive values and those to the left assigned negative values.

In Figure 4.15a, the determinant value of the segment matrix is -4, while the area of ABDC is 5 and area ABFE is -9, thus $-4 = 5 + (-9)$. In Figure 4.15b, the segment matrix yields 14, while the area of ABDC is 5 and area ABFE is 9, thus $14 = 5 + 9$. In Figure 4.15c, the segment matrix yields -12, while the area of AGC is -8, area GBD is 2, area AHE is 2, and area HBF is -8, thus $-12 = (-8) + 2 + 2 + (-8)$.

Since a polygon's boundary may be viewed as a series of directed segments, the above relationship can be extended to obtain the

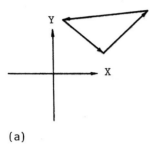

(a)

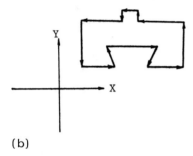

(b)

Figure 4.16   Evaluation of polygon areas via determinants.

area inside the polygon. Consider the two polygons illustrated
in Figure 4.16, with their edges defined in the counterclockwise
direction when viewed from the positive Z axis. Arrows have
been added to indicate the orientation of the directed segments.
Each edge of the polygon will contribute a segment matrix. The
fact that the edges of a polygon always form a closed loop ensures
that the absolute value of the sum of the determinant values of
all the segment matrices is equivalent to two times the area inside
the polygon, for the area inside the polygon will be counted twice
while the projected areas outside will cancel out. It is especially
notable that this approach is applicable to both convex and concave polygons.
    Despite that polygons in CAD-PS may occupy arbitrarily ori-
ented planes, the determinant approach is as effective as ever
since a temporary definition space can always be constructed,
using any two non-collinear edges, such that the polygon under
consideration will lie in its XT-YT plane. The corresponding

XT and YT coordinates in this temporary definition space may
then be plugged into the determinant form to produce the area.

4.7   DISPLAY OF PRODUCT MODELS WITH
HIDDEN LINES REMOVED

Imparting surface definition to a wire-frame allows one to
calculate and display the visible parts of the frame as seen from
orientations specified by viewing directions. As shown in Figure
4.10, edges of certain polygons may be partly or wholly hidden
by other polygons located between the edges and a reference *eye*
plane (see Sec. 3.1) placed at the end of the infinite viewing
axis.

Hidden lines removal procedures often start at a given projectional image, with viewing coordinates registered in blocks
like /XVYVZV/, where edges intersecting with other polygons
are determined and clipped against those polygons. To determine
the visibility of these broken edge segments, one has to trace
them back into the 3-D model or viewing space where depths
from the reference plane can be compared.

This section is to present a practical algorithm for displaying
hidden lines removed images of 3-D surfaces consisting of simple
polygons, convex or concave. Generally speaking, algorithms
for removing the hidden lines in images of convex polygonal surfaces are much simpler than those for concave ones.

Figure 4.17 offers testimony to this. Line segment AB in both
Figure 4.17a and 4.17b is assumed to be farther from the reference plane than the polygons. In order to remove the hidden
parts of AB from a concave polygon, as illustrated in Figure
4.17a, the algorithm must identify all possible intersections with
the polygon and determine that segments CD, EF and GH are
hidden and should be removed. In the case of convex polygons,
as illustrated in Figure 4.17b, a line segment always intersects
with the polygon at no more than two points. Thus a convex
algorithm need only determine the visibility of a single clipped
segment against each polygon.

The approach presented here is unique in that it is able to
handle both convex and concave polygons, while taking advan-
tage of the simplicity of the convex algorithm. The procedure
is twofold. A *triangulation* processor first converts given polygons into adjoining triangles, which are inherently convex. The
triangulated polygons are then passed to a hidden lines removal
procedure that handles only convex polygons. The triangulation

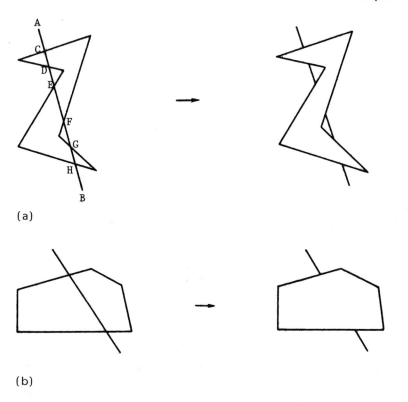

(a)

(b)

Figure 4.17   Removal of hidden lines.

edges or T-edges used to divide polygons into triangles will not
be displayed on the resultant image. The hidden lines removed
images in Figure 4.10 are obtained with this approach.

4.7.1   Triangulation of Polygons

This subsection presents a practical triangulation procedure consisting of four major steps. The algorithm presumes that the
polygon has already been placed in an XT-YT or XV-YV plane,
which reduces the trinagulation to a 2-D undertaking. To facilitate discussion, we shall consider a concave polygon, as shown
in Figure 4.18, whose edges are stored in proper order. The
algorithm examines the first vertex (V) of each edge (E) in
sequence to:

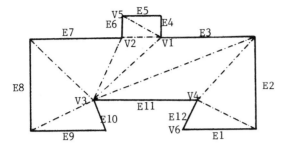

Figure 4.18   Triangulation of concave polygon.

1. Find a concave vertex at which the preceding edge on the
    boundary lies on the right hand side of the active edge
    (with the observer standing upright in the direction of the
    outer normal of the polygon and facing the second vertex of
    the active edge).   There are four such vertices in the polygon
    shown in Figure 4.18:   V1 on E4, V2 on E7, V3 on E11, and
    V4 on E12.   If no concave vertices could be found, go directly to
    Step 4.
2. Construct a forward T-edge across the active concave vertex
    and the farther vertex of the following edge (from V1 to V5,
    for instance) provided that the T-edge does not intersect
    with other edges or lie outside the polygon (no T-edge from
    V3 to V6); update the edge list to exclude the two edges
    used to form a triangle with the T-edge and include the
    T-edge; then go back to Step (1).
3. If concavity still exists after a full cycle around the boundary,
    construct a backward T-edge across the active concave ver-
    tex and the farther vertex of the second preceding edge
    (from V1 to V3 in Fig. 4.19); then go back to Step (1).
4. After removing all concavities, simply construct T-edges
    between the active vertex and all the other vertices but the
    neighboring ones (See Fig. 4.20).   This completes the tri-
    angulation process.

    The above algorithm is also applicable to multiple-loop polygons
connected by B-edges.   The triangulation process requires a
systematic approach to determining whether a point in the plane
containing a polygon is on the inside of the polygon.   This can
be achieved most conveniently by emanating a semi-infinite line
from the point and identifying all intersections between this line

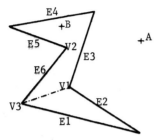

Figure 4.19   Construction of backward T-edge.

and the boundary of the polygon. The point under consideration is on the inside if the emanated line produces an odd number of intersections, otherwise the point is on the outside. In Figure 4.19, any emanating line from point A will produce either no intersection or an even number of intersections while an emanating line from point B will always produce an odd number of intersections.

It ought to be noted that the last step of the foregoing triangulation procedure is not necessary for hidden lines processing since the algorithm delineated in the next subsection is able to handle non-triangulated, convex polygons. It is included here because the volumetric Boolean operations to be discussed in the next chapter will require complete triangulations.

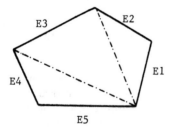

Figure 4.20   Triangulation of convex polygon.

4.7.2   A Practical Hidden-Line Algorithm

The hidden lines or edges processing for displaying realistic images of 3-D models on the computer screen is a well studied subject in the published literature.   The amount of computations required by a particular hidden-line technique is generally commensurate with its capacity in dealing with the various types of polygon.   Powerful algorithms usually require deeper logic loops to support their generality.   The interested reader is referred to the Bibliography for pointers to further studies on this subject.

Since CAD-PS is concerned only with the display of well-formed polyhedral surfaces, and the triangulation processor presented earlier will provide only convex polygons as input to the hidden-line processor, certain assumptions may be made to reduce the complexity of the hidden-line processor.   The practical algorithm presented here is derived from a procedure published in Angell's text on computer graphics [1981].

The algorithm assumes that no edges or line segments in the data base pierce through any polygons.   This assumption relieves the algorithm of the task of checking for such irregularities and determining the results of possible intersections.   The algorithm will be discussed based on the concave, but triangulated polygon shown in Figure 4.21.   Line segment **AB** shown there is to represent a typical edge to be processed against the polygon.

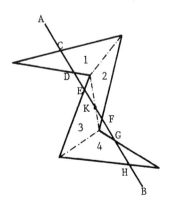

Figure 4.21   Hidden lines or edges removal.

The viewing system under consideration is an orthographic projection with images displayed in the XV-YV plane. The reference eye plane in such a viewing system is theoretically located in infinity in positive ZV direction, but in practice it may be regarded as being located at a finite point on the ZV axis far away from the region occupied by the geometric model. Thus hidden line segments can be identified when interfering polygons lie between the line segments and the reference plane.

We shall process all line entities except in the data base, except B-edges and T-edges which are not displayed, against all the polygonal face entities, either convex or triangulated, starting in the XV-YV plane. Since efficiency will be gained by sifting out non-interfering lines and faces in the beginning of the process, a number of sifters may be implemented in the processor.

A line segment need not be clipped against the faces containing the line segment as an edge, for it will not be obscured by these faces no matter what viewing direction was specified. When processing a line entity against the face data block, such faces should be ignored.

Three other sifters can be built based on the projections of the line and face combination being considered. If the projection of the line does not intersect with that of the face, then the face will have no effect on the line. Figure 4.22 illustrates such cases. It occurs when the vertices of the face all lie (1) on the same side of the line (see Fig. 4.22a); (2) on the opposite side of a reference line, which is perpendicular to and passes through the first vertex of the target line segment, to the seccond vertex of the target line (see Fig. 4.22b); or (3) on the opposite side of a reference line, which is perpendicular to and passes through the second vertex of the target line, to the first vertex of the target line (see Fig. 4.22c).

Any line and face combination that passes through these sifters must be considered in detail. Consider the projected line segment **AB** and face 1 in Figure 4.21. The first step is to find the intersections of **AB** with the edges of face 1. Notice that only 2-D operations need be applied to these 2-D image elements, and that there can *at most* be two such intersections. If no intersection is found, then the face is ignored. In Figure 4.21, C and D are the two intersections. The next step is to determine whether CD is hidden by face 1.

The intersected segment is not visible if its mid-point is on the opposite side of the face to its corresponding point in the reference plane (intersection of the projector through this mid-point

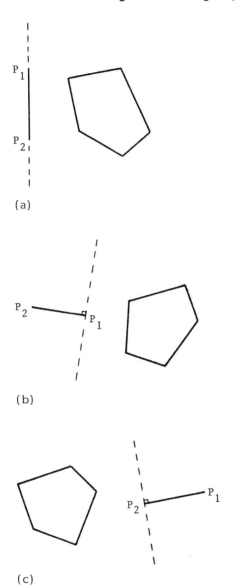

(a)

(b)

(c)

Figure 4.22   Cases of non-intersecting line and convex polygon.

and the reference plane far away). This can be checked by
plugging the viewing space coordinates of the mid-point and its
reference point into the 3-D plane equation of the face in the
viewing space and comparing the signs of the results. They
are on the opposite sides if the signs differ.

If the intersected segment is not visible, then the break points
on the line of the visible parts are registered. The visible segments may be represented as parts of the target line in parametric form and a buffer can be created to store the beginning
and ending parameters (between 0 and 1) of the break points.

This completes a hidden-line routine against a face, the next
face is then fetched and the procedure is repeated. The visible
parts of the target line produced by following faces are compared
with the existing parts in the buffer and necessary adjustments
are made to further break these parts. After processing the
last face, the visible parts of the target line stored in the buffer
are displayed. This completes the processing of a target line,
the next line is then fetched and the procedure is repeated. The
loop terminates when all the lines have been processed.

Consider Figure 4.21 again, assuming that AB is behind the
triangulated faces 1, 2, 3, and 4. Processing of AB against
face 1 would result in two visible segments AC and DB. Then
processing of AB against face 2 would lead to modifying the
visible segment DB into two visible segments DK and FB. Next,
line segment AB is clipped against face 3 which would result in
shortening DK to the visible DE. Finally, AB is clipped against
face 4 which would require that FB be broken into two visible
segments FG and HB. At this point, the buffer should register
four visible segments: AC, DE, FG, and HB. Only these segments
should be drawn in displaying the hidden lines removed image.
The images shown in Figures 4.6b, 4.10, and 4.11 are produced
with a combined triangulation and hidden lines removal algorithm.

A FORTRAN program module implementing the above hidden lines
removal approach can be found in Angell's book.

4.8 SUMMARY

This chapter presents a number of program modules for the
editing and transformation of points, lines, and polyhedral surfaces in a 3-D design space, as well as modules for forming polygonal face entities over wire-frame models. A simple algorithm
for computing the area of polygons based on the segment matrix

is described. Also presented is a practical algorithm for generating hidden-line images of general polyhedral models.

The next chapter will focus on the construction of solid entities and the utility of Boolean operations in designing solids with complex forms.

Chapter 5

Polyhedral Solid Modeling

In Chapter 4 we added the FACE module to CAD-PS to allow formation of polygonal faces from wire-frames created with the POINT, LINE and TRANSF modules introduced earlier. In this chapter we shall begin with the implementation of the last major design module required to construct polyhedral solid entities from existing polygonal face entities. It will be followed by discussions on a determinant-based algorithm for evaluating the volume of a polyhedral solid, and on generation of volumes of revolution. Then we will present a subroutine module for analyzing geometric entities created with CAD-PS.

The principles of Boolean volumetric operations will then be discussed, in the context of forming complex shapes with existing CAD-PS solid primitives. A practical algorithm for the Boolean solid modeling approach will be delineated. We shall conclude this chapter with a discussion on the display of realistic, perspective images of CAD-PS solids.

5.1 MODELING OF POLYHEDRAL VOLUMES

A polyhedral volume or solid, or simply polyhedron, is a *closed* 3-D region bounded by an arrangement of connected, but non-intersecting polygonal faces. A polyhedron is *convex* when it lies entirely on one side of each of its faces. A non-convex or *concave* polyhedron will have *reentrant* faces. The topology of the polyhedron dealing with the connectivity of its component entities and other mathematical consequences is too abstract a

subject to be discussed in a practical guide like this, we shall
therefore limit our discussions to regularly-shaped polyhedra.

A basic rule for validating whether a list of polygons defines
a *simple* polyhedron, convex or cancave, can be derived from
the facts that every edge of a simple polyhedron is shared by
exactly two faces of the polyhedron, and that the whole surface
of the polyhedron can be traversed by a continuous path moving
from one polygonal face to another through a common edge.

A variety of established algorithms are available for simulating
polyhedral solids on the computer, the interested reader should
refer to the Bibliography if he or she wishes to investigate further into this subject. The current state of the art of solid
modeling through constructive geometric primitives is based on
the Euler and the Boolean operations.

The Euler polyhedron construction procedure is built on the
Euler's formula which states in precise terms the relationship
between the numbers of vertices, edges, faces, and holes in a
polyhedral volume. An Euler polyhedron must be well-formed
and compliant with the Euler's formula. Implementation of the
strict mathematical formulation requires an interweaving, and
oftentimes oversized data structure to support the incremental
construction of a polyhedron's geometric primitives. Several
commercially available CAD systems are based on the Euler approach, they all require large amounts of CPU memory and often
demand sophisticated user interfaces.

The Boolean approach is based on the geometric set operations
for forming complex shapes from solid primitives by taking the
union, intersection, or difference between them. The term
constructive solid modeling has been used to describe the Boolean
approach. A constructive solid modeler usually provides the
user with simple-shape solid primitives such as blocks, cylinders,
spheres, and wedges, that he or she can use to construct desired shapes, somewhat like playing the game of wooden blocks
in a hyperspace where blocks can penetrate other blocks. Such
systems are easy to use, but their design abilities are limited
to shapes that can be achieved by the constructing primitives.

The PC-based CAD-PS system integrates computer-aided drafting
with constructive solid modeling. It offers a computer-aided
drafting front-end with which the designer can document his or
her product models first as conventional, skeletal wire-frames.
To construct a solid primitive from a wire-frame, the designer
would invoke the FACE and VOLUME (see Sec. 5.1.2) utilities
to define polygonal faces and eventually a well-formed polyhedron.
Solid primitives may also be created with advanced utilities such

as generators of surfaces (see Sec. 4.5.4) and volumes (see
Sec. 5.1.5) of revolution which usually do not require forming
intermediate wire-frames. These polyhedral solid primitives may
then be combined or intersected to form complex-shape polyhedral solids by means of Boolean operations (see Sec. 5.3).

5.1.1 Representation of Polyhedral Volumes

Representing a polyhedron in the computer requires a well organized data base. In current literature, the most discussed
data structure for representing polyhedra seems to be the
Winged-Edge data structure, first proposed by Baumgart [1974].
A number of papers on this subject are included in the Bibliography for the interested reader. The Winged-Edge structure
defines the interweaving relationships between every edge and
all the geometric entities surrounding it: the two vertices, the
two polygons meeting at the edge, and the preceding and following edges on each of the two polygons. This arrangement
provides direct access to particular geometric entities without
lengthy searches, but it requires large memories to accommodate
the apparent redundancy in the data base.

 CAD-PS adopts a simple pointer-based data structure which
accommodates the minimum data required for representing polyhedra. We have already allocated data blocks for the point, line
and face entities. The /POINTS/ block is used to register definition space coordinates of point or vertex entities, as well as
pointers indicating the specific definition space associated with
each point entity. The /LINES/ block is used to store pointers
to the end points of line segment or edge entities. The /FACET1/
block is used to store pointers to the boundary edges of polygonal face entities.

Sitting at the top of the data structure is the polyhedral volume
entity. A volume entity may be defined through pointers to its
boundary polygonal faces. The following data block is designed
to register up to five volume entities, each can have up to 50
polygonal faces, and the values of their volumes and surface
areas.

```
COMMON /VOL/ NVOS,NFACE(5),IDFACE(50,5),VOLVAL(5),SAREA(5)
```

Again we have included a counter variable, NVOS, to register
the number of existing volume entities.

5.1.2 The VOLUME Module

In modules VOLUME and MKVOL, listed at the end of this subsection, a polyhedron is defined from selected polygons. No
specific order is needed in grouping the boundary polygons to
form a polyhedron. In forming a polyhedral volume, the user
may first instruct the CAD-PS system to display labels of existing
polygonal faces on the computer display, then either select individual faces by pointing the Mouse Cursor at their labels or
elect to include all of the existing faces.

The system then checks the *closedness* of the selected polygonal faces by validating the requisite interrelationship between
the edges and faces as described earlier in this chapter. A
volume entity is created and its label displayed if the specified
polygons form a closed polyhedron. Values of the volume of
such polyhedral solids can be evaluated by an efficient determinant
approach to be discussed in Section 5.1.4.

Figure 5.1a shows polygonal faces defined over a CAD-PS wire-
frame, and Figure 5.1b displays a volume or solid entity defined
by the faces in Figure 5.1a with hidden edges removed. An
image of the same solid after rotating the whole model space
about the Y axis is shown in Figure 5.1c. Figure 5.2 presents
another solid entity created with CAD-PS.

The utilities provided in the VOLUME module include creating
polyhedral volume or polyhedron entities, displaying values of
the surface area and volume of selected polyhedra, deleting polyhedron entities from the data base, displaying hidden lines removed images of existing data base against existing polygonal
faces, displaying face or volume labels, and producing rotated
views about the X, Y or Z axis of the model space with hidden
lines removed. These utilities are implemented in the form of
building blocks, some of which are listed below following the
VOLUME module. Module VOLUME may be included in the MAIN
module in Section 3.5 to provide a basic solid-modeling facility.

```
*
*    Definition and editing of Volume entities
*
     SUBROUTINE VOLUME
     CHARACTER*8 MENUV(14)
     CHARACTER*40 BUFFER
     COMMON /FACET1/ NFAS,NEDGE(100),IDEDGE(30,100)
     COMMON /FACET2/ FX(100),FY(100),FZ(100)
     COMMON /VOL/ NVOS,NFACE(5),IDFACE(50,5),VOLVAL(5),SAREA(5)
     DATA MENUV/'\VOLUME\','\Create\','\Value \','\Delete\',
    &  '\Hidden\','\Show F\','\Show V\','\Mod Sp\','\Def Sp\',
```

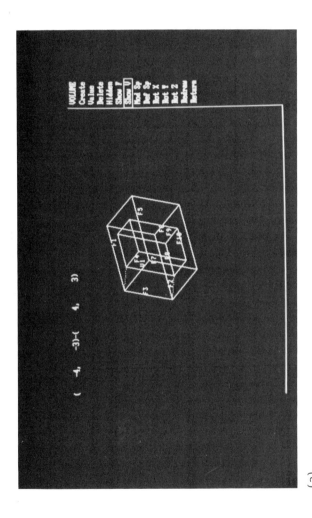

(a)

Figure 5.1   Display of face and volume labels.

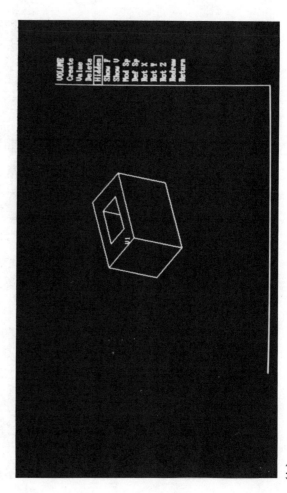

(b)

(c)

Figure 5.1   (Continued)

Figure 5.2   A solid entity constructed with CAD-PS.

```
    &    '\Rot X \','\Rot Y \','\Rot Z \','\Redraw\','\Return\'/
         DATA IC0/0/,IC1/1/,IC2/2/,IC3/3/
         NFAS0=0
         ITEMV=14
         RADDEG=3.141593/180.0
         IF(NFAS.EQ.0) RETURN
         CALL DMENU(ITEMV,MENUV)
30       CALL USELOC(X,Y,IBUTT)
         IF(IBUTT.EQ.1 .OR. IBUTT.GE.128) GOTO 30
         IF(IBUTT.GE.ITEMV) RETURN
         ITEM=IBUTT-1
         CALL SMENU(ITEM)
         GOTO (100,200,300,400,500,600,700,800,900,900,900,1000),ITEM
100      CALL MKVOL
         GOTO 9000
200      IF(NVOS.LE.0) GOTO 9000
210      CALL RESET
         CALL PROMPT('\Enter Vol ID ->  \')
         CALL INPSTR(BUFFER)
         CALL PROMPT('\ \')
         IF(BUFFER .EQ. ' ') GOTO 9000
         READ(BUFFER,*,ERR=210) NV
         IF(NV.GT.NVOS) GOTO 9000
*
*   Volume and Surface Area of a Polyhedron are evaluated
*   with a determinant approach presented in Sec. 5.1.2
*
         WRITE(*,220) NV,VOLVAL(NV),SAREA(NV)
220      FORMAT('+VOL',I1,'-> Vol=',F9.2,'; Area=',F9.2,' <L>')
         CALL USELOC(X,Y,IBUTT)
         CALL PROMPT('\ \')
         GOTO 9000
300      CALL DELVOL
         GOTO 9000
*
*   HIDDEN utilizes the hidden lines removal algorithm
*   presented in Sec. 4.7 to display solid images
*
400      CALL HIDDEN
         GOTO 9000
500      CALL SHOFAC
         GOTO 9000
600      CALL SHOVOL
         GOTO 9000
700      CALL SHOXYZ
         GOTO 9000
800      CALL SHODEF
         GOTO 9000
900      CALL RESET
         IAXIS=ITEM-8
         CALL PROMPT('\Enter Angle ->  \')
         CALL INPSTR(BUFFER)
         CALL PROMPT('\ \')
         IF(BUFFER .EQ. ' ') GOTO 9000
         READ(BUFFER,*,ERR=9000) THETA
```

```
 920   CALL  ROTXYZ(IAXIS,THETA*RADDEG)
       CALL  VSPACE
       CALL  HIDDEN
       CALL  PROMPT('\Continue Rotation with <L>\')
       CALL  USELOC(X,Y,IBUTT)
       CALL  PROMPT('\ \')
       IF(IBUTT.NE.132) GOTO 9000
       GOTO 920
1000  CALL  REDRAW
9000  CALL  SMENU(ITEM)
       GOTO 30
       END




*
*   Formation of Volume entities
*
       SUBROUTINE MKVOL
       COMMON /FACET1/ NFAS,NEDGE(100),IDEDGE(30,100)
       COMMON /FACET2/ FX(100),FY(100),FZ(100)
       COMMON /VOL/ NVOS,NFACE(5),IDFACE(50,5),VOLVAL(5),SAREA(5)
       DATA IC0/0/,IC2/2/,IC3/3/,MAXVOS/5/,MAXFAC/50/
 10    IF(NVOS.GE.MAXVOS) THEN
          CALL  MESSAG('\Number of Volumes overflows!\')
          RETURN
       ENDIF
       IUNDO=0
       ICLOSE=0
       NVOS=NVOS+1
       NFACE(NVOS)=0
100   CALL  PROMPT('\All Faces? <L>-Yes; <M>-End; <R>-No\')
       CALL  USELOC(X,Y,IBUTT)
       CALL  PROMPT('\ \')
       IF(IBUTT.EQ.130 .OR. IBUTT.LT.128) GOTO 900
       IF(IBUTT.EQ.132) THEN
         IF(NFAS.GT.MAXFAC) THEN
            CALL  MESSAG('\Number of Faces overflows!\')
            GOTO 100
         ENDIF
         NFACE(NVOS)=NFAS
110      DO 120 I=1,NFACE(NVOS)
            IDFACE(I,NVOS)=I
            CALL  MARKFA(I,IC2)
120      CONTINUE
       ELSE
130      CALL  PROMPT('\Faces: <L>-Sel; <M>-End; <R>-Undo\')
         CALL  USELOC(X,Y,IBUTT)
         CALL  PROMPT('\ \')
         IF(IBUTT.EQ.130 .OR. IBUTT.L1.1∠8) GOTO 160
         IF(IBUTT.EQ.129) THEN
           IF(IUNDO.EQ.0) GOTO 130
           CALL  MARKFA(NF,IC2)
           NFACE(NVOS)=NFACE(NVOS)-1
           IUNDO=0
         ELSE
```

```
            IF(NFACE(NVOS).GE.MAXFAC) THEN
              CALL MESSAG('\Number of Faces overflows!\')
              GOTO 130
            ENDIF
            CALL SRCHFA(NF,X,Y)
            IF(NF.EQ.0) GOTO 130
            DO 150 I=1,NFACE(NVOS)
            IF(NF.EQ.IDFACE(I,NVOS)) GOTO 130
150         CONTINUE
            CALL MARKFA(NF,IC2)
            NFACE(NVOS)=NFACE(NVOS)+1
            IDFACE(NFACE(NVOS),NVOS)=NF
            IUNDO=1
          ENDIF
          GOTO 130
        ENDIF
160     IF(NFACE(NVOS).GE.3) GOTO 170
162     DO 165 I=1,NFACE(NVOS)
          J=IDFACE(I,NVOS)
          CALL MARKFA(J,IC2)
165     CONTINUE
        GOTO 900
*
*  Check if selected Faces form a closed Volume, calculate
*  its surface area and volume if they do (See Sec. 5.1.4)
*
170     CALL VCLOSE(NVOS,IYES)
        IF(IYES.EQ.0) THEN
          CALL PROMPT('\Volume Not Closed! <L>\')
          CALL USELOC(X,Y,IBUTT)
          CALL PROMPT('\ \')
          GOTO 162
        ENDIF
        ICLOSE=1
        CALL MARKVO(NVOS,-IC3)
        WRITE(*,175) NVOS,VOLVAL(NVOS),SAREA(NVOS)
175     FORMAT('+VOL ',I2,': Vol=',F8.2,'; Area=',F8.2,'  <L>')
        CALL USELOC(X,Y,IBUTT)
        CALL PROMPT('\ \')
900     IF(ICLOSE.EQ.0) NVOS=NVOS-1
        RETURN
        END


*  Option for deleting user-selected Volumes
*
        SUBROUTINE DELVOL
        INTEGER IDTEMP(50)
        COMMON /FACET1/ NFAS,NEDGE(100),IDEDGE(30,100)
        COMMON /FACET2/ FX(100),FY(100),FZ(100)
        COMMON /VOL/ NVOS,NFACE(5),IDFACE(50,5),VOLVAL(5),SAREA(5)
        DATA IC0/0/,IC1/1/,IC2/2/,IC3/3/
        IUNDO=0
100     IF(NVOS.EQ.0) RETURN
        CALL PROMPT('\Delete: <L>-Sel; <M>-End; <R>-Undo\')
        CALL USELOC(X,Y,IBUTT)
        CALL PROMPT('\ \')
```

```
      IF(IBUTT.EQ.130 .OR. IBUTT.LT.128) RETURN
      IF(IBUTT.EQ.132) THEN
        CALL SRCHVO(NV,X,Y)
        IF(NV.EQ.0) GOTO 100
*
*  Remove old Volume labels
*
        DO 120 I=1,NVOS
          CALL MARKVO(I,IC0)
120     CONTINUE
        NVTEMP=NV
        NFA=NFACE(NVTEMP)
        DO 150 I=1,NFA
          IDTEMP(I)=IDFACE(I,NVTEMP)
150     CONTINUE
        VTEMP=VOLVAL(NVTEMP)
        STEMP=SAREA(NVTEMP)
        CALL RMVOL(NV)
*
*  Display new Volume labels
*
        DO 160 I=1,NVOS
          CALL MARKVO(I,-IC3)
160     CONTINUE
        IUNDO=1
      ELSE
        IF(IUNDO.EQ.0) GOTO 100
        DO 170 I=1,NVOS
          CALL MARKVO(I,IC0)
170     CONTINUE
        DO 180 I=NVOS,NVTEMP,-1
        NFACE(I+1)=NFACE(I)
        VOLVAL(I+1)=VOLVAL(I)
        SAREA(I+1)=SAREA(I)
        DO 180 J=1,NFACE(I)
          IDFACE(J,I+1)=IDFACE(J,I)
180     CONTINUE
        NVOS=NVOS+1
        NFACE(NVTEMP)=NFA
        DO 200 I=1,NFA
          IDFACE(I,NVTEMP)=IDTEMP(I)
200     CONTINUE
        VOLVAL(NVTEMP)=VTEMP
        SAREA(NVTEMP)=STEMP
        DO 210 I=1,NVOS
          CALL MARKVO(I,-IC3)
210     CONTINUE
        IUNDO=0
      ENDIF
      GOTO 100
      END



*
*  Remove Volume N from data base
```

```
*
      SUBROUTINE RMVOL(N)
      COMMON /VOL/ NVOS,NFACE(5),IDFACE(50,5),VOLVAL(5),SAREA(5)
      NVOS=NVOS-1
      IF(N.GT.NVOS) RETURN
      DO 20 I=N,NVOS
        DO 10 J=1,NFACE(I+1)
          IDFACE(J,I)=IDFACE(J,I+1)
10      CONTINUE
        NFACE(I)=NFACE(I+1)
        VOLVAL(I)=VOLVAL(I+1)
        SAREA(I)=SAREA(I+1)
20    CONTINUE
      RETURN
      END



*
*   Display Volume labels
*
      SUBROUTINE SHOVOL
      COMMON /VOL/ NVOS,NFACE(5),IDFACE(50,5),VOLVAL(5),SAREA(5)
      DATA IC0/0/,IC2/2/,IC3/3/
      IF(NVOS.EQ.0) RETURN
      DO 100 I=1,NVOS
      CALL MARKVO(I,IC3)
100   CONTINUE
      RETURN
      END
```

5.1.3   Identification of Volume Entities

Similar to the facilities implemented in the FACE module for labeling and identifying individual faces, this subsection presents three
submodules for labeling volume entities and identifying specific
volumes on the display via the Mouse Cursor.

Note that in common block /VOL/ no variables were declared
for the location of volume labels. As stated in the submodules
given below, the label of a volume entity is displayed at the
mid-point between the labels of its first two faces.

```
*
*   Identify user-selected Volume
*
      SUBROUTINE SRCHVO(NV,X,Y)
      COMMON /WINDOW/ XW1,YW1,XW2,YW2
      COMMON /FACET1/ NFAS,NEDGE(100),IDEDGE(30,100)
      COMMON /FACET2/ FX(100),FY(100),FZ(100)
      COMMON /VOL/ NVOS,NFACE(5),IDFACE(50,5),VOLVAL(5),SAREA(5)
      NV=0
```

```
      DEL=(XW2-XW1)/20
      DO 100 I=1,NVOS
        J=IDFACE(1,I)
        CALL MTOV(FX(J),FY(J),FZ(J),FX1,FY1,FZ1,0)
        J=IDFACE(2,I)
        CALL MTOV(FX(J),FY(J),FZ(J),FX2,FY2,FZ2,0)
        DST=(X-.5*(FX1+FX2))**2+(Y-.5*(FY1+FY2))**2
        IF(DST.GE.DEL) GOTO 100
        DEL=DST
        NV=I
100   CONTINUE
      RETURN
      END




*
*   Highlight Volume N
*
      SUBROUTINE MARKVO(N,IC)
      CHARACTER*5 VID
      COMMON /FACET2/ FX(100),FY(100),FZ(100)
      COMMON /VOL/ NVOS,NFACE(5),IDFACE(50,5),VOLVAL(5),SAREA(5)
      DATA IC3/3/
      ICT=IC
      IF(IC.LT.0) ICT=-IC
      CALL GCOLOR(ICT)
      IF(IC.GT.0) CALL GXOR(1)
      J=IDFACE(1,N)
      CALL MTOV(FX(J),FY(J),FZ(J),FX1,FY1,FZ1,0)
      J=IDFACE(2,N)
      CALL MTOV(FX(J),FY(J),FZ(J),FX2,FY2,FZ2,0)
*
*   Label of Volume displayed at mid-point between labels of
*   its first two Faces
*
      CALL VLABEL(N,VID)
      CALL GWGCSR(.5*(FX1+FX2),.5*(FY1+FY2))
      CALL GWTEXT(VID)
      IF(IC.GT.0) CALL GXOR(0)
      CALL GCOLOR(IC3)
      RETURN
      END




*
*   Prepare Volume label N; N < 100
*
      SUBROUTINE VLABEL(N,VID)
      CHARACTER*5 DUMMY,VID
      CHARACTER FEQ(5)
      EQUIVALENCE (DUMMY,FEQ(1))
      DATA FEQ(1)/'\'/,FEQ(2)/'V'/,FEQ(5)/'\'/
      I1=MOD(N,10)
```

```
I2=N/10
IF(I2.NE.0) THEN
  FEQ(3)=CHAR(I2+ICHAR('0'))
  FEQ(4)=CHAR(I1+ICHAR('0'))
ELSE
  FEQ(3)=CHAR(I1+ICHAR('0'))
  FEQ(4)=' '
ENDIF
VID=DUMMY
RETURN
END
```

5.1.4 Volumetric Properties of a Polyhedron

The term *volumetric properties* generally refers to the surface
area, volume and mass, center of gravity, and moments of inertia of a solid object. Such properties of a CAD-PS polyhedral
solid can be evaluated from its geometric data blocks. This subsection presents a simple determinant approach to evaluating the
surface area and volume of polyhedral solids.

The surface area of a polyhedral solid can be determined by
summing the areas of the polygonal faces enclosing the polyhedron. As discussed in Section 4.6, the area of a polygon can
be obtained by a simple determinant approach within a local coordinate system in which the polygon being considered lies in
the XT-YT plane.

A polygonal face entity defined with CAD-PS is composed of
a list of consecutive edges, each of which is bounded by two
vertex or point entities whose coordinates are defined within
specific definition spaces. To establish the temporary local coordinate system for evaluating the area of a given polygon, we
may apply the three-point approach described in Section 4.2 to
any three non-collinear vertices of the polygon. This local coordinate system will assume the form of a definition space in
which the transformed coordinates of each vertex of the polygon
have zero coordinate value in ZT direction. Thus the new XT
and YT coordinates of these vertices can be used to evaluate
determinants of the segment matrices. The area of the polygon
is equivalent to half the absolute value of the algebraic sum of
these determinants. The total surface area of a polyhedron
can be obtained by repeating this procedure on all the polygons
defining the polyhedron.

This useful relationship beyween determinant values of segment
matrices and areas of underlying polygons also exists in three

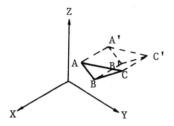

Figure 5.3   A triangle parallel to the Y-Z plane and its projected prism on to the Y-Z plane.

dimensions in a similar form.   Consider a triangle ABC parallel
to the Y-Z plane, as shown in Figure 5.3.   The coordinates of
the three vertices are, respectively, (x_1, y_1, z_1), (x_1, y_2, z_2),
and (x_1, y_3, z_3).   An identical triangle A'B'C' may be projected
along the X axis on to the Y-Z plane and the two triangles may
be used to form a triangular prism ABCA'B'C'.   The definition
of the 2-D segment matrix may be extended to define a 3-D segment matrix made up of the X, Y and Z coordinates of the three
vertices of a triangle, starting from the bottom row, namely

$$\begin{bmatrix} x_1 & y_3 & z_3 \\ x_1 & y_2 & z_2 \\ x_1 & y_1 & z_1 \end{bmatrix}$$

The determinant value of this segment matrix is equivalent to
the product of x_1 and the sum of the determinants of the 2-D
segment matrices of A'B'C', namely

$$\begin{bmatrix} x_1 & y_3 & z_3 \\ x_1 & y_2 & z_2 \\ x_1 & y_1 & z_1 \end{bmatrix} = x_1 \cdot \begin{bmatrix} y_2 & z_2 \\ y_1 & z_1 \end{bmatrix} + \begin{bmatrix} y_3 & z_3 \\ y_2 & z_2 \end{bmatrix} + \begin{bmatrix} y_1 & z_1 \\ y_3 & z_3 \end{bmatrix}$$

$$(5.1)$$

The sign of the above determinant value is determined by the
arrangement of the 3-D segment matrix.   The value is negative

when the three vertices constituting the segment matrix are
arranged in a counterclockwise order when viewed from outside
the prismatic volume. It is positive when the vertices are arranged in a clockwise order. Since the absolute sum of the 2-D
determinants of A'B'C' is equivalent to two times the area of
A'B'C', as indicated in Section 4.6, we may equate the 3-D determinant value to two times the *signed volume* of prism ABCA'B'C'.

It is evident that the projections of ABC in the X-Y and Z-X
planes would degenerate into overlapped line segments. Extending triangle ABC to these projections would produce degenerate, zero-volume prisms. The above analysis indicates that
the determinant of the specific 3-D segment matrix is equivalent
to two times the algebraic sum of the signed volumes of the
three *projected prisms* defined by triangle ABC. Without providing rigorous mathematical proofs, we note that this observation can be generalized to any arbitrarily oriented triangles.

This rule of thumb is more useful when taken one step further
by considering a tetrahedron bounded by four triangles as
shown in Figure 5.4. Each triangular face consists of three
properly ordered edges (counterclockwise when viewed from outside the tetrahedron) which define a 3-D segment matrix and a
resultant determinant value. Since each determinant value is
related to the signed volumes of the three projected prisms with
respect to the three principal planes, the algebraic sum of the
four determinants defined by the four faces bounding the tetrahedron would relate to the volume within the tetrahedron. The
prismatic volumes outside the tetrahedron would cancel out during
the summation process.

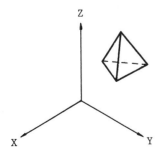

Figure 5.4   A tetrahedron in the X-Y-Z space.

In fact, the *absolute value* of the algebraic sum of the four determinants is equivalent to six times the volume of the tetrahedron. The value *six* comes from counting the signed, doubled volume within the tetrahedron three times (one along each projected prism).

A number of illustrative examples testifying to the above determinant-based formulas can be found in an interesting monograph on matrix and geometry by Kopcsak [1968] which offers many other matrix-based analyses of geometry. No rigorous mathematical proofs to the relationships existing between matrix determinants and analytical geometry are given in Kopcsak's monograph. However, a recent paper by Lien and Kajiya [1984] provides a complete theoretical basis for these relationships, as well as bases for evaluating other integral properties of polyhedra. Both works are included in the Bibliography.

The determinant characteristics of triangles and tetrahedra can be expanded into an efficient algorithm for determining the volume of a polyhedral solid, either convex or concave. A polyhedron is bounded by a finite number of polygonal faces. Let us consider a convex and a concave polygon as shown in Figure 5.5. The dash-dot lines emanating from the starting vertices dissect the polygons into three and four triangles, respectively. Note that the procedure of dissecting polygons is different from the triangulation procedure described in Section 4.7.1 which divides a polygon into wholly contained triangles. The triangles in this case may cross the boundary of the underlying polygon in its reentrant region, as depicted in Figure 5.5. The number of triangles obtained with this procedure is always equal to the number of vertices forming the polygon less two.

Each of the dissected triangles with its edges properly ordered constitutes a 3-D segment matrix. For any given polygon the algebraic sum of the determinants of its 3-D segment matrices (one for each dissected triangle) is equivalent to two times the algebraic sum of the signed volumes of the three projected prisms originated from the polygon being considered. This observation is evident in the case of a convex polygon since all concerned triangles may be regarded as *segments* constituting the whole polygon.

In the case of a concave polygon like the one shown in Figure 5.5b, one has to reason that the prismatic volumes implied by the segment matrices in the reentrant regions would cancel out during the summation process before drawing the same conclusion. The canceling-out is caused by the fact that determinants produced by triangles in the reentrant regions have different signs

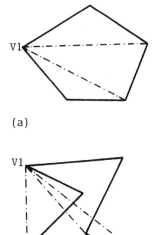

(a)

(b)

Figure 5.5   Dissection of polygons into triangles.

from those produced by the other triangles.   To obtain the volume of a polyhedron, we may follow the same line of argument used in dealing with tetrahedra and conclude that the volume can be obtained by repeating the determinant procedure on all the polygons enclosing the polyhedron and taking the *absolute value* of the accumulated sum divided by six.

The foregoing determinant-based algorithm for evaluating the volume of a polyhedron is summarized as follows:

1.   Assign zero to variable SUM.
2.   Dissect the next n-sided polygon of the polyhedron into n-2 triangles with dissecting edges originating from the first vertex of the polygon.
3.   Evaluate determinants of the segment matrices of the dissected triangles and add the values to SUM.
4.   Go to Step 2 if there are unprocessed polygons left in the polygon list of the polyhedron.
5.   Take the absolute value of SUM/6.0 and terminate the procedure.

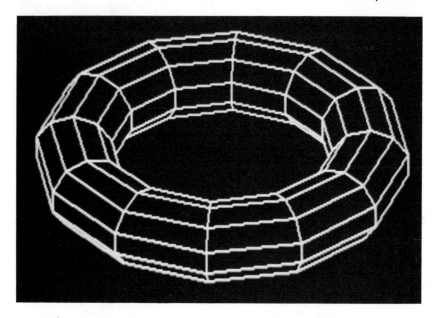

Figure 5.6   A polyhedral volume of revolution.

At this point, the reader should be able to implement the missing submodule VCLOSE incorporated in the MKVOL module which was to check the closedness of a set of selected polygonal faces and to evaluate the surface area and volume of the resultant polyhedron.

5.1.5 Volume of Revolution

In Section 4.5.4 we discussed the prospects of extending the EDROTA module to provide a tool for constructing polyhedral surfaces by revolving a polygonal profile curve about selected axes of rotation, under a single user command. This approach will revolve the selected polygonal edges in increments, using the procedure implemented in EDROTA, into a specific number of rows of polygonal faces.

This polyhedral surface of revolution approach can be extended to create a polyhedral volume under a single user command, by revolving a closed-loop polygonal profile curve about an axis of

rotation by 360° and defining a volume entity from the resultant
closed polygonal faces. Figure 5.6 illustrates a polyhedral volume of revolution.

5.2   ANALYSIS OF POINT, LINE, FACE, AND
VOLUME ENTITIES

During an interactive design session, it is not unusual that at
times the designer wishes to examine coordinate values of specific points or to identify edges of specific polygonal faces. This
section presents a subroutine module, ENTITY, that may be
added to CAD-PS to provide facilities for the user to analyze
all geometric entities created in modules POINT, LINE, FACE,
and VOLUME.

In analyzing point entities, the user should be able to examine
both model and definition space coordinates. ENTITY provides
separate menu items for examining these coordinate values of
selected point entities.

Since the ordering in the edge list of a face entity determines
the orientation of the face, module ENTITY includes two submodules, MARKED and ELABEL, to display sequence numbers of
the edges of selected face entities. The source code of modules
ENTITY, MARKED, and ELABEL is given as follows.

```
*
*    Analysis of geometric entities
*
     SUBROUTINE ENTITY
     CHARACTER*8 MENUE(9)
     CHARACTER*40 BUFFER
     COMMON /POINTS/ NPTS,XT(300),YT(300),ZT(300),IPTDEF(300)
     COMMON /XVYVZV/ XV(300),YV(300),ZV(300)
     COMMON /LINES/ NLNS,IDPT1(400),IDPT2(400),LNFONT(400)
     COMMON /FACET1/ NFAS,NEDGE(100),IDEDGE(30,100)
     COMMON /VOL/ NVOS,NFACE(5),IDFACE(50,5),VOLVAL(5),SAREA(5)
     COMMON /LNGRP/ NLNGP,LNGP(50)
     DATA MENUE/'\ENTITY\','\Pt Mod\','\Pt Def\','\Line  \',
    &  '\Face  \','\Volume\','\Group \','\Redraw\','\Return\'/
     DATA IC1/1/,IC2/2/
150  FORMAT('+',I3,'->',F8.1,',',F8.1,',',F8.1)
     ITEME=9
     CALL DMENU(ITEME,MENUE)
10   CALL USELOC(X,Y,IBUTT)
     IF(IBUTT.EQ.1 .OR. IBUTT.GE.128) GOTO 10
     IF(IBUTT.GE.ITEME) RETURN
     ITEM=IBUTT-1
     CALL SMENU(ITEM)
     GOTO (100,105,200,300,400,500,600),ITEM
```

```
*
*  Analysis of Model Space coordinates of selected Points
*
100   IMOD=1
      GOTO 110
*
*   Analysis of Definition Space coordinates of selected Points
*
105   IMOD=0
110   CALL PROMPT('\Point: <L>-Sel; <M>-End; <R>-Key #\')
      CALL USELOC(X,Y,IBUTT)
      CALL PROMPT('\ \')
      IF(IBUTT.EQ.130 .OR. IBUTT.LT.128) GOTO 999
      IF(IBUTT.EQ.132) THEN
        CALL SRCHPT(N,X,Y)
        IF(N.EQ.0) GOTO 110
      ELSE
120     CALL RESET
        CALL PROMPT('\Enter Point # ->  \')
        CALL INPSTR(BUFFER)
        CALL PROMPT('\ \')
        IF(BUFFER.EQ.' ') GOTO 999
        READ(BUFFER,*,ERR=120) N
      ENDIF
      IF(N.GT.0 .AND. N.LE.NPTS) CALL MARKPT(N,IC1)
      IF(IMOD.NE.0) THEN
        CALL DTOM(XT(N),YT(N),ZT(N),XM,YM,ZM,IPTDEF(N))
        CALL GTTCSR(1,1)
        WRITE(*,150) N,XM,YM,ZM
      ENDIF
      GOTO 110
*
*   Analysis of selected Lines
*
200   CALL PROMPT('\Line: <L>-Sel; <M>-End; <R>-Key #\')
      CALL USELOC(X,Y,IBUTT)
      CALL PROMPT('\ \')
      IF(IBUTT.EQ.130 .OR. IBUTT.LT.128) GOTO 999
      IF(IBUTT.EQ.132) THEN
        CALL SRCHLN(N,X,Y)
        IF(N.EQ.0) GOTO 200
      ELSE
220     CALL RESET
        CALL PROMPT('\Enter Line # ->  \')
        CALL INPSTR(BUFFER)
        CALL PROMPT('\ \')
        IF(BUFFER.EQ.' ') GOTO 999
        READ(BUFFER,*,ERR=220) N
      ENDIF
      IF(N.GT.0 .AND. N.LE.NLNS) CALL MARKLN(N,IC1)
      GOTO 200
300   CALL PROMPT('\Face: <L>-Sel; <M>-End; <R>-Key #\')
      CALL USELOC(X,Y,IBUTT)
      CALL PROMPT('\ \')
      IF(IBUTT.EQ.130 .OR. IBUTT.LT.128) GOTO 999
      IF(IBUTT.EQ.132) THEN
```

```
             CALL SRCHFA(N,X,Y)
             IF(N.EQ.0) GOTO 300
          ELSE
   *
   *   Analysis of Edges of selected Faces
   *
   320    CALL RESET
          CALL PROMPT('\Enter Face # ->  \')
          CALL INPSTR(BUFFER)
          CALL PROMPT('\ \')
          IF(BUFFER.EQ.' ') GOTO 999
          READ(BUFFER,*,ERR=320) N
          ENDIF
          IF(N.GT.0 .AND. N.LE.NFAS) THEN
            DO 340 I=1,NEDGE(N)
              CALL MARKLN(IDEDGE(I,N),-IC2)
              CALL MARKED(N,I,-IC2)
   340    CONTINUE
          CALL MARKFA(N,IC1)
          ENDIF
          GOTO 300
   *
   *   Analysis of Faces of selected Volumes
   *
   400    CALL PROMPT('\Volume: <L>-Sel; <M>-End; <R>-Key #\')
          CALL USELOC(X,Y,IBUTT)
          CALL PROMPT('\ \')
          IF(IBUTT.EQ.130 .OR. IBUTT.LT.128) GOTO 999
          IF(IBUTT.EQ.132) THEN
          CALL SRCHVO(N,X,Y)
          IF(N.EQ.0) GOTO 400
          ELSE
   420    CALL RESET
          CALL PROMPT('\Enter Volume # ->  \')
          CALL INPSTR(BUFFER)
          CALL PROMPT('\ \')
          IF(BUFFER.EQ.' ') GOTO 999
          READ(BUFFER,*,ERR=420) N
          ENDIF
          IF(N.GT.0 .AND. N.LE.NVOS) THEN
            DO 440 I=1,NFACE(N)
              CALL MARKFA(IDFACE(I,N),-IC2)
   440    CONTINUE
          CALL MARKVO(N,IC1)
          ENDIF
          GOTO 400
   *
   *   Analysis of Lines in the Group buffer
   *
   500    DO 520 I=1,NLNGP
          CALL MARKLN(LNGP(I),IC1)
   520    CONTINUE
          GOTO 999
   600    CALL REDRAW
   999    CALL SMENU(ITEM)
          GOTO 10
          END
```

```
*
*   Highlight Edge N of Face M
*
      SUBROUTINE MARKED(M,N,IC)
      CHARACTER*5 EID
      COMMON /POINTS/ NPTS,XT(300),YT(300),ZT(300),IPTDEF(300)
      COMMON /XVYVZV/ XV(300),YV(300),ZV(300)
      COMMON /LINES/ NLNS,IDPT1(400),IDPT2(400),LNFONT(400)
      COMMON /FACET1/ NFAS,NEDGE(100),IDEDGE(30,100)
      DATA IC3/3/
      ICT=IC
      IF(IC.LT.0) ICT=-IC
      CALL GCOLOR(ICT)
      IF(IC.GT.0) CALL GXOR(1)
      CALL ELABEL(N,EID)
      NPT1=IDPT1(IDEDGE(N,M))
      NPT2=IDPT2(IDEDGE(N,M))
*
*   Display Edge number at mid-point of the Edge
*
      CALL GWGCSR(.5*(XV(NPT1)+XV(NPT2)),.5*(YV(NPT1)+YV(NPT2)))
      CALL GWTEXT(EID)
      IF(IC.GT.0) CALL GXOR(0)
      CALL GCOLOR(IC3)
      RETURN
      END




*
*   Prepare Label for Edge N; N < 100
*
      SUBROUTINE ELABEL(N,EID)
      CHARACTER*5 DUMMY,EID
      CHARACTER FEQ(5)
      EQUIVALENCE (DUMMY,FEQ(1))
      DATA FEQ(1)/'\'/,FEQ(2)/'E'/,FEQ(5)/'\'/
      I1=MOD(N,10)
      I2=N/10
      IF(I2.NE.0) THEN
        FEQ(3)=CHAR(I2+ICHAR('0'))
        FEQ(4)=CHAR(I1+ICHAR('0'))
      ELSE
        FEQ(3)=CHAR(I1+ICHAR('0'))
        FEQ(4)=' '
      ENDIF
      EID=DUMMY
      RETURN
      END
```

5.3 BOOLEAN VOLUMETRIC OPERATIONS

Current applications of computer-aided design and computer-aided manufacturing (CAD/CAM), including automated drafting and analysis, numerically controlled tools programming, parts inspection and assembly, computer vision, and robots programming, owe much of their existence to developments in geometric modeling in the last decade. The subject of geometric modeling deals with the construction of computer-based geometric models of real world products in the hope that these models may be used to facilitate the design and manufacturing processes.

Starting with modeling of 2-D drawings on the computer display, geometric modeling has gone through several stages of maturity. The methodology for 2-D and 3-D wire-frame modeling is now well developed. Currently, research efforts in this area are centered at the modeling of sculptured solids. These models contain smoothly blended, curved surface patches representing the boundary of arbitrarily curved shapes.

However, due to high computational overhead associated with sculptured solid modeling, polyhedra-based solid modeling is widely used in exploratory and preliminary design stages, although it does not produce the smooth surfaces needed in computer-aided manufacturing. In addition, polyhedral solid modeling has found many direct applications in the areas of engineering analysis, robot systems simulation, computer vision, and animated motion pictures.

The following subsections are to present a constructive solid modeling scheme that will allow one to form complex shapes by applying Boolean operations to polyhedral solid primitives.

5.3.1 Constructive Solid Geometry and
Boundary Representations

Constructive Solid Geometry or CSG refers to a representation scheme of solid modeling which uses geometrically simple primitives, such as rectangular blocks, cylinders, spheres, and wedges, to represent complex shapes by intersecting, unionizing, or differencing these primitives. These three solid construction procedures are known as Boolean volumetric operations.

The CSG concept was originally developed by Voelcker and his coworkers at the University of Rochester. The CSG representation of a solid takes the form of a *binary tree* structure in which

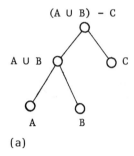

(a)

Figure 5.7 Binary tree of a CSG solid model.

each *node* represents a particular stage during the incremental solid construction and the lowest level nodes represent the required primitives.

Figure 5.7a shows the binary tree of a CSG solid model. The primitive nodes A, B and C represent the primitive solids depicted in Figure 5.7b, from left to right. The intermediate node, A ∪ B, represents the solid depicted in Figure 5.7c which is the result of unionizing solids A and B. The top node, (A ∪ B) − C, represents the CSG solid shown in Figure 5.7d which is the result of subtracting primitive C from the intermediate solid represented by A ∪ B.

An adjunct representation scheme in constructive solid modeling is boundary-representation or B-rep. B-rep defines a solid region with its bounding faces. For the case of polyhedral solids defined with CAD-PS, the bounding faces are the polygons stored in the face list of each polyhedron. As shown in Figure 5.8, the six bounding faces can be used to define the left solid depicted in Figure 5.7b. The order in the edge list of each face entity, counterclockwise when viewed from outside the polyhedron, allows one to distinguish the inside from the outside of the polyhedron.

5.3.2 Boolean Operations Based on Connected Intersections Loops

This subsection is to present an algorithm for performing basic Boolean operations: Union (∪), Intersection (∩), and Difference (−), on CAD-PS solid primitives. The union of bounded solids

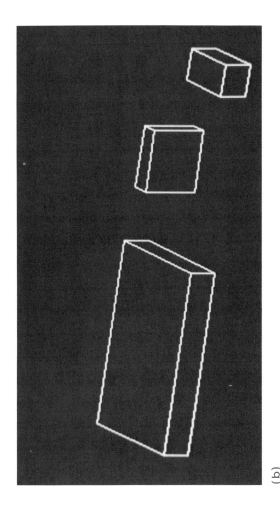

(b)

Figure 5.7   (Continued)

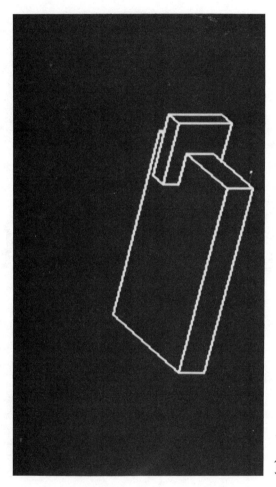

(c)

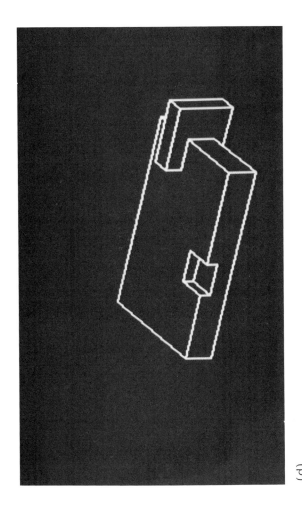

(d)

Figure 5.7   (Continued)

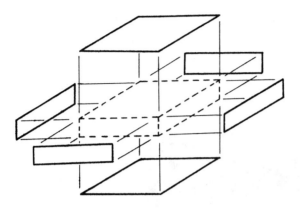

Figure 5.8   B-rep definition of solid depicted in Figure 5.7b.

S1 and S2 corresponds to a bounded solid region whose boundary
and interior is enclosed by either S1 or S2. The intersection
of S1 and S2 corresponds to a solid region whose boundary and
interior is enclosed by S1 and S2 simultaneously. The difference
of S1 and S2, or the remainder of S1 after subtracting S2, corresponds to a solid region whose boundary and interior is enclosed by S1 but not by S2. The algorithm to be presented is
derived from work published by Yamaguchi and Tokieda [1984].
The Boolean processor will be able to take two polyhedra defined
with CAD-PS, in a B-rep form, as input and produce a resultant solid in the same B-rep form.
     When two polyhedra intersect, the intersections between the
intersecting face pairs may be called *surface edges* because they
will become edges of the new polyhedron. The basis of this
Boolean processor lies in the fact that these surface edges always
form *connected loops*. Figure 5.9 illustrates three possible intersections between two rectangular blocks. The connected loops
are highlighted at the right of each intersection. Multiple loops
occur when faces of one polyhedron operand completely separate
the other polyhedron operand, as shown in Figure 5.9c where
two connected loops can be identified.
     Let us consider the intersection between solid operands S1 and
S2 as shown in Figure 5.9a. Edges E1, E2 and E3 of S1 intersect with faces F4, F5 and F6 of S2 at points A, C and E respectively. It is evident that part of E1 is located inside the

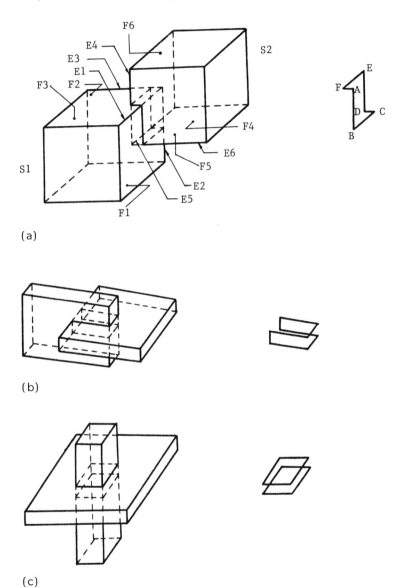

Figure 5.9   Connected loops of surface edges.

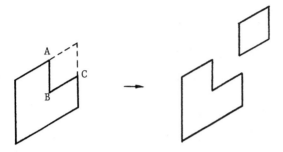

Figure 5.10   Dissection of a polygon into exterior and interior
faces.

opposite polyhedron with respect to face F4.   Similarly both E2
and E3 may be broken into two parts each classified as an interior or exterior edge with respect to their dividing face.

The new exterior, interior, and surface edges in a face, along
with the remaining non-intersecting edges, constitute new boundaries for separating the original face into an exterior face and
an interior face with respect to the opposite polyhedron.   Face
F1 in Figure 5.9a is redrawn in Figure 5.10, where the interior
edges are dashed and edges **AB** and **BC** are the two surface
edges located in F1.   Face F1 is shown to be dissected into an
exterior face and an interior face.   These dissected faces are
represented in the same form as the original face, with their
bounding edges registered in the same order.

Suppose we have identified the connected loop and dissected
all the intersecting faces into exterior and interior faces for the
case depicted in Figure 5.9a, the new solids corresponding to
the three Boolean operators can now be constructed.   The union
of S1 and S2 corresponds to the solid region bounded by all the
exterior faces associated with S1 and all the exterior faces associated with S2.   Figure 5.11a shows the resultant solid from
unionizing S1 and S2.

The intersection of S1 and S2 is equivalent to the solid region
bounded by all the interior faces associated with both S1 and
S2.   Figure 5.11b shows the resultant solid that is the intersection of S1 and S2.   Note that the outer normals of the interior
faces need not be inverted because they still point to the outside of the new polyhedral solid.

The difference of S1 and S2 (S1−S2) corresponds to the solid
region bounded by all the exterior faces associated with S1 and

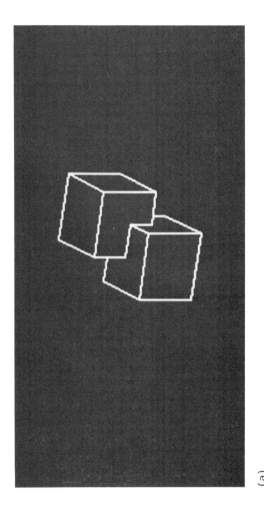

(a)

Figure 5.11   Union, intersection, and difference of two blocks.

(b)

(c)

Figure 5.11   (Continued)

all the interior faces associated with S2, with the outer normals of the interior faces inverted (see Fig. 5.11c). The inversion of face normals is necessary since the original outer normals to these interior faces now point to the inside of the new solid. In CAD-PS, the direction of the outer normal to each face is embedded in the list of edges attached to each polygonal face entity (counter-clockwise when viewed from outside the solid), thus inversion of the outer normal to a face can be achieved by simply reversing the order of entry of its boundary edges.

5.3.3   A Practical Algorithm for Tracing Connected Loops

Tracing all the connected intersection loops between two inter-secting polyhedra is the major task of the Boolean processor. Since intersection of two triangles is a much simpler problem to deal with than intersection of two arbitrary polygons, we shall use the triangulation processor described in Section 4.7.1 to convert the intersecting polygons into triangles prior to initi-ating the loop-tracing procedure.

For any two interfering triangular faces, these can at most be two intersection points. Generally, the two intersection points are contributed either by two edges of one of the triangular faces, when one face pierces through the other face as shown in Figure 5.12a, or by one edge of each face, when one face cuts into the other as shown in Figure 5.12b. This character-istic provides an efficient route for tracing the connected inter-section loops of two interfering polyhedra, for boundaries of the

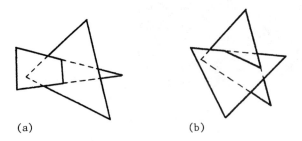

(a)   (b)

Figure 5.12   Intersection of two triangles.

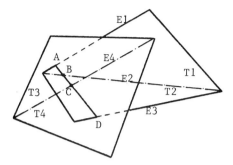

Figure 5.13   Intersection of two polygons.

polyhedra can be reconstructed with triangular faces and an
intersecting edge between two triangular faces can lead to the
next intersecting triangular face pair and thus the next segment
of a connected loop.

Figure 5.13 illustrates a pair of interfering polygons of two
intersecting polyhedra which have been reconstructed by triangular faces or triangles T1, T2, T3 and T4. Suppose we have
already identified that there are three pairs of intersecting triangles: T1 with T3, T2 with T3, and T2 with T4, and that edge
E1 of T1 intersects T3 at point A. Thus the loop-tracing procedure may begin with the *initial intersection point* A and the
first intersecting triangle pair T1 and T3. The triangle containing the cutting edge will be called the *subject* triangle and
the target triangle under consideration the *object* triangle. Thus
T1 is the subject triangle and T3 the object triangle of the first
intersecting triangle pair.

Since it is possible that another edge of T1 might intersect T3,
we try out E2 and realize that it indeed intersects T3 at B.
Thus AB must be a part of the underlying connected loop. However, segment AB is not a full surface edge because edge E2 is
only a Triangulation edge or T-edge which is not a real boundary
edge of the polygon replaced by T1 and T2. The rest of this
surface edge still needs to be found.

Since E2 of T1 is the last intersecting edge with T3, the next
triangle pair that would produce the rest of the surface edge
must be T2 and T3. The choice of the T2/T3 pair, instead of
the T2/T4 pair, guarantees a right track because the subject
triangle T2 shares E2 with the preceding subject triangle T1 and
the object triangle T3 is unchanged so segment AB can be

extended to trace out the surface edge. This shows how the current intersecting edge may be used to identify the next intersecting triangle pair.

The next step is to identify the other possible edge of the current subject triangle T2 that will intersect with the current object triangle T3. As illustrated in Figure 5.13, it is evident that E2 is the only edge of T2 intersecting with T3. This implies that the intersection between T2 and T3 is similar to the one depicted in Figure 5.12b. At this point, the functional statuses of T2 and T3 are swapped so T3 becomes the subject triangle and T2 the object triangle and T3 now should have that *other* edge intersecting with the current object triangle T2. In fact, E4 of T3 intersects with T2 at C as shown in Figure 5.13. Segment AB may now be extended to AC, noting that AC is not a full surface edge yet because E4 is, again, a T-edge.

The procedure for getting the next triangle pair just described is again applied, and this would lead to the T4/T2 pair. The fact that the other two edges of T4 do not intersect with T2 would require another swapping of triangle status between T4 and T2 so T2 becomes the current subject triangle and T4 the current object triangle. It is found that edge E3 of T2 produces an intersection point D with T4. Thus segment AC may be extended to AD, which is a full surface edge because E3 is a regular boundary edge of the polygon made up of T1 and T2. This completes the process of identifying a surface edge of the connected loop.

At this point, we can dissect the polygon made up of T1 and T2 into an exterior face and an interior face with respect to the opposite polyhedron, as depicted in Figure 5.10. Then the above procedure can be repeated to trace out the next surface edge of the connected loop and create consequent exterior and interior faces. For instance, edge E3 can be used to identify the next pair of intersecting triangles and point D will be the beginning point of the next surface edge. The loop is completed when the current surface edge ends at the initial intersection point A.

However, it is possible that the exterior and interior faces defined at the end of each surface edge still intersect with other polygons of the opposite polyhedron. This situation occurs in the cases depicted in Figures 5.9b and 5.9c. Since the dissection of a polygon into an exterior and an interior face removes the original triangulation on the polygon and thus the pairing relationships between the original triangles in the polygon with the intersecting triangles of the opposite polyhedron, the new

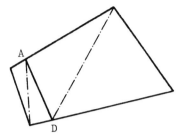

Figure 5.14   Re-triangulation of dissected polygons.

exterior and interior faces must be re-triangulated and the
pairing of these new triangles with those intersecting triangles
of the opposite polyhedron must be re-established before tracing
the next surface edge. The re-triangulation of the polygon
shown in Figure 5.13 due to surface edge AD is illustrated in
Figure 5.14.

Special attention must be paid to cases involving mutiple-loop
polygons defined with B-edges. A B-edge always appears twice
in the edge list of the underlying polygon. Consider a double-
loop polygon as shown in Figure 5.15. If the surface edges in
the polygon do not cross the loops nor the B-edges, then no
special treatment is needed, as illustrated in Figure 5.16. If
the surface edges cut across an outer and an inner loop, as
shown in Figure 5.17a, then the B-edge connecting the two loops

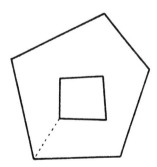

Figure 5.15   A double-loop polygon.

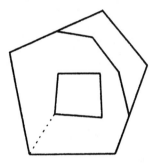

Figure 5.16   Dissection of a double-loop polygon.

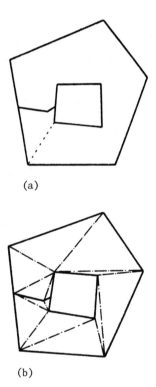

Figure 5.17   Re-triangulation of a double-loop polygon.

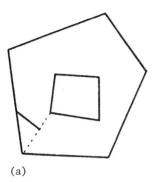

(a)

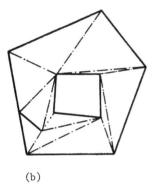

(b)

Figure 5.18   Re-triangulation of a double-loop polygon.

is removed and the polygon re-triangulated as shown in Figure
5.17b. The connected loop-tracing process continues with the
rematched intersecting triangle pairs. When the surface edges
cross a B-edge, as illustrated in Figure 5.18a, part of the B-
edge is removed. The polygon is then re-triangulated, as shown
in Figure 5.18b, and the loop-tracing process continues.

In the case that a polygon of a polyhedron cuts through the
other polyhedron and multiple connected loops exist, as shown
in Figure 5.9c, the polygon is split into an interior face and a
double-loop exterior face after closing the connected loop. The
split faces are re-triangulated and new intersecting triangle
pairs added to the current triangle list after removing the triangle pairs associated with the pre-split polygon from the triangle list.

The foregoing loop-tracing algorithm is summarized as follows:

1. Compute the rectangular bounding boxes of the two polyhedra being considered, by finding the minimum and maximum
   values of the X, Y and Z coordinates of the polyhedra.
2. Compute a common rectangular box which is the intersection
   of the two boxes obtained in Step 1. The two polyhedra
   will not intersect if they do not share a common box. If
   so, exit.
3. Establish a stack of pairs of intersecting polygons by
   computing the bounding box of each polygon and testing it
   against the common box obtained in Step 2 and, if it intersects with the common box, testing it against the
   bounding boxes of the possible intersecting polygons of
   the opposite polyhedron. The polygon pairs between the
   two polyhedra with intersecting bounding boxes are registered in the polygon stack. Then classify those polygons
   located inside the opposite polyhedron as interior faces.
4. Triangulate each polygon pair in the polygon stack and register all intersecting triangular pairs in the intersecting
   triangle list. An intersecting triangle pair is found by
   testing each edge of one triangle against the other triangle.
   If any edge intersects the other triangle, then the two
   triangles are included in the triangle list. An edge does
   not intersect a triangle if it lies in the plane of the triangle.
   Equation of the plane containing a triangle can be derived
   from the vertices of the triangle, as described in Section
   4.5.2. An edge will intersect the target triangle if the intersection point between the edge and the plane containing
   the triangle lines inside the triangle. The two polyhedra
   do not intersect if the intersecting triangle list is empty.
   If so, exit.
5. Compute and record the initial intersection point, starting
   with the first triangle pair, between a regular boundary
   edge of the initial subject triangle and the initial object triangle; register the current intersecting edge and the underlying subject and object polygons. Mark the initial intersection point as the starting point of a new connected loop.
6. Find the other intersection point between the current subject
   and object triangles and extend the surface edge; swap triangle statuses if necessary.
7. If the current surface edge ends at a boundary edge, prepare the current subject polygon for splitting by removing
   those triangles of the opposite polyhedron which still

intersect with the current subject polygon from the intersecting triangle list and placing them in a temporary buffer.
Split the current subject polygon into an exterior and an
interior face with respect to the object polyhedron. If the
temporary buffer is not empty, re-triangulate the split faces,
match the resulting triangles with the triangles in the buffer,
and add the new intersecting pairs to the triangle list.

8. If the existing surface edges already cut the current object
   polygon once before and the current surface edge ends at
   one of its boundary edges, split the object polygon as described in Step 7.

9. If the current surface edge cuts across an outer and an
   inner loop or ends at a B-edge of the current subject polygon, as shown in Figures 5.17 and 5.18, re-triangulate the
   subject polygon and modify the triangle list. Apply the
   same procedure to the current object polygon.

10. Close a connected loop of surface edges if the new inter-
    section point coincides with the initial intersection point.
    Split the current object polygon if it is not yet split.

11. Remove the current triangle pair from the intersecting tri-
    angle list and find the next triangle pair based on the cur-
    rent intersecting edge.

12. Go to Step 6 if existing surface edges are not closed.

13. Go to Step 5 if the intersecting triangle list is not empty.

14. Remove degenerated edges bounded by identical vertices.
    and degenerate polygons bounded by overlapped edges.

15. Construct specific solids from the lists of exterior and
    interior faces. This completes the solid-modeling algorithm.

It ought to be noted that, in the above procedure, an edge is
considered to have intersected an object triangle when it merely
touches the triangle. This enables the algorithm to handle face-
to-face touching polygons, an example is given in Figure 5.19.
Also note that the Boolean processor may be applied to the sec-
tioning of solid entities where rectangular blocks are subtracted
from a solid entity to reveal cross sections or interiors of the
solid entity.

The part of the algorithm where surface edges are obtained from
intersecting polygons and intersecting polygons are dissected
into separate face entities, may be separately implemented to
provide design options for identifying intersections between selected face entities and for dividing face entities into separate
faces.

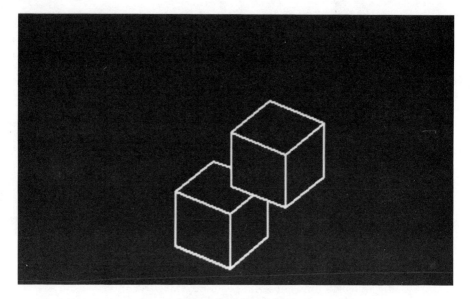

Figure 5.19   Polyhedron with face-to-face touching polygons.

Examples of Boolean operations on CAD-PS solid primitives
are shown in Figures 5.20 and 5.21.

5.4 DISPLAY OF PERSPECTIVE IMAGES

All 3-D images presented thus far are 2-D orthographic views
projected on to user-specified XV-YV planes. Such 2-D projections are suitable for interactive design purposes because parallel lines in the 3-D design space will remain parallel in an
orthographic projection, hence related line entities can easily be
identified. However, in the real world our eyes do not receive
orthographic images from our environment.

We visualize our surroundings in the form of perspective images,
in which parallel rails of a railroad may appear converging into
a single point far away and sizes of objects farther away from
the eyes are always smaller than sizes of same objects near by.
Perspective drawings are commonly used in presenting architectural designs. In this section we shall compute such perspective
images of solid entities created with CAD-PS.

The perspective effect is a result of placing an image-receiving
device at a finite point (the eye point) in a 3-D environment.

(a)

Figure 5.20   (a) A block less a smaller block and a cylinder; (b) solid in (a) less another cylinder.

(b)

Figure 5.20   (Continued)

(a)

Figure 5.21 Union of four cubes: (a) wire-frame; (b) hidden lines removed Image.

(b)

Figure 5.21   (Continued)

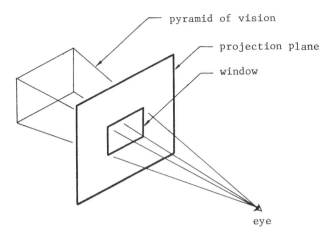

Figure 5.22   An orthographic view of a perspective projection system.

Figure 5.22 provides an orthographic view of a perspective projection system, in which a projection plane with a rectangular
window is placed in front of the *eye* device. The eye can only
see through the window. The locations of the eye and the window
define a pyramid of vision which contains all visible objects. The
perspective image of an object point is the intersection of the
projector line, connecting the eye point and the object point, and
the projection plane.

   To facilitate discussion of a perspective viewing algorithm in
the CAD-PS environment, we shall consider a perspective projection system defined in an active XV-YV-ZV (orthographic)
viewing space as shown in Figure 5.23a. The rectangular box
represents the current window.

   Imagine that an orthographic image of a solid entity is displayed
in the XV-YV plane and we would like to visualize the solid entity in perspective at an eye point located at a distance z_e away
from the center, (x_c, y_c), of the window. The window on the
XV-YV plane coincides with the window on the projection plane
of the perspective system. This defines a rectangular perspective system, for the projector passing through the center of the
window is perpendicular to the window. In this simplified system,
the perspective image projected on to the projection or XV-YV
plane would be a function of only one parameter, z_e.

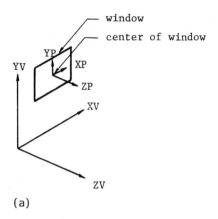

(a)

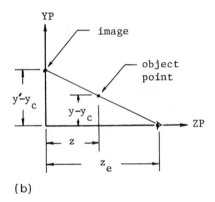

(b)

Figure 5.23   A perspective system defined in an XV-YV-ZV Space.

The XP, YP and ZP axes mark the projection reference space, with the XP and YP axes lying in the XV-YV plane and the ZP axis lying parallel to the ZV axis. Since we are not interested in seeing a solid entity from inside the solid, the distance z_e may be assumed to be positive and greater than the maximum ZV coordinate occupied by the model. This assumption precludes the singular cases where images may be projected to infinity in the projection plane, or where objects exist behind the eye point. Although parts of the product model may be located on the outside of the pyramid of vision and thus resulting in images outside the window, clipping of the image against the window is not required because the GGI routines used to display the image would perform such clipping automatically.

Figure 5.23b illustrates the relationship between the YV coordinate of an object point and that of its image point in the projection plane. The relationship may be referred to as a perspective transformation. It is evident that

$$y' = (y - y_c) \cdot z_e/(z_e - z) + y_c \qquad (5.2)$$

Similarly, the XV coordinates can be related by

$$x' = (x - x_c) \cdot z_e/(z_e - z) + x_c \qquad (5.3)$$

The assumption that z_e is positive and greater than the maximum ZV coordinate would result in a positive denominator for the above equations.

The point of convergence of the perspective images of a set of infinitely long parallel lines is known as the vanishing point. The vanishing point of parallel lines in any direction can be calculated from the above perspective transformation.

Consider a set of parallel lines represented in a general parametric form in the XV-YV-ZV space, that is

$$x = x_b + t \cdot x_d$$

$$y = y_b + t \cdot y_d \qquad (5.4)$$

$$z = z_b + t \cdot z_d$$

where (x_b, y_b, z_b) is a base point and (x_d, y_d, z_d) the directional vector of a general line, and t is the parameter whose value approaches infinity at the vanishing point.

The perspective image of the point (x, y, z) in the XV-YV plane may then be obtained as

$$x' = z_e(x_b/t + x_d - x_c/t)/(z_e/t - z_b/t - z_d) + x_c$$

$$y' = z_e(y_b/t + y_d - y_c/t)/(z_e/t - z_b/t - z_d) + y_c \qquad (5.5)$$

The vanishing point (x_v, y_v) corresponding to $t \to \infty$ would be

(a)

Figure 5.24   Perspective images of the solid entity shown in Figure 5.21.

$$x_v = -z_e \cdot x_d/z_d + x_c$$

$$y_v = -z_e \cdot y_d/z_d + y_c \qquad\qquad (5.6)$$

It should be noted that the location of the vanishing point depends only on the directional vector of the parallel lines, and that for parallel lines in planes parallel to the XV-YV plane, $z_d = 0$ and their images remain parallel and converge at infinity.

Perspective images received at specific distances away from the projection plane, with hidden lines removed, can be obtained by applying the algorithm described in Section 4.7.2 using the x' and y' coordinates of projected images. The reader should note that the reference *eye plane* used in computing orthographic images now reduces to a single eye point. Figure 5.24 shows two perspective images of the solid entity illustrated in Figure 5.21.

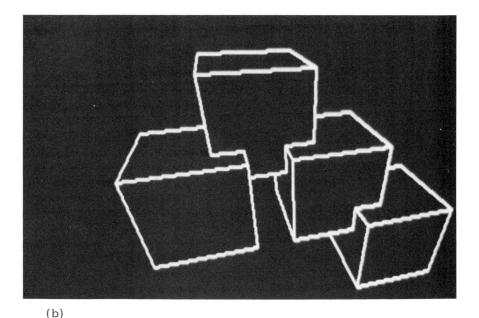

(b)

Figure 5.24   (Continued)

5.5 CLOSING THE CHAPTER

This chapter presents the VOLUME and ENTITY modules, along
with their supporting submodules, for creating polyhedral solid
entities from existing polygonal face entities. These modules,
together with the modules described in the preceding chapters,
provide basic building blocks for implementing 3-D CAD systems
in a typical PC environment. The CAD-PS system is created with
a typical PC environment. The CAD-PS system is created with
these building blocks for the IBM PC, PC/AT and PS/2 level
machines.

As an introduction to advanced solid modeling, this chapter
also touches on several related topics. A procedure for creating
volumes of revolution by simple user commands is delineated.
The volume of a solid entity is evaluated with an efficient determinant-based algorithm. Also presented is a practical algorithm
for performing Boolean operations on polyhedral solid primitives
in order to obtain complex-shape solid entities.

The display of realistic, perspective images of solid entities
is discussed in the context of deriving the perspective transformation from the current orthogrpahic viewing space to a
perspective viewing space whose axes are affixed to the center
of the current window. This allows the system to display a
computer generated solid entity in forms similar to images of
real life objects perceived by human eyes.

Appendix A

Assembly-Language Programming on the IBM PC

This appendix provides a practical guide to the assembly language of the IBM PC and its compatibles based on the 8086/88 CPU. The machine instructions for the IBM PC are a subset of those for the IBM PC/AT. An assembly language is a redefinition of a CPU's binary instruction codes in a more understandable mnemonic form. Every machine instruction is represented by a mnemonic term so algorithms can be readily coded by the human programmer. Although assembly-language source codes must be translated back to binary machine codes by an *assembler* for execution, this programming approach effectively relieves the human programmer of the tedium of working with binary codes.

A computer program is generally made up of two intermixed elements: Algorithm and Data. An algorithm lays down the procedures for processing information, while a data base provides the information to be processed. A data base may be static as stored on magnetic tapes or disks, or dynamic as obtained in real time from the environment surrounding the computer system.

Before attempting to write any 8086/88 assembly-language programs, we first examine the types of data that a typical PC can handle.

A.1 DATA TYPES

A CPU or processor is driven by machine instructions coded in strings of zeros and ones to process information coded also in strings of zeros and ones. The ways the instructions are coded

are defined by the manufacturer of a specific processor according to its electronic architecture. They usually vary from one
processor to another. In practice, a programmer utilizes a set
of keywords to code the necessary machine instructions for a
particular processor. However, the ways data are coded should
be universal so that the coded data can be exchanged between
different computers. The formats for coding numeric and non-
numeric data described below are widely accepted and practiced
by the industry.

A.1.1   Unsigned Integers

Computers work in binary. An eight-bit byte may be used to
code 256 (in decimal) different machine instructions, it may also
be used to represent 256 whole numbers from 0 to 255. These
non-negative whole numbers are called *unsigned integers*. The
most common unsigned integers are two-byte long, representing
whole numbers from 0 to 65,535. When numbers beyond the two-
byte range need to be dealt with, most microcomputers allocate
four bytes to store an unsigned integer with a value between 0
and 4,294,967,295.

In writing binary numbers, programmers prefer to group the
value of four consecutive bits into one *hexadecimal* digit to simplify interpretation of strings of zeros and ones. Table A.1
lists the hexadecimal digits and their values.

Both binary and decimal numbers are *positional number systems*
in that their values are determined by the positions of the digits.
The value of a positional number is the sum of the products of
each digit and an associated weight. For example, the value V of
a 3-digit decimal number $d_2 d_1 d_0$ is

$$V = d_2 \cdot 10^2 + d_1 \cdot 10^1 + d_0 \cdot 10^0$$

Thus the value of 615 (in decimal) is evaluated as

$$615 = 6 \cdot 10^2 + 1 \cdot 10^1 + 5 \cdot 10^0$$

The value of a binary number can be similarly computed,
noting there are only two legitimate digits, 0 and 1, and the
progressive weighting factor is now 2, instead of 10 for decimal
numbers. In a general positional number system, this factor,

Table A.1   Hexadecimal digits and their values.

Four-bit group	Value	Hexadecimal Digit
0000	zero	0
0001	one	1
0010	two	2
0011	three	3
0100	four	4
0101	five	5
0110	six	6
0111	seven	7
1000	eight	8
1001	nine	9
1010	ten	A
1011	eleven	B
1100	twelve	C
1101	thirteen	D
1110	fourteen	E
1111	fifteen	F

known as the *base* (b) or *radix*, defines the range of legitimate digits. The value of a general positional number can be computed through the following summation procedure:

$$V = \sum_i d_i \cdot b^i$$

A.1.2   Signed Integers

Representation of negative integers is required for arithmetical operations. In representing signed integers with one byte, most computers assign the most significant (leftmost) bit as the sign bit, and utilize the remaining seven bits to represent the value. An intuitive approach would be to apply the so-called *sign-magnitude* representation, which singles out the sign bit and uses the remaining bits to represent 0 through 127. For example, 0000 0111 represents +7, 1000 0111 would be −7, and 1111 1111 would be −127. However, the sign-magnitude approach is not consistent with binary arithmetic, for example

```
  0000 0111
− 0001 0000
  1111 0111
```

The above binary operation states that $7 - 16 = -119$, which should have been -9.

In order to use the same arithmetic circuits on both unsigned and signed integers, we need another representation in which 1111 0111 represents -9, not -119. This representation scheme is called the *two's complement* representation, in which a negative integer is obtained as the complement of the corresponding positive integer (including the sign bit), plus one. Thus -9 would be the two's complement of 0000 1001, which is 1111 0110 plus 1, resulting in 1111 0111. Note that in the two's complement format the meaning of the sign bit remains unchanged, and that positive integers are also two's complements of their negative counterparts.

The above single-byte two's complement approach is directly applicable to two-byte, four-byte, or eight-byte integers. Furthermore, converting signed integers to larger size signed integers requires only copying the sign bit to all the additional bits on the left side. For example, the single-byte integer 0000 0111 can be converted to a two-byte integer by duplicating the sign bit (0) throughout the additional eight bits on the left hand side, thus resulting in 0000 0000 0000 0111. Similarly, converting 1111 0111 to a two-byte integer would result in 1111 1111 1111 0111. This process is referred to as *sign extension*.

A.1.3   Binary-Coded Decimals

It is typical that computers convert the more human decimal numbers into binary, process them, and convert the results back to decimals for human users. Such conversions not only take time, but also incur roundoff errors for fractional numbers. One way to avoid this is to code the ten decimal digits (0–9) using four bits and to apply the decimal arithmetic directly to the binary-coded decimals (BCD).

The BCD is equivalent to the first ten values of a hexadecimal digit, 0000 for one and 1001 for nine. Thirty-nine (39) would be coded as 0011 1001, instead of 0010 0111 in binary. This BCD format is referred to as *packed* BCD because two decimal digits are packed into one byte. Another format, known as *unpacked* BCD, uses one full byte for one decimal digit. The four least significant, or rightmost, bits contain the decimal digit, and the four most significant bits do not affect the value of the coded number.

A.1.4   Floating-Point Numbers

In the practical world we often are required to deal with fractional or real numbers. In the decimal system, 13.52 represents the value of thirteen and a certain fraction of one; the "." is known as the *decimal point*. Real numbers encompass integer or whole numbers, 13. is exactly thirteen. Integers are a special kind of *fixed-point numbers* because the decimal point is always fixed to the right of the rightmost digit.

For a general positional number $d_{m-1}d_{m-2} \cdots d_1 d_0 . d_{-1}$ $\cdots d_{-n}$ the "." is referred to as the *radix point*. The formula for computing the value of a general positional number still applies; the fractional parts are obtained from negative exponents.

A binary integer has an implicit radix or binary point affixed to the rightmost digit. Fractional numbers can be represented by relocating the binary point, for example "0010 0111." represents 39; while "0010 01.11" yields

$$V = 1 \cdot 2^3 + 1 \cdot 2^0 + 1 \cdot 2^{-1} + 1 \cdot 2^{-2} = 9.75$$

The range of representation from manipulating the binary point is rather limited, however. By letting the binary point *float* around the binary digits according to an exponent, we can expand this range significantly. Thus came the term *floating-point numbers*. The following describes a standard 32-bit floating-point format proposed by the Institute of Electrical and Electronics Engineers (IEEE).

The 32-bit string is divided into three fields as shown in Figure A.1. The rightmost 23 bits constitute the *mantissa* or *significand*, the next 8 bits the *exponent*, and the leftmost bit is the *mantissa's sign bit*. The value of such a floating-point number is:

$$(-1)^{sgn} \cdot M \cdot 2^E$$

where sgn is the value of the sign bit, M the value of the mantissa, and E the value of the exponent. The value of M is represented in a fixed-point fromat where the binary point is affixed to the right of a *hidden bit* that is implicitly located to the left of the M-field. So the M-field has, in fact, 24 bits. The value of the hidden bit is assumed one, thus the value of M is always between one and two.

The E-field gives a specific power of two by which the mantissa must be multiplied to yield the value of the real number; it determines the final location of the binary point. The E-field uses the *excess-127* notation: an E-field of 0000 0101 (5) represents an exponent of -122 ($5-127$) and an E-field of 1111 1110 (254) represents an exponent of +127 (154 $-$ 127).

The values represented by the 32-bit floating-point format range from $-3.37 \cdot 10^{38}$ to $3.37 \cdot 10^{38}$. The precision and range of the floating point representation may be increased by using larger numbers of bits. A 64-bit format was also proposed

```
31 30                23 22                                          0
|MS|    Exponent (E)   |          Mantissa (M)                     |
```

Figure A.1   IEEE 32-bit floating point format.

by the IEEE to *double* the precision of the 32-bit floating-point format.

It is obvious that the binary arithmetic for integers would not work for real numbers as represented above. However, by treating each field separately, we are able to customize the binary arithmetic to perform real number operations. Moreover, dedicated floating-point processors can be adapted to handle real numbers directly and more efficiently. The Intel 8087 is a floating-point or math coprocessor that operates in conjunction with either an Intel 8086 or 8088.

The concept of using a finite number of bits to form floating-point numbers in an attempt to represent the continuum of all real values inevitably leads to certain *approximation* or *roundoff* errors. Not every real number is representable in a floating-point format with a finite number of bits. For example, a representation of the value one-third in a floating-point format might take the form

0 01111101 01010101010101010101010101010101 . . .

which requires an infinite number of bits for the mantissa field. In the 32-bit floating-point format, the value may be approximated by either

0 01111101 01010101010101010101010

or

0 01111101 01010101010101010101011

both of which involve a roundoff error occurred at the least significant bit of the mantissa field.

Analysis of roundoff errors is not an easy task, particularly so when large numbers of multiplications or divisions have to be performed. Here it can only be mentioned that the art of number crunching demands a solid understanding of what the numbers reveal.

A.1.5   Characters

The most widely practiced coding system for characters is ASCII, the American Standard Code for Information Interchange. ASCII defines a set of 128 different characters including alphabets, numerals, and commonly used symbols, each coded by a 7-bit

Table A.2   ASCII Character Codes.

Decimal	Character	Decimal	Character	Decimal	Character
0	NUL	43	+	86	V
1	SOH	44	,	87	W
2	STX	45	–	88	X
3	ETX	46	.	89	Y
4	EOT	47	/	90	Z
5	ENQ	48	0	91	[
6	ACK	49	1	92	\
7	BEL	50	2	93	]
8	BS	51	3	94	^
9	HT	52	4	95	_
10	LF	53	5	96	`
11	VT	54	6	97	a
12	FF	55	7	98	b
13	CR	56	8	99	c
14	SO	57	9	100	d
15	SI	58	:	101	e
16	DLE	59	;	102	f
17	DC1	60	<	103	g
18	DC2	61	=	104	h
19	DC3	62	>	105	i
20	DC4	63	?	106	j
21	NAK	64	@	107	k
22	SYN	65	A	108	l
23	ETB	66	B	109	m
24	CAN	67	C	110	n
25	EM	68	D	111	o
26	SUB	69	E	112	p
27	ESC	70	F	113	q
28	FS	71	G	114	r
29	GS	72	H	115	s
30	RS	73	I	116	t
31	US	74	J	117	u
32	SP	75	K	118	v
33	!	76	L	119	w
34	"	77	M	120	x
35	#	78	N	121	y
36	$	79	O	122	z
37	%	80	P	123	{
38	&	81	Q	124		
39	'	82	R	125	}
40	(	83	S	126	~
41	)	84	T	127	DEL
42	*	85	U		

Table A.3   Control Codes in Table A.2.

NUL	= Null	DC1	= Device control 1
SOH	= Start of heading	DC2	= Device control 2
STX	= Start of text	DC3	= Device control 3
ETX	= End of text	DC4	= Device control 4
EOT	= End of transmission	NAK	= Negative acknowledge
ENQ	= Enquiry	SYN	= Synchronize
ACK	= Acknowledge	ETB	= End transmitted block
BEL	= Bell	CAN	= Cancel
BS	= Backspace	EM	= End of medium
HT	= Horizontal tab	SUB	= Substitute
LF	= Line feed	ESC	= Escape
VT	= Vertical tab	FS	= File separator
FF	= Form feed	GS	= Group separator
CR	= Carriage return	RS	= Record separator
SO	= Shift out	US	= Unit separator
SI	= Shift in	SP	= Space
DLE	= Data link escape	DEL	= Delete or rubout

string. Most computers use one byte to store one character,
leaving an extra bit for system-dependent usage. A list of
ASCII characters is given in Table A.2. The control codes
used in Table A.2 are listed in Table A.3.

A.2   ARCHITECTURE OF THE PC

An assembly language is an abstraction of the machine language
or instructions through use of mnemonics. Learning any particular assembly language should always start with an examina-
tion of the underlying hardware structure.

   Figure A.2 illustrates a system block diagram of the IBM PC.
An Intel 8088 chip serves as the operation center of the PC
system, coordinating all the attached devices. For intensive
number crunching tasks like computer-aided design (CAD), the
Intel 8087 Math Coprocessor can improve the response time. Although not part of the standard configuration, an 8087 can
easily be plugged into a pre-assigned socket on the system board
of most IBM PC level machines. Note that the 8088 differs from
the 8086 only in the size of their data bases: 8-bit for the 8088
and 16-bit for the 8086.

   In just a few years since its birth, the PC has been adopted
by all kinds of users: office white collars, shop floor blue collars, school teachers, students, and homemakers, to name a

```
: 8088        :  Cassette :_____:  Cassette  :
: CPU         :  Adapter  :       :_____:
: 8 Interrupt :  Speaker  :_____:  Speaker   :
: Levels      :  Adapter  :       :_____:
: 4 Channels  :  Keyboard :_____:  Keyboard  :
: DMA         :  Adapter  :
: Memory      :  Read-Only :
: Bank        :  Memory    :
: Math        :
: Coprocessor :
             :
             :  5 Slot
             :  I/O Channel
    _____:
   : : : : : :
   : : : : : :
   :_:_:_:_:_:
```

Figure A.2   System block diagram of the IBM PC.

General Registers

```
        7          0 7           0
AX -> |    AH     |     AL      |   (Accumulator)
BX -> |    BH     |     BL      |   (Base)
CX -> |    CH     |     CL      |   (Counter)
DX -> |    DH     |     DL      |   (Data)
```

Pointer and Index Registers

```
       15                       0
SP -> |_____|   (Stack Pointer)
BP -> |_____|   (Base Pointer)
SI -> |_____|   (Source Index)
DI -> |_____|   (Destination Index)
```

Segment Registers

```
CS -> |_____|   (Code Segment)
DS -> |_____|   (Data Segment)
SS -> |_____|   (Stack Segment)
ES -> |_____|   (Extra Segment)


IP -> |_____|   (Instruction Pointer)

FLAG -> |_____|   (Flags)
```

Figure A.3   The 8086/88 registers and flags.

few. A warm reception for PC or any other tool by people
from varied walks always hinged on its ease of use. The success of the IBM PC owes dearly to its easily adaptable PC-DOS
operating system.
    An operating system (OS) is a special computer management
program that shields the user from the complex electronics within the computer and offers a simple user interface. By entering
simple commands, the user can direct the computer, via an OS,
to create and store files (sets of data), to check the available
memory size, to display a directory for the files on a disk, to
load a compiler from a disk, and to perform many other functions.
The PC-DOS is produced by Microsoft Corp., which also produces MS-DOS for many IBM compatible micros. The user

interfaces of the PC-DOS and the MS-DOS are virtually identical.
In this book the DOS 2.1 version is used in developing the programs.

The 8086/88 processor contains a total of thirteen 16-bit registers and nine 1-bit flags. Based on their specific functions,
the registers may be categorized into four sets. As illustrated
in Figure A.3, the general registers include four 16-bit registers
which can also be used as 8-bit registers for byte opertions.
The pointer and index registers refer to two pointer and two
index registers. The segment registers are, respectively, the
Code, Data, Stack, and Extra registers. The thirteenth register, the instruction pointer, is a set by itself and is used by
the processor to fetch the machine instructions stored in memory.
The nine flags are placed in a 16-bit FLAGS register and used
to reflect the current processor status and to control certain
machine operations.

A unique feature of the 8086/88 processor is its segment-
based memory structure. At any point in time, the 8086/88 is
able to access four segments of memory each of which can be up
to 65,536 or 64K bytes long. The four-segment memory space is
accessed or *addressed* via an offset sum of two 16-bit registers:
a Code, Data, Stack, or Extra *segment* register and an *offset*
register. The offset sum is obtained by first loading the 16-bit
value of the segment register into the leftmost 16 bits of a 20-bit
physical address indicator, with the rightmost four bits padded
with zero, then adding the 16-bit value of the offset register to
the rightmost 16 bits of the indicator. The provision of a 20-bit
physical address indicator limits the physical memory space of
an 8086/88-based system to about one million bytes (2^{20}). Figure A.4 illustrates how physical addresses are computed from
segment and offset register pairs.

Segment Register:	0100 0111 0010 1101
Physical Address Indicator:	0100 0111 0010 1101 0000
Offset Register:	1001 0010 1001 1110
Physical Address:	0101 0000 0101 0110 1110

Figure A.4   Formation of physical address.

It is clear that the physical address indicator at the first stage points to the first byte of a physical *segment*, and that the range of a segment is limited to the 64K bytes addressable by an offset register. It should also be noted that the four memory segments are allowed to overlap one another, as long as the programmer juggles them properly. In practice, the assignment of memory blocks to the various segments may be left to the assembler and linker so the programmer need not be concerned with such details.

In addition to the memory addressing channel, the 8086/88 also supports other input/output channels for communications with attached peripheral devices, such as mouse and plotter for CAD applications. The processor is able to address any of the allowable 65,536 I/O devices through the same number of 8-bit I/O ports or half of that through 16-bit I/O ports. These I/O ports may be regarded as special memory cells within an implicit I/O segment. The RS-232C standard serial port is the most common interface for general-purpose communications.

The 8086/88 system is equipped with an *interrupt* mechanism for attending external devices and handling emergency situations, like an unexpected power failure. When an interrupt signal is generated by a device or event, the processor responds by putting aside the current task and *jumping* to a service routine requested by the interrupt. The processor will resume the disrupted task as soon as the *interrupt service routine* is completed.

There are two kinds of interrupt: plain interrupt (INTR) and non-maskable interrupt (NMI). The processor can be programmed to allow or disallow external devices to send plain interrupt signals, but the NMI is not maskable hence emergencies such as a power failure can always interrupt the system to perform salvaging routines such as stashing away important data before a *system crash* occurs.

There are 256 types of plain interrupt and only one type of NMI. The processor distinguishes the type of an interrupt by demanding a *type number* (0—255) from the interrupting device after acknowledging the receipt of the interrupt signal. The processor regards the first 1,024 bytes of the memory map as an interrupt table in which the location of each of the 256 types of interrupt is stored as two 16-bit addresses (for a segment and offset pair).

Several type numbers are reserved for special uses. Type 0 is reserved for a routine dealing with the arithmetic error of dividing by zero, type 1 is for the single stepping mode allowing

the processor to execute the instructions one at a time, which
is useful in finding and correcting program errors, or *debugging*.
Type 2 is reserved for the NMI interrupt, type 3 for a special
interrupt with no type number, type 4 for a routine handling the
arithmetic error of overflowing the specific size of a variable.
Types 6 through 31 are reserved for future versions of the 8086/
88. Types 32 through 255 are for user-specified interrupts.

A.3 IMPLICIT PAIRING OF SEGMENT AND OFFSET REGISTERS

The unique segment-based memory structure of the 8086/88
processor is accompanied by certain implicit binding between the
four segment registers and the eight data and pointer registers.
The processor uses the contents of the Code Segment (CS) register to identify the *current* code segment in the memory space
containing mainly coded machine instructions. The contents of
the Data Segment (DS) register indicate the *current* memory
segment containing only data, the contents of the Stack Segment
(SS) register indicate the *current* memory segment containing
stacked parameters, and the contents of the Extra Segment (ES)
indicate the *current* memory segment containing mainly intermediate computational results. The four segment registers cannot
be used interchangeably.

The current code segment contains the program being executed. The offset pointer for identifying the next instruction
to be executed in the segment is stored in the Instruction
Pointer (IP) register. The CS:IP pair provides the physical
address of the next instruction.

The concept of using a *stack* to transfer parameters between
tasks is common in computer architectural design. A computer
seldom executes every instruction in a code segment in sequence
without branching to other parts of the segment or other segments. In order to fly freely within the memory space without
going astray and to be able to communicate between different
tasks, the processor leaves or *pushes* necessary parameters
and its current position or address on a stack before branching
and, after executing the intervening task, fetches or *pops* the
returning address from the stack to continue the previously disrupted task. A stack may be regarded as a reserved array
of memory locations used to store transient parameters and addresses.

The 8086/88 system implements its stacking mechanism in a top-down fashion, assuming the memory arranged in a vertical array with higher addresses lying above lower addresses. The first location in the stack segment starts from the high-end address of the memory segment, pointed to by the combination of SS and the Stack Pointer (SP) register. After *pushing* a word (two bytes) on to the stack, the processor automatically decrements the contents of SP by two to point to the new top of the stack. Conversely, *popping* a word from the stack would trigger the processor to increment the contents of SP by two to update the location of the current top of the stack. Since the stack contains parameters meant to be passed along to various tasks, the programmer should exercise caution in synchronizing the *pushing* and *popping* of parameters.

With instructions and stack parameters properly arranged, all that is left is the data. The processor fetches data from the current data segment unless the offset address was stored in either SP or BP register, for which case the current stack segment is used. The Base Pointer (BP) register is useful in retrieving the parameters sent through stack. Another exception to assuming the current data segment for data storage occurs when using a byte-string operation to copy a block of bytes from one location (source) to another (destination). In this case the processor assumes the DS:SI pair to be the source pointer and the ES:DI pair to be the destination pointer.

The segment for data-fetching can also be specified by using a *prefix* to override the implicitly assumed data segment. For instance, consider an ADD instruction that adds the contents of a memory word, located in the current data segment and addressed by an offset stored in SI, to the contents of AX and leaves the result in AX. In an assembly language, this instruction may look like:

ADD AX, [SI]

Note that the implicit segment assignment need not be mentioned and the square brackets indicate that the contents in SI is an offset pointer to the operand, not the operand itself. If the source operand is located within the current code segment at the same offset, then the instruction would be

ADD AX, CS:[SI]

The CS prefix will instruct the processor to fetch the operand
from the same offset location within the memory segment specified
by the CS register.

A.4   USE OF FLAGS

Six of the nine flag bits on the 8086/88 are used to record the
current processor status (status flags) and the other three to
control certain CPU operations (control flags).
   The status flags provide the programmer with information
about the results of arithmetic or logical operations so he or she
can properly direct the program flow. The carry flag (CF) indicates if the instruction just executed generated a carry out
of the most significant bit; the auxiliary carry flag (AF) indicates if a carry was generated out of the four least significant
bits. The overflow flag (OF) is turned on when the operation
results in a number that cannot be accommodated by the specified
size. The zero flag (ZF) indicates if the operation generated a
zero result; the sign flag (SF) indicates a negative result.
And the parity flag (PF) indicates if the binary result has an
even number of ones.
   The control flags include the direction flag (DF), which specifies the direction (incrementing or decrementing of address) of
the byte-string operations; the interrupt-enable flag (IF), which
is used to allow or disallow external interrupts; and the trap
flag (TF), which forces the processor to execute one instruction
at a time so the program can be closely examined.

A.5   ADDRESSING OF INSTRUCTION OPERANDS

Most 8086/88 machine instructions perform operations on one or
two *operands*. There are many different ways for the 8086/88
to obtain operands. They may be directly attached to the instruction, stored in specific registers, or stored in memory. This
section examines these operand-addressing modes.
   We will use the increment (INC) instruction as an example of
those working withone operand. To increment the contents of
register AX, we write

```
INC    AX
```

This addressing mode is referred to as the *register mode*. To increment the contents of the 8-bit AL register, we would write

```
INC   AL
```

The two INCrement operations are obviously different, one operates on a 16-bit value and the other on an 8-bit value. However, since an assembler is designed to distinguish an 8-bit register (AL) from a 16-bit one (AX) and generate correct machine codes accordingly, the programmer need not distinguish such variations explicitly.

We may also INCrement a value in the memory. In an assembly-language program, a memory location for storing a value is designated by a *symbol*, or *name*. While allocating the storage location, the program also defines the size of the location. Consider a part of a program:

```
:
:
SUM_BYTE      DB      0FEH
SUM_WORD      DW      01234H
:
:
INC           SUM_BYTE
INC           SUM_WORD
:
:
```

The symbol SUM_BYTE is used to define a byte-location (DB) with an initial value of 1111 1110 (FE), SUM_WORD defines a word-location (DW) with an initial value of 0011 0100 (34) 0001 0010 (12), in low to high address order. Note that a zero is used to start a hexadecimal number in the assembly-language program to avoid confusion between a value and a symbol, and an "H" ends every hexadecimal value. Also note that the 8086/88 treats two consecutive bytes as one *word* with the low-address byte storing the least significant eight bits, and the high-address byte storing the most significant eight bits. Thus the high-byte and the low-byte are reversed when listed in low to high address order.

Since the assembler has been instructed to allocate specific numbers of bytes to specific symbols, it has no problem generating the correct codes for the byte-INCrement and word-INCrement.

This mode of operand addressing is known as *direct memory addressing.*

Next, let's consider instructions having two operands, such as ADD. The ADD instruction adds the value of a *source* operand to that of a *destination* operand, and stores the result in the destination operand. Although either of the two operands may be residing in the memory, the 8086/88 does not allow the case of having both operands stored in the memory; at least one operand must be in a register. For example,

```
ADD     AX, DX

ADD     AL, 0A9H

ADD     AX, SUM_WORD

ADD     SUM_BYTE, AH

ADD     AX, [SI]

ADD     [BP+DI+6], DX
```

are all legitimate ADD operations. The 8086/88 convention is to put the destination operand in front of the source operand, thus the first statement adds the contents of DX to that of AX, and leaves the result in AX. The second operation obtains its source operand using *immediate mode*, which attaches a numeric operand to the instruction code so the processor receives the operand as part of the instruction. It is obvious that an instruction like "ADD 0A9H, AL" is meaningless since the result cannot be stored in a numeric operand.

The last two ADD operations obtain their operands using *indirect memory addressing.* The square brackets direct the assembler to use the sum of the contents of the bracketed register or registers, and an immediate displacement (for example, [BP + DI + 6]) as the offset pointer to the operand. Because of implicit binding, the "[SI]" symbol would direct the processor to look up the operand in the current data segment, while the "[BP + DI + 6]" notation would tell the processor to look up the operand in the current stack segment.

A.6   THE 8086/88 INSTRUCTION SET

According to their specific functions, the 8086/88 instructions may be classified into eight groups: data movement, arithmetic,

Table A.4   Data movement instructions (dst = destination, src = source, reg = register, ptr = pointer).

Mnemonic	Operands	Comments
MOV	dst,src	;Copy src to dst, for BYTE or WORD operands
PUSH	src	;Push src onto stack, for WORD operands
POP	dst	;Pop stack top into dst, for WORD operands
XCHG	dst,reg	;Exchange dst with reg, BYTE or WORD

(a)   General Purpose Data Transfer

Mnemonic	Operands	Comments
IN	accum,port#	;Load data in port (0-255) into AL or AX
IN		;Load data in port (# in DX) into AL or AX
OUT	port#,accum	;Transfer AL or AX to port (0-255)
OUT		;Transfer AL or AX to port (# in DX)
XLAT		;Load AL with [BX+AL]

(b)   Accumulator (AX or AL) Specific Data Transfer

Mnemonic	Operands	Comments
LEA	reg,ptr	;Load offset or effective address of ptr into reg
LDS	reg,ptr	;Load double-word pointer (ptr) into DS:reg
LES	reg,ptr	;Load double-word pointer intq ES:reg

(c)   Address Pointer Transfer

Mnemonic	Comments
LAHF	;Load low byte of FLAGS into AH
SAHF	;Store AH into low byte of FLAGS

Table A.4   (Continued)

PUSHF	;Push FLAGS onto top of stack
POPF	;Pop top of stack into FLAGS

(d)   Flag Transfer

---

logical, string manipulation, program flow control, interrupt control, flag control, and coprocessor synchronization. This section examines each of these classes.

Data Movement Instructions. Table A.4 summarizes the data
transfer instructions, which may be subdivided into four sub-
classes. The entries of the table follow the basic line format
of the MASM Macro Assembler, an 8086/88 assembler published
by Microsoft Corp. and to be discussed in Section A.7. A statement or instruction line contains label, opcode (*operation code*)
mnemonic, operand, and comments, in that order. Since labels
are optional and used to identify particular statements in a program, the table does not provide a label field. Comments start
with semicolons, they are used only to help the reader of a program understand the underlying logic of program statements and
are not regarded by the assembler as part of the program.

Arithmetic Instructions. As expected, there are four kinds of
arithmetic instructions: addition, subtraction, multiplication,
and division. Table A.5 lists the 8086/88 arithmetic instructions.
It ought to be noted that Table A.5 does not include the instructions for converting binary numbers to and from BCD numbers.
    In practice, program flows are generally dependent on the
types of results of arithmetic operations, which manifest themselves as *flags*. The six status flags are set or reset to indicate specific properties of the results of most arithmetic and
logical operations: CF is set to indicate an unsigned result
being out of range; OF set to indicate a signed result being out
of range; ZF set when the result is zero; SF set to indicate
a negative result; PF set to indicate a binary result having an
even number of "1" bits; and AF is set when the least significant four bits or *nibble* of the result is out of range.

Table A.5   Arithmetic instructions.

Mnemonic	Operands	Comments
ADD	dst,src	;Add src to dst, for BYTE or WORD operands
ADC	dst,src	;Add src and the carry bit to dst
INC	dst	;Increment dst by 1
SUB	dst,src	;Subtract src from dst
SBB	dst,src	;Subtract src with borrow from dst
DEC	dst	;Decrement dst by 1
NEG	dst	;Negate dst
CMP	dst,src	;Compare src with dst (subtract src from ;dst, but keep dst intact)
MUL	src	;Unsigned multiply AL by src leaving the ;result in AX, or multiply AX by src leaving ;the result in both DX and AX
IMUL	src	;Signed multiply (see above)
DIV	src	;Unsigned divide AX by src leaving quotient ;in AL and remainder in AH, or divide DX,AX ;by src leaving quotient in AX and remainder ;in DX
IDIV	src	;Signed divide (see above)
CBW		;Sign extend AL to AX
CWD		;Sign extend AX to double-word DX,AX

Table A.6   Logical and shift instructions.

```
AND    dst,src    ;Logical AND src on to src

OR     dst,src    ;Logical OR src on to dst

XOR    dst,src    ;Logical Exclusive OR src on to dst

NOT    dst        ;Invert all bits of dst

TEST   dst,src    ;Perform src AND dst, leave dst unchanged,
                  ;but set FLAGS

SHL    dst,cnt    ;Logical shift dst left cnt bits, the right-
                  ;most bit padded with zero and the leftmost
                  ;bit replaces CF (cnt is either 1 or CL, which
                  ;contains the shift count)

SHR    dst,cnt    ;Logical shift right cnt bits

SAL    dst,cnt    ;Same as SHL

SAR    dst,cnt    ;Arithmetic shift right cnt bits, SF shifted
                  ;into the leftmost bit and the rightmost bit
                  ;replaces CF

ROL    dst,cnt    ;Rotate dst operand left cnt bits, the left-
                  ;most bit rotated into the rightmost bit

ROR    dst,cnt    ;Rotate dst operand right cnt bits, the right-
                  ;most bit rotated into the leftmost bit

RCL    dst,cnt    ;ROL with CF at the left of dst

RCR    dst,src    ;ROR with CF at the left of dst
```

Logical Instructions. The 8086/88 logical operations comprise
Boolean and shift/rotate operations as summarized in Table A.6.
The bit-by-bit Boolean AND, OR, XOR, and NOT operations
may be described with a True/False table as follows:

dst	src	AND	OR	XOR	NOT dst
0	0	0	0	0	1
1	0	0	1	1	0

dst	src	AND	OR	XOR	NOT dst
0	1	0	1	1	1
1	1	1	1	0	0

Like arithmetic operations, the logical operations can operate on byte- or word-size operands, treating all the bits in parallel, and set the status flags according to the resultant byte or word. Note that the NOT operator has only one operand.

String Manipulation Instructions. A string is a specific number of consecutive bytes or words in memory. String instructions operate on each item in the string, they are summarized in Table A.7. The source string is always assumed to begin at location DS:SI and the destination string at location ES:DI.

Table A.7   String manipulation instructions.

MOVS	dst,src	;Copy the contents of location DS:SI to ;ES:DI, update SI and DI according to DF ;(increment SI and DI if DF=0, decrement ;if DF=1); dummy dst and src are used to ;determine operand size
CMPS	dst,src	;Compare src with dst, update SI and DI
SCAS	dst	;Scan dst and compare AL or AX with dst, ;update DI
LODS	src	;Load AL or AX with src, update SI
STOS	dst	;Store AL or AX at dst, update DI
REP	instr	;While CX <> 0, repeat (1) decrement CX ;by 1 and (2) instr (a MOVS or STOS ;instruction)
REPZ	instr	;While CX <> 0 and ZF = 0, repeat (1) ;decrement CX by 1 and (2) instr (a CMPS ;or SCAS instruction)
REPNZ	instr	;While CX <> 0 and ZF = 1, repeat (1) ;decrement CX by 1 and (2) instr (a CMPS ;or SCAS instruction)

Table A.8   Program control instructions.

JMP	addr	;Jump unconditionally to address addr
CALL	addr	;Call subroutine or procedure at address addr; ;current IP will be pushed onto current stack ;for <u>intrasegment</u> calls, current CS:IP will be ;pushed for <u>intersegment</u> calls
RET		;Pop return address and return from subroutine ;or procedure
RET	n	;Return from subroutine, add n to SP to delete ;parameters passed through stack
Jxx	addr8	;Jump conditionally to address IP + addr8, ;addr8 is an 8-bit displacement with a value ;between -128 and +127; condition determined ;by the preceding arithmetic or logical ;operation; there are 16 conditional jumps: ; JE or JZ — jump on equal or zero (ZF=1) ; JNE or JNZ — jump on not equal or not zero ; JL — jump on less than (in the preceding ; <u>signed</u> integer comparison, SF xor OF ; = 1) ; JGE — jump on greater than or equal ; (SF xor OF = 0) ; JG — jump on greater than [(SF xor OF) or ; ZF = 0] ; JLE — jump on less than or equal ; [(SF xor OF) or ZF = 1] ; JB — jump on below (in the preceding ; <u>unsigned</u> integer comparison, CF = 1) ; JAE — jump on above or equal (CF = 0) ; JA — junp on above (CF or ZF = 0) ; JBE — jump on below or equal (CF or ZF ; = 1) ; (the following six conditional jumps ; concerns <u>only</u> with the setting of a ; particular flag) ; JS — jump if SF = 1 ; JNS — jump if SF = 0 ; JO — jump if OF = 1 ; JNO — jump if OF = 0 ; JP — jump if PF = 1 ; JNP — jump if PF = 0
LOOP	addr8	;Decrement CX, jump to IP + addr8 if CX <> 0

Table A.8   (Continued)

LOOPZ	addr8	;Decrement CX, jump to IP + addr8 if CX <> 0 ;and ZF = 1
LOOPNZ	addr8	;Decrement CX, jump to IP + addr8 if CX <> 0 ;and ZF = 0
JCXZ	addr8	;Jump to IP + addr8 if CX = 0

Program Control Instructions. An important part of virtually all programs, the program control instructions provide traffic-light and road-block devices for programming flexibility, since the flow of a program generally varies with the input information. Conditional transfers of the flow of program are performed by the processor based on the state of the flag bits. Table A.8 summarizes the program control instructions.

Interrupt Control Instructions. When the IF-bit is set, interrupt service routines can be activated by the interrupt instructions summarized in Table A.9.

Flag Control Instructions. The flag instructions, as summarized in Table A.10, are used to set or clear the flags.

Coprocessor Synchronization Instructions. In order to work in sync with coprocessors like the 8087 math coprocessor, the 8086/88 is equipped with instructions for monitoring coprocessor

Table A.9   Interrupt control instructions.

INT		;Jump to the interrupt routine pointed to by ;interrupt vector 3
INTO		;Jump to the overflow routine pointed to by ;interrupt vector 4
INT	n	;Jump to the interrupt routine pointed to by ;interrupt vector n (between 0 and 255)
IRET		;Return from interrupt
HLT		;Stop the processor, leave CS:IP pointing to ;the next instruction, and wait for an interrupt

Table A.10   Flag instructions.

CLC	;Clear CF (load zero into CF)
CMC	;Complement CF (invert CF bit)
STC	;Set CF (load one into CF)
CLD	;Clear DF
STD	;Set DF
CLI	;Clear IF
STI	;Set IF

activities. The 8087 has its own instruction set, these instructions are embodied in special ESCape code. The 8087 is able to
monitor the instructions being received and executed by the
8086/88. When the central processor detects an ESC instruction,
it proceeds to help the 8087 to obtain specified operands, while
the 8087 takes over the ESC instruction and performs the necessary operations. After properly reacting to the ESC instruction,
the central processor may wait for the 8087 to finish its task or
proceed to execute, in parallel, the following instructions.

The WAIT instruction allows the programmer to implement
the parallel processing. When the 8086/88 receives a WAIT instruction, it will stop and wait for as long as the 8087 is busy
executing. Only after receiving a task-complete signal from the
8087 can the 8086/88 proceed to execute the next instruction.
Thus placing a WAIT instruction *after* each ESC instruction
would ensure that the central processor does not execute any
instructions while the coprocessor is executing the preceding
ESC instruction. Conversely, placing a WAIT *before* each ESC
would allow parallel processing and, in the same time, ensure
that the central processor does not execute the next ESC instruction while the coprocessor is still executing the previous one.

Since most high-level language compilers provide floating-
point operation routines for the 8087 in their math libraries, we
will not attempt to program the 8087 directly and the reader is
referred to an 8087 user's manual for listings of its instruction
set.

A.7   MASM: MICROSOFT MACRO ASSEMBLER

This section is about writing and executing assembly-language programs on the PC. To do this we need an assembler that will translate assembly-language programs into machine codes. In this book we utilize the Microsoft Macro Assembler (MASM) to develop assembly routines for the PC. This section examines the basic features of the MASM.

In developing CAD application programs on the PC, assembly-language programming is important because it provides the programmer with access to the innards of the PC that a high-level language like FORTRAN does not. Since most of the number crunching tasks of CAD applications can be programmed in FORTRAN, we shall focus on the organization of assembly-language routines or procedures that perform tasks not feasible with FORTRAN. Such routines may be attached to a FORTRAN program and *called* from within the FORTRAN program.

As will be detailed in Appendix B, the MS-FORTRAN compiler from Microsoft Corp. is used in developing the CAD programs presented in this book. The rules for interfacing assembly-language routines with FORTRAN programs will be discussed there.

A complete assembly-language program module consists of up to four segment sections each of which is made up of *instructions* and *directives*. An instruction is to instruct the processor to perform specific machine operations and a directive is to direct the assembler to perform one of its own functions. Consider the following program:

```
DATA_SEG  SEGMENT                 ;Start of data segment
X         DB          58H         ;Define Byte with initial value
Y         DW          5A59H       ;Define Word
DATA_SEG  ENDS                    ;End of data segment

EXTRA_SEG SEGMENT
A         DB          ?           ;Define Byte, no initial value
B         DW          ?           ;Define Word
EXTRA_SEG ENDS

STACK_SEG SEGMENT
          DW          200 DUP (?);Define 200-Word stack
STACK_TOP EQU         THIS WORD   ;Locate top of stack
STACK_SEG ENDS

DOS       EQU         21H   ;Assembler will replace DOS with 21H
CONSOLE   EQU         06H
RETDOS    EQU         4CH
```

```
CODE_SEG    SEGMENT
            ASSUME      CS:CODE_SEG,DS:DATA_SEG
            ASSUME      ES:EXTRA_SEG,SS:STACK_SEG
START:      MOV         AX,DATA_SEG      ;Initialize DS
            MOV         DS,AX
            MOV         AX,EXTRA_SEG     ;Initialize ES
            MOV         ES,AX
            MOV         AX,STACK_SEG
            MOV         SS,AX
            MOV         SP,STACK_TOP     ;Initialize top of stack
            MOV         DL,X             ;Transfer data in X to A
            MOV         ES:A,DL
            MOV         AH,CONSOLE       ;Output data in X to screen
            INT         DOS              ; via an MS-DOS interrupt
            MOV         DX,Y             ;Transfer data in Y to B
            MOV         ES:B,DX
            INT         DOS            ;Output low byte of Y to screen
            MOV         DL,DH          ;Copy high byte of Y to DL
            INT         DOS            ;Output high byte of Y to screen
            MOV         AH,RETDOS ;Interrupt to return to MS-DOS
            INT         DOS
CODE_SEG    ENDS
            END         START     ;Begin execution at label START
```

In the above *source* file all the non-instruction symbols are *directives*. A Macro Assembler directive statement comprises four fields: Name, Action, Expression, and Comment. For example:

```
X           DB          58H        ;Define Byte with initial value
```
(Name) (Action)   (Expression)   ;(Comment)

A Macro Assembler instruction statement consists of up to the same four fields, for example:

```
START:             MOV        AX,DATA SEG     ;Initialize DS
```
(Name/Label) (Action)   (Expression)   ;(Comment)

In an instruction statement, the Action and Expression fields contain, respectively, the mnemonics and operands discussed in the previous section. Note that the Name or Label field in an instruction ends with a ":" while the Name field in a directive ends with a " " (blank).

Each statement line is assembled as either a free-format directive or instruction. The format is free in that only *spaces* are needed to separate each field and the number of spaces is

Table A.11   Basic MASM directives.

\<segname\> SEGMENT   [\<align\>] [\<combine\>] [\<'class'\>]
    ⁞
\<segname\> ENDS

; \<align\> may be PARA (paragraph - default), BYTE, WORD, or PAGE.
; \<combine\> may be PUBLIC, COMMON, AT \<exp\>, STACK, MEMORY, or
;   no entry (Not Combinable or Private).
; \<'class'\> provides a Name for Linker to group segments.

        ASSUME   \<seg-reg\>:\<seg-name\> [,...]

; This directive directs the assembler to assemble variable
; references, such as X, Y, A, and B in the foregoing example,
; under proper segment registers.

[\<var-name\>]   DB   \<value\>

; This directive tells the assembler to allocate one or more
; byte-locations with or without initial values. The values can
; be expressions and the assembler will evaluate the expressions
; before assigning initial values. When a \<var-name\> is speci-
; fied, the assembler will associate the starting address with
; the byte-variable symbol. Multiple entries may be specified
; using the DUP function, for instance "100 DUP (?)" would
; allocate 100 byte-size locations with no initial values.

[\<var-name\>]   DW   \<value\>

; This directive tells the assembler to allocate one or more
; word-size memory locations with or without initial values.

\<symbol\>   EQU   \<value\>

; The assembler associates \<value\> with \<symbol\> and replaces
; \<symbol\> entries in the program with \<value\>. \<value\> can be
; another symbol, an instruction mnemonic, or a text string.

        END   [\<exp\>]

; This statement specifies the end of the assembly process, and
; passes the optional \<exp\> to MS-LINK as the starting location
; of the program.

Table A.11   (Continued)

        PUBLIC   <symbol> [,...]

; The PUBLIC directive makes the listed symbol(s) available for
; use by modules in other code segments.

        EXTRN   <symbol or name>:<type> [,...]

; The EXTeRNal directive declares the listed symbols as <u>external</u>
; which must have been declared PUBLIC in the module where the
; symbols are defined. <type> may be (1) BYTE, WORD, or DWORD
; (Double Word); (2) NEAR or FAR for Labels or Procedures; or
; (3) ABS for pure numbers.

<proc-name>   PROC   [NEAR or FAR]
     ┆
              RET
<proc-name>   ENDP

; The PROCedure block defines a callable subroutine. The default
; is a NEAR procedure, which may be <u>called</u> only from locations
; inside the same code segment (an <u>intrasegment</u> call). A FAR
; procedure is to be called as an <u>intersegment</u> call from loca-
; tions outside the current code segment. The distinction is
; important because both CS and IP have to be <u>pushed</u> as a return
; address for a FAR procedure call, while only IP needs to be
; <u>pushed</u> for a NEAR procedure call.

---

arbitrary. However, the order of the fields is fixed and all
assembler-specific keywords must appear in the Action field.
The fact that the ";" symbol signals the beginning of the Comment field should also be noted. Comments are used to document
the logic of program design so the source code is more human-
readable.

The function of the foregoing example program is to copy
the character codes stored in X (one byte) and Y (two bytes)
within the current data segment to locations represented by A
and B in the current extra segment, and to output the data to
the console or the PC screen. Because X contains 58H (88 in
decimal) which is the ASCII code for "X", and Y contains 59H
in the low byte and 60H in the high byte, executing the program would display "XYZ" on the screen. The program can be
executed on either the IBM PC or the TI PC since no IBM-spe-
cific BIOS routines were used.

The MASM Macro Assembler is too complicated a system to be completely covered even in a dedicated chapter, it seems sensible to refer the reader to the Macro Assembler Manual for details and to summarize only the more frequently used *directives* here so we shall be familiar with assembly-language programming enough to proceed to develop CAD related programs. Table A.11 lists these basic MASM directives. In this table, the parameters enclosed by angled brackets are user-specified parameters and those enclosed by square brackets are optional parameters.

The MS-DOS environment provides a number of utility routines useful for monitoring and maneuvering the inner workings of a PC, as demonstrated in the foregoing example. These service routines can be accessed through the interrupt vectors reserved by Microsoft Corp. It only takes a few machine instructions to invoke these service routines. Generally, a high-level language like FORTRAN does not provide, in its standard library, access to these DOS routines. However, specific assembly-language procedures can be built to bridge the gap.

The next example assembly-language procedure module, called DCIO, would allow a FORTRAN program to perform Direct Console I/O (Keyboard for input and Screen for output) through the service routine associated with the Interrupt Vector 21H (33 in decimal) of MS-DOS. A listing of procedure DCIO is given as follows.

```
CODE_SEG   SEGMENT
;
           ASSUME    CS:CODE_SEG
           PUBLIC    DCIO
;
DCIO       PROC      FAR              ;For intersegment calls
           PUSH      BP               ;Save Frame Pointer on stack
           MOV       BP,SP            ;Copy current SP to BP
           LES       DI,DWORD PTR [BP+6] ;Load First Argument into
           MOV       DX,ES:[DI]   ;  DL register (DH = 0)
           MOV       AH,06H           ;Set up for Function 06H
           CMP       DL,0FFH          ;Input or Output?
           JZ        DCIN             ;Go to Input sequence
           INT       21H              ;MS-DOS Function Request (Output)
           JMP       DCRET            ;Clear stack and Return
DCIN:      INT       21H              ;Console-input a character in AL
           XOR       AH,AH            ;Clear AH
           MOV       ES:[DI],AX  ;Return AL via the input Argument
DCRET:     POP       BP               ;Restore BP
           RET       4
DCIO       ENDP
;
CODE_SEG   ENDS
           END
```

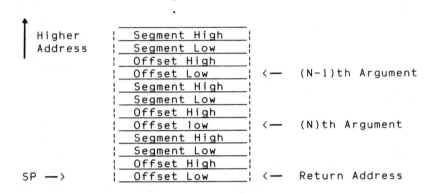

Figure A.5   Stack at beginning of FORTRAN calls.

The above procedure assumes that the physical address (Segment:Offset) of a two-byte integer argument or parameter will be *pushed* on to the stack by the *caller* program before it *jumps* to the procedure.   This is exactly how an MS-FORTRAN module *calls* a subroutine.   The procedure picks up the integer parameter from the current stack defined by the *caller* program and performs the requested console I/O.

In the foregoing procedure, "DWORD PTR" is a *reserved word* used to tell the assembler that the following *address* "[BP + 6]" points to a Double Word.   At the entry to the procedure, SP (top of stack contains the low byte of the Offset pointer of the return address, as illustrated in Figure A.5.   After *pushing* BP on to the same stack, we realize that the address of the only parameter is stored in "SP + 6".   The "RET 4" statement adds 4 to SP to clear the four bytes used to store the address of the parameter.   It should follow that for N parameters 4 · N bytes should be cleared.   Note that the last statement "END" is not followed by a label because the procedure is expected to be activated by a *caller* program.

The DCIO procedure may be *called* by the FORTRAN statement

```
CALL   DCIO(VALUE1)
```

with VALUE1 declared as a two-byte integer variable and assigned a value between 0 and 255.   FORTRAN statements are discussed in Appendix B.

An assembler cannot, by itself, transform source code to *executable* machine code, however. The assembling process produces a so-called *object* code module, which contains individual segments in a binary form. There may be more than one object module in a complete program. To produce an executable code, a linking program or *linker* is called upon to combine object modules to form a *Run file* (executable image).

The MASM assembler is accompanied by a linker called MS-LINK. An output file from MS-LINK can be loaded and executed by entering the file name following the MS-DOS prompt. Procedures for operating MASM and MS-LINK can be found in an MASM manual.

The strength of assembly-language programming in developing micro-CAD software is in providing direct links between a high-level language and machine-level I/O devices, and, in some cases, in speeding up inefficiently compiled high-level language routines. Of course it is possible to develop CAD or any other application programs solely in an assembly language, but the coding of such would be a very tedious and error-prone process. Using high-level languages to implement problem-solving algorithms can save precious development time, simplify system maintenance, and enhance program portability. Therefore, being multilingual is a requisite toward effective PC programming.

FORTRAN Programming
on the IBM PC

Invented in 1957, FORTRAN is still the most widely used computer language for scientific and engineering applications. The standard FORTRAN has gone through two large-scale revisions since its inception. The early one was released in 1966 and known as FORTRAN IV. Since then its popularity among engineers and the ever increasing rate of advancement in computer hardware and software technology have coupled to create a good deal of dialectal improvements on the language structure and, consequently, incompatibility between varied systems seemed to be plaguing certain software development. In order to avoid further aggravation in software portability, the American National Standards Institute (ANSI) released an updated definition of FORTRAN in 1977 which has become known as FORTRAN-77.

In this book, the MS-FORTRAN version 3.3 Compiler from Microsoft Corp. is used in developing CAD application programs on the IBM PC and PC/AT and the TI PC. A FORTRAN compiler is a translation program for converting symbolic FORTRAN programs into modules of machine codes. The MS-FORTRAN language conforms to the ANSI X3.9-1978 subset FORTRAN specifications. Many other features of the full language are also supported.

This appendix provides a brief account of the MS-FORTRAN environment. FORTRAN statements or instructions will be classified according to their specific uses. Examples will be given to emphasize the interfacing of FORTRAN and assembly-language program modules in the PC environment.

B.1   STRUCTURE OF FORTRAN PROGRAMS

Let us consider a complete FORTRAN program:

```
      PROGRAM SAMPLE
C
C   This program computes the area of an N-sided polygon
C
      REAL X(10),Y(10)
      INTEGER NVERTX,I
C
C   Prompt for input of N and (X(N),Y(N))
C
      WRITE(*,*) ' Enter Number of Vertices: '
      READ(*,*) NVERTX
      DO 10 I=1,NVERTX
        WRITE(*,*) ' Enter (X,Y) of Vertex ', I
        READ(*,*) X(I),Y(I)
10    CONTINUE
C
C   Call Subroutine AREANP to compute the area
C
      CALL AREANP(NVERTX,X,Y,AREA)
C
C   Display the result on the screen
C
      WRITE(*,*) ' AREA = ',AREA
      STOP
      END


      SUBROUTINE AREANP(N,X,Y,A)
      REAL X(N),Y(N),A,DET
      INTEGER N,I,J
C
C   Area of a polygon equals to half the sum of the determinants
C      of all 2*2 matrices formed by consecutive vertices
C
      A=0.0
      DO 10 I=1,N
        J=MOD(I,N)+1
        A=A+DET(X(J),Y(J),X(I),Y(I))
10    CONTINUE
      A=ABS(A)/2.0
      RETURN
      END

      REAL FUNCTION DET(X1,Y1,X2,Y2)
      REAL X1,Y1,X2,Y2
C
C   Compute the determinant of a 2 * 2 matrix
C
```

```
DET=X1*Y2-X2*Y1
RETURN
END
```

A FORTRAN program may take the form of a deck of computer cards, or simply a text file stored on a magnetic medium.
In the PC environment programs are usually stored as text files
on floppy disks. A *modular* FORTRAN program is usually composed of a number of *program modules* each performing specific
tasks. The foregoing example contains three program modules.
There is always a chief module (Main Program) to coordinate
the interplay of all the other subordinate modules (Subprograms),
by *calling* subordinate modules with parameters passed through
arguments. An argument is a symbol representing a *pointer* or
address to a specific memory location (see Fig. A.5). The *arguments* constitute the only explicit passage between modules,
and the symbols of the arguments used in the *caller* and *called*
modules may vary.

The structural similarity between FORTRAN and assembly-
language programs (the Main and Procedure code segments) is
worth noting. Under MS-FORTRAN, individual FORTRAN modules can be created and compiled separately and then *linked*
together to form a complete program.

There are two kinds of FORTRAN subprogram: Subroutine
and Function. When a Subroutine module is *called*, it receives
parameters via the arguments, performs specific computations
on the parameters, and transfers the results back to the *caller*
module via the arguments. A Function module cannot be *called*.
When the name of a Function module appears in an expression
consisting of FORTRAN operators and operands, the module is
activated to do the same things a Subroutine module would do
and, in addition, to attach a resultant value to the Function
name serving as a variable. Thus the expression can use the
returned value directly.

Each *statement* line in a FORTRAN file has 80 columns, which
correspond to the 80 columns in a computer card. A FORTRAN
program module consists of four parts: header, data declaration,
algorithmic statements, and terminator. The first and the last
parts may be regarded as directives used to inform the compiler
of the range of the program module. Data base and algorithm
are the two major players in all computer programs.

Each 80-column statement line is divided into four fields.
Most compilers associate these four fields with specific columns.

Columns 1–5 form the statement number field for labeling individual statements with positive integer constants. There is
another special use of column 1: A "C", "c", or "*" in column
1 initiates a *comment line* which may be used to document the
logic flow of the program; comment lines are not processed by
the compiler. Column 6 is used to indicate a *continuation line*,
and is left blank if a statement can be completed in one line.
When any character other than a blank or a zero appears in
column 6 and the first five columns are blanks, the compiler
will regard this line as a mere continuation of the preceding
statement line. Columns 7–72 constitute the statement field,
containing FORTRAN-specific instructions and operands. Columns
73–80 constitute the identification field used to identify individual
cards or lines; they are not processed by the compiler.

In the foregoing example, the three program modules are
enclosed, respectively, by three pairs of header and terminator:

```
PROGRAM <name>

     <Main Program Body>

END

SUBROUTINE <name> [( <arg1> [, ...] )]

     <Subroutine Body>

RETURN

END
```

and

```
FUNCTION <name> [( <arg1> [, ...] )]

     <Function Body>

RETURN

END
```

The Functions as defined above are *external functions*. It's
typical for a FORTRAN compiler to predefine a set of *intrinsic
functions* available for use in a FORTRAN program to evaluate
frequently used mathematical functions such as sine, cosine,
absolute value, logarithm, and many others.

B.2   DATA TYPE AND ASSIGNMENT
STATEMENTS

Data types include integer, real (floating-point) number, logical
value, and character. Data expressed in explicit forms are
called *constants*, for example:

Integer constants: 123, 0, −59825, . . .
Real constants: 38.987, −0.00345, 6.28E13, . . .
Logical constants: .TRUE. or .FALSE.
Character constants: 'A', 'a', 'I am a String', . . .

Constants represent values of certain type of data. Data stored
in specific memory locations are called *variables*. The name of
a variable is a user-defined symbol indicating a memory location.
The value of a variable refers to the contents of a specific memory location which may vary during program execution. Since
different types of data are stored under different rules, as discussed in Section A.1, variables must be defined with specific
types.
    A user-specified variable symbol or name contains up to six
characters each being either a letter (A–Z) or a digit (0–9).
The first character of a name must be a letter. The MS-FORTRAN
compiler makes no distinction between uppercase and lowercase
letters, except when they are parts of character constants.
    FORTRAN statements are generally composed of *keywords, sym-
bolic names, constants, labels,* and *operators*. Keywords look
like variable names but have special meaning in the language.
INTEGER, REAL, LOGICAL, and CHARACTER are keywords
used to declare the corresponding types of variables. For example,

```
INTEGER  I, KOUNT, NUMBER

REAL  COUNT, YOU, TIME

DOUBLE PRECISION  DETAIL, X, Y

LOGICAL  COM1, COM2

CHARACTER  ANS, YES, ONECHR

CHARACTER*2  TWOCHR, ANSWER
```

In MS-FORTRAN, an integer variable has a default size of four
bytes. However, two-byte integers can be declared with the

keyword INTEGER*2. The DOUBLE PRECISION type declares floating-point variables with two times the number of *bytes* for storing a standard or single precision real variable. The IEEE specification defines a REAL on four bytes, and a DOUBLE PRECISION on eight bytes. Also note that CHARACTER declares locations for storing single-character code, while CHARACTER*n allocates locations for storing n-character code (each variable is n-byte long).

The special keyword IMPLICIT can be used to associate a data type to all variable names starting with a particular letter. For example,

IMPLICIT INTEGER(A-K, Z)   REAL (R)

declares that all variables starting with A through K and with Z are integer variables, excepting those individually declared in following declaration statements. It also specifies those starting with R to be real variables. It is important to note that the compiler automatically inserts the following IMPLICIT statement as the first data declaration statement to provide an *implicit typing*:

IMPLICIT REAL(A-H,O-Z)   INTEGER(I-N)

The data type keywords can be used to declare *arrays* of data elements as well. An array refers to a group of data elements by a single symbol; it distinguishes its individual elements by *subscripts*. For example,

INTEGER COUNT(10)

declares an array of ten integer elements (the lower bound is always one in MS-FORTRAN), and COUNT(5) would refer to the fifth element in the array. COUNT(10) is a one-dimensional array.

Multi-dimensional arrays can be similarly declared, with multiple subscripts. For example,

REAL THING(5,10), PEOPLE(100,20)

CHARACTER*8 NAME(10,100), NUMBER(100,2)

declare four two-dimensional arrays. All the data type statements are *non-executable* statements because they do not call
for any CPU actions.

Arithmetic and logical operations perform all the number
crunching in FORTRAN programs. An arithmetic or logical expression comprises variables, constants, parentheses, and operators. The arithmetic operators include addition, subtraction,
multiplication, division, and exponentiation, which are respectively represented by +, −, *, /, and **.

The object of a logical expression is to produce a result of
either .TRUE. or .FALSE. from comparing numerical or logical
values. *Relational* operators are used to compare numerical
values. They include:

.EQ.—for *Equal to*
.NE.—for *Not Equal to*
.LT.—for *Less Than*
.LE.—for *Less than or Equal to*
.GT.—for *Greater Than*
.GE.—for *Greater than or Equal to*

Thus the expression *A .GT. B* will yield a value of .TRUE. if
the value of A is greater than that of B, otherwise a .FALSE.
will result. Logical values themselves (.TRUE. and .FALSE.)
can be compared with *logical* operators. The .OR. operator is
used to test two logical values and produce a .TRUE. result if
at least one of the two is .TRUE., .FALSE. if none of them is
.TRUE.. The .AND. operator is used to test two operands and
produce a .TRUE. result only if both operands are .TRUE..
The last logical operator .NOT. is used to negate a .TRUE.
value into .FALSE. and vice versa. Following are some possible
logical expressions:

SUM .LE. DIFF .OR. A .NE. 13

(A .LT. (B+3.9)*C) .AND. XYZ .GE. 5.5

C .AND. LG .OR. BB

.NOT. ((S .LT. T) .OR. (ABC/2.0 .LE. XYZ))

TEST .LT. 0.000001

A FORTRAN compiler always observes the following priority order
in executing the arithmetic and logical operators in an expression:

(1)   **
(2)   * and /
(3)   + and −
(4)   relational operators
(5)   logical operators

unless parentheses are used to enforce certain execution order.
In the case of multiple nested parentheses, the inner ones will
be evaluated first. For operators at the same level the left-to-
right rule is applied.
   An assignment statement has the following general form:

   <symbol> = <expression>

The special symbol "=" should read: *is assigned the value of*.
Thus, $A = B + CD$ would direct the machine to add the values
of variables B and CD, and assign the result to variable A. It
is clear that assignment statements are *executable* statements.

B.3   TRANSFER STATEMENTS

There are a number of FORTRAN *keywords* for regulating the
logic flow of a program module. The *unconditional* GO TO is
the simplest transfer mechanism. Such a GO TO statement has
the form:

```
GO TO  <label>
```

which transfers control to the statement with the listed integer
label.
   The *computed* GO TO allows provision of multiple transfer
routes, it has the form:

```
GO TO ( <label1>, <label2>, ..., <labeln> ) <expression>
```

The *expression* should result in an integer value between 1 and
n, leading the program flow to the statement with the corresponding label, otherwise control will be passed to the next
statement.
   The *arithmetic* IF statement provides a similar control mechanism. Its general form is:

```
IF ( <expression> )  <label1>, <label2>, <label3>
```

The value of the expression here can be either integer or real. A negative value will direct the program flow to <label1>; a zero value will transfer control to <label2>; and a positive value will transfer control to <label3>.

The CALL statement can be used to temporarily disrupt the program flow. The procesor first *pushes* the arguments, if any, saves the return *address*, and then jumps to the *called* subroutine. It has the form:

```
CALL  <subroutine_name> [ (arg1, arg2, ..., argn) ]
```

The *called* subroutine must provide a RETURN statement in order to transfer control back to the statement following the CALL.

FORTRAN *calls* pass parameters between program modules via *address*, as opposed to some languages' passing parameters via *value*. The *arguments* are symbols representing parameter locations. For example, the

```
CALL  EXAMPL(A,BC)
```

statement allows SUBROUTINE EXAMPL to access the values of the variables A and BC directly, thus changes of the values at A and BC locations made in the subroutine will also be effective in the *caller* module. At times this may cause unexpected disruptions in the *caller* module. To prevent unintentional distortion of data due to argument transfers, FORTRAN provides a shielding machanism for guarding data. For example, the

```
CALL EXAMPL(A,2.5)
```

statement would direct the compiler to create a temporary address or location to store the value 2.5 and pass that address to the subroutine. In so doing changes made to the temporary cell will not affect the caller module.

B.4 THE IF-THEN STRUCTURE

The structure involves three or more statements:

```
IF (<logical_expression>) THEN
  <statement1>
  <statement2>
  :
  :
END IF
```

The group of statements between IF and END IF will be executed only if the logical expression yields a .TRUE. value, otherwise control will be transferred to the statement following END IF.

When there is only one statement in the above statement group, the above structure can be simplified to one line:

```
IF (<logical_expression>)  <statement>
```

which is also known as the logical IF statement.

B.5   THE IF-THEN-ELSE STRUCTURE

An IF-THEN structure cannot accommodate the situation where there are statements that need to be executed on a .FALSE. value from the logical expression, for which case an IF-THEN-ELSE should be used. Its general form is:

```
IF (<logical_expression>) THEN
  <statement>
  :
  :
ELSE
  <statement>
  :
  :
END IF
```

in which the statement group following ELSE will be executed when the logical expression yields a .FALSE. value.

A more versatile structure can be constructed by inserting ELSE IF statements in front of ELSE. This enhanced structure allows more than one logical expression to be used as *check points*, which may be illustrated by the following:

```
IF (<logical_expression_1>) THEN
  <statement>
  :
  :
ELSE IF (<logical_expression_2>) THEN
  <statement>
```

```
:
:
ELSE IF (<logical_expression_3>) THEN
  <statement>
:
:
ELSE
  <statement>
:
:
END IF
```

where the statement group between ELSE and END IF will be
executed only when *all* the preceding logical expressions yield
.FALSE.

In a FORTRAN program module IF-THEN-ELSE structures can
be *nested* within other IF-THEN-ELSE structures. In these
cases *indentation* of statements should be used to align individual
structures to ease the debugging and maintenance of the source
code.

B.6   THE DO STATEMENT

Most computer algorithms involve repetitive computations of
some sort. The DO statement is the only repetitive statement in
FORTRAN. Its general form is:

```
DO   <label> <var> = <exp1>,<exp2>,<exp3>
```

where <label> indicates the label of the terminal statement. In
MS-FORTRAN, <exp1>, <exp2>, and <exp3> are integer expressions for, respectively, the initial value, the terminal value, and
the incremental value of the repetition integer variable <var>,
If <exp3> is not given, an increment of one is assumed. In the
complete set of FORTRAN-77, the variable and expressions can
be real.

The term *DO-loop* is used to refer to the block of statements
starting from the DO statement and ending at the labeled terminal statement, which is often a CONTINUE statement just to
mark the end of a DO-loop. In the beginning, the repetition
variable is assigned the value of <exp1>.

In the case of a positive <exp3>, the DO-loop is executed
when the value of <exp2> is greater than or equal to that of
the repetition variable. At the end of each DO loop, the value
of <exp3> is added to the repetition variable before returning
control to the DO statement where the value of <exp2> is again

compared with that of the repetition variable. The loop is terminated when the value of <exp2> is less than that of the repetition variable, and control is then transferred to the statement
following the labeled terminal statement. Conversely, a negative
<exp3> would direct the DO statement to execute the DO-loop
while decrementing the value of the repetition variable. An
example is:

```
      DO  10  I=1,N
        J=MOD(I,N)
        A=A+DET(X(J),Y(J),X(I),Y(I))
 10     CONTINUE
```

which adds N calculated values of function DET to A. It is clear
that a zero <exp3> would result in an infinite loop, and is thus
meaningless.

B.7   INPUT/OUTPUT STATEMENTS

Several I/O statements are available for reading from or writing
to the console (Keyboard/Screen) or a storage disk. The OPEN
statement is used to *open* an external file so data can be transferred between the program and the storage disk. A file can
be opened as a *sequential* file whose data can be accessed only
in sequence, or as a *direct access* file whose data may be accessed at random. This section examines only sequential files.

If we wish to save some data in a new disk file under the
name DATAFILE, we must first *open* the file with

```
OPEN (7, FILE='DATAFILE',STATUS='NEW')
```

The number 7 is a logic unit number we assigned to the file so
later the file can be referred to as a logic unit. Now we may
output the data to the file with

```
WRITE(7, *) ALPHA, BETA, GAMMA
```

The asterisk in the WRITE statement indicates a system-specified
format. User-specified formats can be requested with the
FORMAT statement, to be discussed in the next section. The
above WRITE will output the values of the three variables to
the disk file and store them in a *record* (a storage area generated

by a single WRITE statement) using a format specified by the MS-FORTRAN compiler. There is an implicit record pointer kept to indicate the next available record location.

While residing in the memory in a binary form, the values will, for a formatted WRITE, be converted to decimals before being outputted to the external file. When an output procedure is completed, the file should be *closed* with

```
CLOSE (7)
```

To retrieve data stored in the file DATAFILE, we should first open the file with

```
OPEN (9, FILE='DATAFILE', STATUS='OLD')
```

Note that a logical unit number is used only to designate a logical link between a file and a program, it does not affect the contents of a file. Now we may input the data with

```
READ (9, *) X, Y, Z
```

When a file is just opened, the record pointer points to the first record. The pointer moves forward as records are being read. FORTRAN provides a special statement for *rewinding* a file so its pointer is at the first record, namely

```
REWIND  9
```

The term *console I/O* refers to input/output via system-specified devices. In MS-FORTRAN, keyboard is the input console and display screen is the output console. The logic unit number of these default I/O stations is an asterisk. Thus the following statement would output a text string and two real values to the display screen:

```
WRITE (*, *) 'X and Y: ', X, Y
```

The above READ and WRITE statements are *external* because they are used to transmit information between the memory and external devices. The *internal* READ and WRITE statements perform the same I/O functions between different parts of the memory. Consider the following statements:

```
CHARACTER*40 BUFFER
WRITE(BUFFER,*) A,B
READ(BUFFER,*) X,Y
```

The above CHARACTER statement declares a 40-character variable to serve as an *internal* file. Thus the WRITE and READ
statements perform their I/O duties between variables in the
memory and the internal file BUFFER, which is also in the memory.

B.8   THE FORMAT STATEMENT

Consider a formatted WRITE statement:

```
      WRITE(7, 100) NUMBER, ALPHA, BETA, GAMMA
100   FORMAT(I5, 2X, 'Followed By', 2X, 2F8.2, 3X, E12.5)
```

The second entry in the argument list of WRITE points to a labeled FORMAT statement containing several *edit descriptors*. In
the above example, four values are written to an external file where
the first five columns are used for an integer value, the next
two are left blank, the next eleven for the string within the
quotes, another two for blanks, then two eight-column fields
each for a real value with two digits following the decimal point,
the next three columns are left blank, and then a twelve-column
field for an exponentiated real number with five digits following
the decimal point.
   Assume that NUMBER is 50, ALPHA is 2.3, BETA is -0.1234,
and GAMMA is $0.123*10^{45}$, then the outputted record will be
written as:

^^^50^^Followed By^^^^^^2.30^^^-0.12^^^^^1.23000E+44

where the symbol "^" denotes a blank character.
   Space does not permit detailed descriptions of all available
descriptors. The reader is referred to an MS-FORTRAN manual
for other edit descriptors.

B.9   THE COMMON AND EQUIVALENCE
STATEMENTS

We have learned that the argument list of a SUBROUTINE or
FUNCTION statement constitutes the only explicit passage

between program modules. This facility may not be sufficient when large amounts of data need to be shared by a number of program modules, since it would be very inefficient if all the data have to be passed via the argument list. To avoid such difficulty, FORTRAN provides the COMMON mechanism. A *named COMMON* statement relocates a group of variables to a common area so that other program modules can access them by declaring the same named COMMON. For example,

```
COMMON /TEAM/ NUMBER, NAME, SYMBOL
```

declares a common area of three variables. All program modules having included the same COMMON statement can access the three variables.

The EQUIVALENCE statement allows multiple uses of particular memory locations. For example,

```
CHARACTER  FILEID(14)
CHARACTER*14  FLSTR
EQUIVALENCE  (FLSTR, FILEID(1))
```

The first two statements declare a character array, FILEID, of 14 elements each one-byte long and a 14-byte character variable, FLSTR. The EQUIVALENCE statement forces the array to use the locations used by the variable. In so doing the array can be used to input a string, character by character, while the variable FLSTR can be used in an OPEN statement as a file name composed of the individual characters.

B.10   THE DATA STATEMENT

The DATA statement allows us to assign initial values to declared variables at compilation time, uninitialized variables may have meaningless values after compilation. For example,

```
DATA  NAME, NUMBER, XVALUE /1, 205, 3.14/, SURE / .TRUE./
```

assigns values within the slashes to corresponding variables. Obviously the variable SURE must have been declared LOGICAL. It should be noted that the initialization can also be done in the program using simple assignment statements.

FORTRAN does not allow straightforward initialization for variables in named COMMON blocks, however. They have to be

initialized in a BLOCK DATA subprogram, which contains only
the header, COMMON, DATA, and terminator statements and
may be regarded as a special program module. For example,

```
BLOCK   DATA
COMMON   /TEAM/ NAME, SYMBOL
DATA   NAME, SYMBOL /55, 180.5/
END
```

B.11   INTERFACING OF FORTRAN AND ASSEMBLY-LANGUAGE PROGRAMS

To conclude our discussions on FORTRAN, let us write a
FORTRAN program to interface with the assembly-language module DCIO presented in Section A.7. The following program will
first send characters 'X', 'Y', and 'Z' to the screen, then start
echoing the characters pressed on the keyboard to the screen
until the ESC (Escape) key is pressed.

```
      PROGRAM TEST
      INTEGER*2 DX
C
C  Send 88 (ASCII code for 'X') to screen
C
      DX=88
      CALL DCIO(DX)
C
C  Send 89 (ASCII code for 'Y') to screen
C
      DX=89
      CALL DCIO(DX)
C
C  Send 90 (ASCII code for 'Z') to screen
C
      DX=90
      CALL DCIO(DX)
C
C  Direct DCIO to read a character from keyboard
C
10    DX=255
      CALL DCIO(DX)
C
C  Echo received character to screen
C
      CALL DCIO(DX)
C
C  Compare received code with 27 (ASCII code for ESC key)
C
      IF(DX.NE.27) GOTO 10
      STOP
      END
```

We should note that DX is an arbitrarily defined variable
symbol and has nothing to do with the DX register in the 8088
chip. Since the ASCII character code received from keyboard
was treated as an integer between 0 and 127 in the DCIO procedure, we may compare the value of DX directly with the ASCII
sequence code of the expected ESC key. In other cases when
CHARACTER variables are used to store character codes, they
can only be compared with character constants. However, an
ASCII character and its integer sequence code can be related
through two FORTRAN intrinsic functions:

```
ICHAR ( <single_character> )
```

returns an integer value that is the ASCII sequence code of the
character argument; and

```
CHAR ( <integer> )
```

returns a single-character constant that has the value of the
integer argument as its ASCII sequence code.

The rules we have learned for interfacing assembly-language
modules with FORTRAN modules apply directly to interfacing
assembly-language modules with other high-level languages. The
only variation would be in the way the arguments are transmitted
through the stack.

B.12   CLOSING

This appendix and last present the basic ingredients of microcomputer programming, with specific emphasis placed on programming flexibility through integration of assembly-language
and FORTRAN programming skills. In the dawning and seem-
ingly inescapable microcomputer age, the ability to program the
microcomputer, and program it well, is becoming an indispensable item in an engineer's toolbox.

This book is about CAD, the coverage of the basics of programming here is meant to be supplementary. Nevertheless,
the material presented here should suffice in serving as an introduction to the inner workings of the PC system and the elements
of assembly-language and FORTRAN programming in a PC environment.

Bibliography

1. Angell, I. O., *A Practical Introduction to Computer Graphics*, John Wiley & Sons, New York, 1981.
2. Baumgart, B. G., "Geometric Modeling for Computer Vision," Ph.D. Thesis, Computer Science Department, Stanford University, 1974.
3. Bezier, P., "Mathematical and practical possibilities of UNISURF," in *Computer-Aided Geometric Design*, R. E. Barnhill and R. F. Riesenfeld (eds.), Academic Press, New York, 1974.
4. Braid, I. C., Hillyard, R. C., and Stroud, I. A., "Stepwise Construction of Polyhedra in Geometric Modelling," in *Mathematical Methods in Computer Graphics and Design*, K. W. Brodie (ed.), Academic Press, London, 1980, pp. 123−141.
5. Encarnacao, J. and Schlechtendahl, E. G., *Computer Aided Design*, Springer-Verlag, Berlin Heidelberg, Germany, 1983.
6. Foley, J. D. and Van Dam, A., *Fundamentals of Interactive Computer Graphics*, Addison-Wesley, Reading, Massachusetts, 1982.
7. Groover, M. P. and Zimmers, E. W., Jr., *CAD/CAM*, Prentice-Hall, Englewood Cliffs, New Jersey, 1984.
8. *Initial Graphics Exchange Specification (IGES)*, U.S. National Bureau of Standards, Gaithersburg, Maryland, 1986.
9. Kopcsak, P. J., *Matrix Analysis and Analytical Geometry*, Chemical Publishing, New York, 1968.
10. Lien, S. and Kajiya, J. T., "A Symbolic Method for Calculating the Integral Properties of Arbitrary Nonconvex

Polyhedra," IEEE Computer Graphics and Applications, Vol. 4, October 1984, pp. 35–41.

11. Morse, S. P., *The 8086/8088 Primer*, Hayden Book, 1982.

12. Mortenson, M. E., *Geometric Modeling*, John Wiley & Sons, New York, 1985.

13. Newman, W. M., and Sproull, R. F., *Principles of Interactive Computer Graphics*, 2nd ed., McGraw-Hill, New York, 1979.

14. Osborne, A. and Kane, G., *Osborne 16-Bit Microprocessor Handbook*, McGraw-Hill, New York, 1981.

15. Palmer, J. F. and Morse, S. P., *The 8087 Primer*, John Wiley & Sons, New York, 1984.

16. Ryan, D. L., *Principles of Automated Drafting*, Marcel Dekker, New York, 1984.

17. Tiller, W., "Rational B-Splines for Curve and Surface Representation," IEEE Computer Graphics and Applications, Vol. 3, September 1983, pp. 61–69.

18. Voelcker, H. B. and Requicha, A. A. G., "Geometric Modeling of Mechanical Parts and Processes," Computer, Vol. 10, No. 2, December 1977, pp. 48–57.

19. Wakerly, J. F., *Microcomputer Architecture and Programming*, John Wiley & Sons, New York, 1981.

20. Wei, C., Lee, M., and Thorsen, R., "Integration of Two Geometric Modelers Based on Polyhedra and Rational Parametric Bicubics," Computers in Engineering 1986, the American Society of Mechanical Engineers, New York, Vol. 2, 1986, pp. 85–88.

21. Yamaguchi, F. and Tokieda, T., "A Unified Algorithm for Boolean Shape Operations," IEEE Computer Graphics and Applications, Vol. 4, June 1984, pp. 24–37.

Index